Philosophy in Youth and Community Work

Mike Seal and Simon Frost

First published in 2014 by:
Russell House Publishing Ltd.
58 Broad Street
Lyme Regis
Dorset DT7 3QF

Tel: 01297-443948
e-mail: help@russellhouse.co.uk
www.russellhouse.co.uk

British Library Cataloguing-in-publication Data:
A catalogue record for this book is available from the British Library.

ISBN: 978-1-905541-90-4

Typeset by TW Typesetting, Plymouth, Devon

Printed by IQ Laserpress, Aldershot

About Russell House Publishing

Russell House Publishing aims to publish innovative and valuable materials to help managers, practitioners, trainers, educators and students.

Our full catalogue covers: families, children and young people; engagement and inclusion; drink, drugs and mental health; textbooks in youth work and social work; workforce development.

Full details can be found at www.russellhouse.co.uk and we are pleased to send out information to you by post. Our contact details are on this page.

We are always keen to receive feedback on publications and new ideas for future projects.

Contents

About the Authors

Mike Seal is Principal Lecturer and Head of Youth and Community Work at Newman University, Birmingham. He has written four other books and has worked in he field for over 20 years.

Simon Frost is Programme Director and Senior Lecturer in Youth Work, Community Learning and Development at YMCA George Williams College, London.

Acknowledgements

I would like to acknowledge John Bowden for getting me into philosophy while I was working as a chef, and Caroline and Alan for being there.

Mike Seal

I would like to acknowledge my wife Ruthie and my children Chloe and Sammy.

Simon Frost

Introduction: It's More Than Just Common Sense . . . The Relevance of Philosophy to Everyday Youth and Community Work

Mike Seal

Philosophy likes to keep common sense on the run.

Mason Cooley

The aim of philosophical inquiry is to gain insight into questions about knowledge, truth, reason, reality, meaning, mind and value.

A.C. Grayling

Language is never neutral.

Paulo Freire

Youth and community workers operate through words and ideas. It is the conversations (words) we have and the meanings (ideas) which we help people create in their lives that define us. So, whether we acknowledge it or not, philosophy lies behind everything we do in our work.

When new students question the relevance of philosophy, we ask them to read something out from a daily newspaper and we agree to stop when we reach a philosophical concept. We never get past the first paragraph. If we follow Grayling's lead, youth and community work *is* philosophy, for his concerns are our concerns.

However, philosophy demands that we are precise in our arguments, and analytical and questioning about the assumptions behind our ideas, including the very language we use. Otherwise we stumble along, imprecisely grasping at ideas, communicating at cross-purposes, and in danger of listening to rhetoric – ideas with resonance – but not reason. For without philosophy arguments can easily become sentiment, and sentiment is powerful.

Common sense?

Ideas can also become rigid if they buy into the idea of common sense. We are also in danger of reinforcing the oppressions we are meant to be challenging. If an idea is common sense, it is self-evident; we all agree on it and don't need to question it. That women should not be given the vote, that black people are genetically less intelligent and that different sexualities are inherently wrong have all been common sense ideas at some point in history. Common sense is socially constructed, a tale that a society tells itself, and convinces the people within that society to believe, to justify itself. If youth and community work is about challenging oppression and injustices it needs to challenge common sense, not re-enforce it. As Cooley (1987) says, we need to keep it on the run.

Philosophy for youth (and other people) workers

The aim of this book is to identify in what ways philosophy is relevant for youth and community workers. It explores how philosophical concepts are used, often without thinking, by practitioners in their daily practice. It intends to show how there is value in approaching our practice philosophically and in measured, careful thinking, that identifies and explores the assumptions behind our work. We believe that in doing so we will improve it. The book sets out how philosophy provides a series of questions that apply to youth work and its everyday practice.

As such, the primary audience for this book is youth and community workers, and people undertaking training to become youth and community workers who wish to grapple with ethical issues, to examine their value base and to explore the relevance of philosophical concepts in their work. It should be of use in a wider sense for anyone in the social care sector. It is not primarily intended for philosophers, or philosophy students, but for those who actively work with people – hence the title.

It will not cover all philosophical concepts, but will instead focus on how philosophy can be applied to everyday youth and community work practice. As such it is primarily concerned with people, because youth and community work is primarily concerned with people. Questions about the values we should hold in relating to each other, the nature of these relationships, and what it is to be a person in society, are the fundamental concerns of this book, as, we argue, they are the fundamental concerns of youth and community work. Underlying this, and primarily explored in the first chapter and the conclusion, is a philosophical concern about the nature of knowledge (epistemology), and questions that flow from this, such as who creates knowledge.

A different approach

There are already some publications that examine the relevance of philosophical issues for youth and community workers. The three that are closest to this publication are *Ethical Issues in Youth Work* by Sarah Banks, *The Art of Youth Work* by Kerry Young and a new publication *Ethics in Youth Work* by Jonathan Roberts. We would recommend the reader to look at these books, as our book complements them. Young's book attempts to answer the central questions of 'What is youth work?' and 'What do youth workers do?' We do not seek to explore or define a philosophy of youth work, although we will refer back to her work. Banks analyses some of the core ethical dilemmas facing youth workers in their day-to-day practice such as when to break confidentiality, the ethics of religious conversion, and conflicts between cultures, amongst others. Roberts also looks centrally at ethics and values and considers such issues as the establishment of organisations, the nature of neighbourhoods and networks, where professionals should site their practice within youth work's code of ethics (NYA, 2000) and work within complex and unpredictable contexts.

Our book is complementary to these publications, but has a fundamentally different approach. It explores how philosophical concepts and ways of thinking are pertinent to youth work, and more to the point, what the implications are for workers using these concepts on a daily basis, without necessarily having thought them through thoroughly. We draw on a wide variety of philosophical traditions and do not seek to develop, or push, a certain view, although the conclusion does seek to establish whether there is coherence in the sources we utilise.

Author philosophies

This book has two main authors: we have very different philosophical and political perspectives, and often did not agree when pulling together the ideas for the book. Pete Harris, who contributes to the chapter on conversation, has a different perspective again. However, one thing we do agree on is that knowledge is a dynamic thing, and needs this difference and these tensions to develop. Its dynamism enriches our practice and our theory.

Structure of the book

The structure of the book is based around a series of statements, or sound bites, that the authors have heard practitioners say on a daily basis. In our teaching they have proved to be useful starting points for examining philosophical issues, as opposed to systematically going through the thinking of particular philosophers. We find this a better way of allowing practitioners to see the relevance of philosophy in their everyday practice, and how philosophical concepts underpin the basis of their work. Such phrases include: 'we should be tolerant of others', 'I work in a democratic way', 'young people respect me', 'it's all about getting them to trust you', 'I just talk to young people' and 'we should treat everyone as an individual'. These statements are divided into three sections, focusing on the prime concerns outlined above, preceded by an introductory chapter looking at the privileging of common sense and anti-intellectualism in youth work, linking it to an exploration of our epistemology, and asking what the nature of the knowledge is that can be acquired without rigour and effort.

Simon, in the **first section**, looks at the values that we hold, as workers, regarding how people should relate to each other. It includes chapters on democracy, tolerance and fairness.

In the **second section** Mike will look at three philosophical concepts that underlie the nature of workers' relationships with young people and communities we work with and, by implication, the nature of the relationships young people and communities should have towards each other. This will include chapters on trust, respect and conversation.

The **third section** is slightly different in that it looks at youth and community work views about the world, and the people in it – in short the nature of self and society. It begins with a chapter on individualism and collectivism, looking at different ways of looking at the self and society, and building on previous work on democracy. The subsequent chapter builds on this by looking at autonomy, which is how individuals mediate themselves within communities.

The **final chapter**, which serves as a conclusion, will attempt to bring all these philosophical influences together to see if there is any coherence amongst them, and examines the tensions that arise.

The themes of the book

In the opening chapter of the book, building on this introduction, Mike will examine the accusation that youth and community work is anti-intellectual. He examines some of the dynamics of this anti-intellectual and anti-theoretical stance arguing that, while understandable, it undermines our professionalism. Mike then explores the alternative idea of the 'charismatic, natural worker', who is guided by their instinct for youth work and common sense, arguing again that such a construction often reinforces, rather than challenges, the status quo. To challenge this common sense, challenge oppression and facilitate change we have a duty to question all assumptions, including our own, in a systematic and analytical way, and encourage this facility in others, echoing Gramsci's (1971) idea of the organic intellectual. Finally Mike asks workers to make alliances with academics and theoreticians, as we have a duty to research and create our own models, theories and knowledge, to counter received wisdom that demonises young people and the communities that we work with.

In the first section Simon begins by exploring the concepts of *acceptance* and *tolerance*, considering the conditions that are necessary for tolerance to exist. He argues that tolerance is a more useful concept than acceptance as a way of guiding and explaining the way youth workers think and feel about young people. In building this argument he will consider questions such as how far we should tolerate the intolerant, and whether there are things which should never be tolerated. He will look at this in the context of how youth workers relate to young people, how young people relate to one another and how we relate as practitioners to our peers. Simon demystifies the idea that youth workers have some special gift that means they just 'accept young people for who they are'.

In the chapter on *democracy* Simon considers the different ways in which youth and community workers use the concept, arguing that we use it both as a set of values, and as a way of governing. He will argue that in invoking democracy we are invoking a number of values such as fairness, liberty, rights and so on. He will consider whether democracy is justified as a central value of youth work. Second, using examples from youth and community work practice, he will consider how we discuss, and model the question of who should govern. He will problematise democracy's claim that rule by the people is both the fairest and most effective way of governing in terms of benefiting society, examining ethical and philosophical arguments for others types of government. He argues that the principles and values that provide the necessary conditions of democracy are not exclusive to democracy.

The final chapter in this section, again by Simon, considers the concept of *fairness*, and specifically the fair treatment of young people. He contends that young people often use the idea of fairness when they feel they have been wronged in some way. In response to this commonly held concern by young people, he thinks two questions must be answered. First, what do we mean by fair treatment? And second, what can be done, if anything, to ensure young people are treated fairly? He also considers the idea of equality, seeing it as a separate concept, but one that is often intertwined with fairness, as they strengthen each other. He also considers different dimensions of equality, including equality of opportunity, but also equality of capability. He finishes by taking the debate wider and considering what makes for a 'fair' society, using Rawls' (1999) mechanism of the 'veil of ignorance', to further this debate.

In the second section Mike begins by examining the concept of *respect*. He makes a distinction between three close, but distinct, concepts: awe, a religious view of respect; Respekt (Feinburg, 1970) which is akin to inspiring or feeling fear (a type of respect that some young people he has worked with have sought, but which does not, ultimately, live up to expectations); and respect as generally understood. Confusion between the concepts is not unique to young people as he illustrates when arguing that current measures against those involved in the riots will at best, invoke Respekt, not respect. Importantly, Mike argues that to give respect – true respect – is both a subjective and an objective process and, as such, we can work with young people on defining it for themselves. Finally, he examines self-respect, arguing it to be the bedrock of respect from which respect for others stems. It is, however, a slippery concept, and easily confused with pride and self-esteem, which can have unfortunate consequences for individuals and for us all.

In the chapter on *trust*, Mike makes the argument that it is vital to youth and community workers, as we base our interactions around relationships, which need trust as their basis. Positively, he also argues that one of the unique aspects of youth work relationships is that they allow trust to flourish, including in its most powerful form, mutual trust. Mike asks five vital questions:

1. What is the nature of trust?
2. What is it to be considered trustworthy?
3. Is it reasonable, or a good idea, to trust others?
4. What is the value of trust?
5. How do we cultivate trust, as workers, with the young people and communities we work with?

In doing this he argues that the trust has been eroded in many care professions' relationships in the name of professional boundaries, and through a mechanised view of safeguarding; and that the same thing is in danger of happening in youth and community work – a trend we must counter. We also need to think carefully about trust because it is a slippery concept that is not always used precisely, or even ethically. Reflecting on his own practice, Mike looks at how trust as a concept can be abused, and seeks to outline how we can use it ethically.

In the chapter on *conversation* Mike explores the nature of conversation with a colleague from Newman University, Pete Harris, asking why workers privilege it as one of our primary means of engagement. First, we look at the nature of youth work conversations, something practitioners and authors such as Smith and Jeffs place great emphasis on, asking what we are trying to achieve by them. Second, we highlight why we privilege spontaneous conversation, as opposed to more formalised structures. Lastly, we explore how a youth and community worker develops the skills needed for these spontaneous conversations, as opposed to a reliance on stock responses, arguing that we have lessons to learn from jazz music, using improvisation as a metaphor for our practice.

In the third section's initial chapter Mike examines the concept of *the individual and the self*. He argues that we exist in a society that privileges individualism, and that youth and community workers often reinforce this social construction. Mike contends that from this privileging of the individual stem things that need to be contested: first, a moral stance that independence and self reliance are the highest virtues, as opposed to interdependence and collectivism; second, that individualism underpins many political initiatives and policy considerations for young people and communities that actually demonise them, blaming them for their situations; and third, the assumption that liberal capitalism, politically, and the market, economically, best serve the individual. Mike spends the bulk of the chapter exploring different conceptions of the individual and the self, from 'rugged individualism' to 'collectivism'. Mike takes the stance that youth and community work should be communitarian in orientation, seeing humans as best fulfilled through community, but he considers that we should also value the individual, and embrace notions explored in our first section, such as democracy, tolerance and autonomy, as checks on our collectivist tendencies.

Simon then further explores the concept of *autonomy*. Central to autonomy is the idea that we should be able to live our lives according to what we think is right rather than living under the authority of others, which is what makes this subject an important one. Autonomy relies on the concept of free will, and that we have the ability to reason, which obliges us to take responsibility in determining our actions. Simon considers these claims, and examines the components of autonomy and its alternatives such as coercion. He argues in the conclusion that autonomy should not be equated with rugged individualism, and is compatible with communitarianism. It should be considered as a feature of a collective exercise rather than purely as an act of self-governance.

The conclusion poses the question of whether there is any coherence in our philosophical influence, or whether we just cherry pick. We identify the different philosophical schools that influence youth and community work as humanism, Marxism, existentialism, phenomenology, post-modernist/post-structuralist/post-colonial theory, and feminism. We then identify and evaluate philosophical tensions that may exist between these schools. These tensions are essentialism vs inter-subjectivity, agency vs structure/determinism, utilitarianism vs virtue ethics vs deontological approaches, individualism vs collectivism, pragmatism vs idealism. We explain why we think there is coherence in our positions on these tensions, and that the tensions give us a healthy dynamism. This dynamism is compatible with the commonality between the schools, which is their epistemology, seeing knowledge as an evolving, inter-relational dynamic force between, and through, theory and practice. However we do take the stance that, ultimately, youth and community work is a communitarian project of the left.

CHAPTER 1

'Youth Work is Just Common Sense, You Just Have to Trust Your Instincts'

Mike Seal

The ahistorical, apolitical and anti-intellectual attitude of many in this area has meant that practice is peculiarly prone to influence by moral panics, fads and fashions. Lack of theory in the youth work literature reflects both a dominant anti-intellectualism within youth work and a reluctance to analyse, rather than just record, practice. Without a core theory based on real life experiences of practitioners there has been no base to which these acquisitions can be fixed.

Smith, 1988

As Smith indicates, youth work has a history of being anti-theory and anti-intellectual, with an accompanying emphasis on action. It is just something you do, and this 'doing' is almost on an instinctual level, something we cover elsewhere in the chapter on conversation. In academia there is also the clashing claim that we are not taken seriously as a profession and as a subject of study. As another manifestation of this, amongst youth and community work students I have encountered on my course, there is a common myth that we favour those who can 'write assignments', but can't necessarily 'do the work', and that good 'on the ground' practitioners do not always get through. I do not dispute that many experienced practitioners, particularly those who did not have a good first experience of education, struggle, initially, to do academic work in a way that those who have been through education successfully before do not. However, once the experienced workers gain their academic confidence, they start to shine. Those who can write, but not do, are the ones who flounder. Those who do best can do both practical and academic work. More to the point, when they combine reflection on practice and theory, as Gilmore (1991) notes, both academic work and practice improve. I am confident that those who get Firsts are also those who 'do' some of the best practice. I think youth work is a degree level enterprise – it takes that level of intellectual ability, and this is part of the claim I wish to make in this chapter. This is why once experienced practitioners are able to articulate themselves academically, they fly – because they are already functioning at that level. I am not saying you have to have a degree to be a good practitioner, but I am saying that a good practitioner is capable of getting a degree. I will also argue, later, that they should go and get a degree as developing their intellectual capability will in turn enable them to develop their practice more. Going through the process of getting a degree will make a good practitioner's practice better. The challenge is to create an environment where this flourishing can happen.

Yet the myth continues, and it is a myth I am, or at least was, a part of. I remember going to a conference of youth work lecturers. We were all bemoaning that we did not write and venting our frustration that many of those who did write about young people in academic circles had never worked with them. They were studying them as a phenomenon, not as people they had a relationship with. We talked about the prejudice of academia, whose voices are heard and privileged. However there was also quiet frustration at ourselves for not writing to counter this, in not developing an alternate voice. When we talked about why we were not doing it, we found we did not know where to start, or what to say, or how to say it, just that we knew something needed to be said. At the end of the conference I volunteered to write a piece about why youth work lecturers do not write, which of course, I did not end up writing. Years later I now write, but this took a long time, and I had to overcome many barriers, most of them in myself. I am dyslexic and so struggled at school. It was only years later, while I was qualifying that I encountered something that helped me understand my own reactions to this failure. I had already encountered the Gramscian concept of hegemony, whereby if you are told you are useless for long enough you believe it, but this did not quite fit. I knew I was not thick, despite my difficulties, although my confidence had taken a big knock.

Seligman's (1975) concept of 'learned helplessness' looks at how people react to continuous exposure to adverse events, in my case, as in many of our students, failing in education, and it spoke to me. Firstly he talks about 'permanency', i.e. *I failed this time therefore I will always fail*, which in the context of education became *My last experience of education was bad so this one is going to be*. Then he talks about 'universality' i.e. *I can't do this therefore I cannot do anything*. Interestingly for me, probably because I do have agency, this became externalised to *Some academic ideas are irrelevant therefore they are all irrelevant*, which again has resonance with many student reactions I encounter. Finally he talks about an internalisation/externalisation dynamic whereby one tends to say that *This is my fault/their fault*, rather than *This is something to be worked on together*. In educational terms it becomes *It is all the college's fault/my fault*, both of which I did, and both of which I hear regularly from students and which somewhat explains the dynamic of the lecturers at the conference I described earlier.

This chapter seeks to explore some of the dynamics of our anti-intellectualism, our anti-theoretical stance and the alternative cult of the 'born not bred' (Doyle and Smith, 1999) charismatic leader (Jeff and Smith, 1990). I will argue that this is an understandable, but dangerous, trend, and it both undermines our professionality and denies our history. Such a stance also, as Gilmore implies (1991), is in danger of re-enforcing rather than challenging the status quo. We have a duty to question all assumptions, including our own, in a systematic and analytical way. In fact this facility could be one of the things that is unique about youth work, particularly our ability to foster such abilities in others. Finally I will argue that we have a duty to research and create our own models, theories and knowledge, because if we do not, as we know, there are plenty who will do this in our stead. As Beizerman (1989) argues, we could and should do better, as this is part of what it is to be taken seriously. However before all this I wish to look at the nature of anti-intellectualism, to consider how it manifests in youth workers and to see if it has any validity.

Anti-intellectualism and youth work

Sowell (2010) defines anti-intellectualism in terms of a mistrust of 'intellect, intellectuals and intellectual persuits':

> *Anti-intellectuals usually perceive and publicly present themselves as champions of the common folk – populists against political elitism and academic elitism – proposing that the educated are a social class detached from the everyday concerns of the majority, and that they dominate political discourse and higher education.*
>
> Sowell, 2010

I can see these views in youth workers, as I can see them in myself. Most of the students who come on the course are working class, and the majority have had bad previous experiences of education. Many express views that this bad experience was compounded by tutors and teachers who either did not understand them or did not believe in them. Sowell's views therefore seem to have some truth in them. Going right back to Willis's work in the late seventies (1981) the question is whether the education system is there to deliver the liberal education it often espouses to, or to get working class people ready for working class jobs without questioning this end. More recent work by Evans (2007) and Archer (2003) says this persists, with working class young people still feeling that university is 'not for the likes of us'. When combined with factors like gender and race (the majority of our students being women and black) the exclusion increases exponentially (Perry & Francis, 2010). Recent reports (Pollard et al., 2004) have shown that the New Labour mantra of 'raising aspirations' was most successful for middle class, not working class, families in encouraging entry into higher education. Saddeningly, these same reports have shown that even those working class students who do go to university are still less likely to get a decent job at the end of it. Interestingly these studies talk about how universities are middle (and upper class) culturally as well as demographically, particularly the elite universities. Their rituals, particularly in the elite universities, from exam protocols to tutorial structures to formal dinners, are closer to public school culture than that of state schools, and working class people have a choice of 'standing out', only partially accepting their student status, and consequently getting worse results, or 'fitting in' (Reay, Crosier and Clayton, 2010) and leading a double life, one at home and another at university, or abandoning their roots.

Indeed as a subject, Youth and Community Work reflects this sense of unease, of not fitting in. It has been decidedly ambiguous about where it sits within academia, both structurally in where it is situated, but also in how lecturers within it self-identify. It is almost exclusively taught at post 1992 institutions. Indeed the exceptions at Brunel, Birmingham and Durham have all recently closed down or are in the process of doing so. I talked earlier about the conference with colleagues. The group is called TAG and has only recently changed its name to the Professional Association of Lecturers in Youth and Community Work in Higher Education. TAG stood for Training Agencies Group, revealing how we identify, not as academics, but trainers of workers – deceiving ourselves that we are not that far from practice, as this is where we really belong – and the 'not fitting in' perspective seems to pervade. I have no doubt that this filters down to the messages I give students, both in terms of my own identity, my teaching, and the culture I try to foster. When I taught at the YMCA George Williams College our students graduated through Canterbury Christ Church University and their ceremony was held at Canterbury Cathedral, a place which could be considered elite, or certainly establishment. I remember taking pride in the 'difference' of our students. Before us came primary education whose graduates were almost exclusively young, white women, and I used to sit through a sea of them coming up to graduate. When our subject was called, and the students walked up, the difference was palpable in terms of age, race and background, and I took pride in not fitting in. In inter-departmental meetings when youth work students are mentioned, it is often in their difference from other students, and I take pride in this, and relay these sentiments back to students. So workers are trained in less academic institutions by reluctant lecturers – our own culture may well be one that reinforces anti-intellectual views.

So we can perhaps accept that there is something about universities that is elitist, culturally middle class, and hence re-enforces the power structures that this represents. There is also the charge that the academic world is distant from the views of the majority and wields unfair power – beyond the class dimensions noted. Sowell suggests 'intellectuals have few disincentives for speaking outside their expertise, and are less likely to face the consequences of their errors'. Is this a fair accusation? As a way of framing this I will consider two concepts, indeed holy cows, of academia – 'academic freedom' and 'peer review'. Academic freedom is defined by the AFAF (Academics for Academic Freedom – a UK based campaign group) in its founding principles as:

1. That academics, both inside and outside the classroom, have unrestricted liberty to question and test received wisdom and to put forward controversial and unpopular opinions, whether or not these are deemed offensive.

2. That academic institutions have no right to curb the exercise of this freedom by members of their staff, or to use it as grounds for disciplinary action or dismissal.

Indeed these rights are embodied in the 1988 Education Reform act. These are hard won rights that are in continual danger of being eroded (UCU, 2009) and are intended to stop political and commercial pressure from determining what research can be conducted and published. While censorship is of prime concern here, there are also indirect impacts of things like the Research Excellence Framework (REF) which determines which institutions or departments are funded to conduct research. Of particular concern has been the introduction of 'social impact' as a criterion, which some see as a curtailment of academic freedom with governmental and political definitions of what constitutes this 'social impact' dominating (UCU, 2009). Although others may see the academics' communities reaction as evidence of their wish to be distant from the society in which they live.

However there have been a number of academics who have invoked academic freedom to defend views which are contradictory to youth and community work values. Dr Satoshi Kanazawa at the LSE has a history of producing research relating to the IQ levels of black people and their 'attractiveness'. Similarly St Andrews recently appointed Roger Scruton, a moral philosopher, who has argued in several books that homosexuality is 'not normal'. There have also been a variety of historians who deny the Holocaust, such as David Irving, who still speaks at universities. Without wanting to repeat Simon's arguments in the chapter about tolerance, there would seem to be a question about the degree to which we tolerate the presence of such opinions. LGBT groups have worried about the power that Scruton's presence will have in putting off LGBT students from studying philosophy at St Andrews, despite the institution's assurances that he will have to abide by their diversity policy. Hopefully there are enough mechanisms in place to reassure students and allow for academic debate. Two other debates come to mind. First, the degree to which research still has to be valid and second, the degree to which one can speak outside of one's own subject.

In America there has been an interesting debate around the idea of intelligent design (ID). This theory believes that 'certain features of the universe and of living things are best explained by an intelligent cause, not an undirected process such as natural selection' (Padian and Matzke, 2009), i.e. that evolution cannot explain our development completely. Proponents say that alternatives to evolution need to be taught in schools and universities in the name of academic freedom. However opponents say that ID is simply creationism-lite. They state that the overwhelming evidence is that it is not a sound theory, with the few published articles on it not standing up to scientific scrutiny, as they are being published by religiously biased authors, and in some cases in biased publications. Debates centre on whether the view is just controversial, and should be defended, or whether it is simply wrong. In

America a number of 'academic freedom' bills have appeared in state legislatures on the basis on ID's claims. To date only one bill has been passed in Louisiana.

So it seems that academic freedom may need to extend quite far, but there are limits, normally of method. Controversial ideas can be defended, but this must be done so rigorously. Who then will ensure this rigour? Traditionally most new academic knowledge is produced in journals that are peer reviewed, i.e. your academic peers ensure that your claims have validity and can be substantiated. Funding and status for researchers in the UK is largely determined by how much you are published in such journals. Yet how rigorous is it? Rennie et al., at a conference in 2003, commented:

> There seems to be no study too fragmented, no hypothesis too trivial, no literature too biased or too egotistical, no design too warped, no methodology too bungled, no presentation of results too inaccurate, too obscure, and too contradictory, no analysis too self-serving, no argument too circular, no conclusions too trifling or too unjustified, and no grammar and syntax too offensive for a paper to end up in print.

This would seem a little harsh given that a recent study (Bornmann et al., 2010) showed that around 50% of articles are rejected. However the same study showed that the consistency between feedback from reviewers (most journals have two reviewers for each article) is very low. Whether you are accepted for a journal may well be dependent on whether you are pleasing to your individual reviewers, but also on how many potential articles have been submitted that month for that particular journal. Other authors question whether peer reviewers actually pick up on errors, or ensure quality of methods (Jefferson et al., 2002, 2007). Others have criticised the peer review process for suppressing non mainstream knowledge, and being overly conservative (Martin, 1997; Campanario, 2004) although some of these accusations have come from the aforementioned supporters of intelligent design. A recent report (Ware, 2008) found that despite it faults, most academics valued it and found reviewers' comments improved their pieces. The question remains as to whether youth workers and the wider public should value it, and believe that it is an accurate mechanism for testing knowledge. An interesting comparison, and a source regularly used by many of my students, and even myself, is Wikipedia. Many universities advise against it as a source and have even banned it. Wikipedia is an open editing source, meaning anyone can edit anyone else's posting, so inaccurate information can be put up there, but it relies on the community, including the academic community, to re-edit this. Interestingly several studies (Leithner et al., 2010; Clauson & Polen, 2008; Reavley at al., 2012) have found Wikipedia's articles to compare favourably with peer reviewed articles in terms of accuracy. Giles in 2005 found that its entries were as accurate as the *Encyclopaedia Britannica*, and has defended this finding since. Interestingly in its own guidance on using itself as an academic source (http://en.wikipedia.org/wiki/Wikipedia:Academic_use) Wikipedia recommends that it should be seen only as a starting point, as should any encyclopaedia, and that students should still evaluate the sources of the article – this would seem to be valuable advice for reading any article, even those that are academically peer reviewed.

How about Sowell's claim about academics speaking outside of their area and having undue influence? Authors such as Carey (1992) and Johnson (1988), examining the number of intellectual figures in the 20th Century history, discuss how intellectuals have championed innumerable disastrous public policies beyond their expertise. However, their claims have been disputed (Collini, 2006) as being over claimed, personal attacks and biased against left wing thinkers, belying a conservative anti-intellectualism, and a covert attack on left wing ideological views. Collini finds in British intellectual life the opposite. He notes a publicly espoused British pragmatism that does not trust intellectualism, rejecting the 'intellectual as rock star' of such continental figures as Foucault, Marcuse and Sartre. Ironically Collini traces a strong intellectual tradition, British pragmatism having origins in Hume, but one that the intellectuals deny. Outside of Britain there is a larger tradition, and valuing of the intellectual, and speaking outside of their 'subject', is seen positively.

For Bourdieu (1989) and Burawoy (2005), public intellectuals bridge the gap between academia and public debate, and were more accountable and in touch because 'participation in open, contemporary public debate separates intellectuals from academics; by venturing from academic specialism to address the public, the academic becomes a public intellectual'. Other authors feel that they should not be bound by a 'partial preoccupation of one's own profession' (Furedi, 2004: 23). For Furedi this was something to be 'risen above' in order to 'engage with the global issues of truth, judgement, and taste of the time'. For Bourdieu (1977), it is essential in a democracy for the public intellectual to be 'independent of those in power'. They were to be 'critical of received ideas, demolishers of "simplistic either-ors" and respecters of "the complexity of problems" . . . to raise embarrassing questions, to confront orthodoxy and dogma, to be someone who cannot easily be co-opted by governments or corporations' (Bourdieu, 1977). There is, however, another tradition going back to Socrates: rejection of the Sophist idea of a public market place of ideas, that is prevalent in the modern thinking of people like Collini (2006) and Bender (1993). For them, for academics to engage in public debates would entail an inevitable dumbing down of their academic rigour, and they should indeed retreat from it, Bender distinguishing between a professional sphere of knowledge and a civic one. Another question is who should become such 'public intellectuals'. For authors such Furedi (2004) and Collini (2006), they need to achieve 'success' either academically or creatively, and then use the media to engage in wider public debate. Again, for academics we can see how this is class bound, and Bourdieu (1977) and others (Anyon, 1981) have written about how creativity, or creative capital, is similarly class bound, at least in terms of who is successful and makes a career out of it. Others, such as Posner (2002), still feel that insufficient attention is given to how transferable the skills of analysis for, say, a scientist, are to engage in social science debates, or even those from a moral philosophy background to social policy debates. He worries it makes 'their declarations untidy and biased in ways which would not be tolerated in their academic work'. (Posner, 2002: 43). He also thinks that the debates they are allowed to engage in are narrow – proclamations on social policy – rather than wider moral, ethical and political issues. Public intellectuals have been co-opted rather than having their independent status affirmed.

It seems then that there is a wide debate about the role and definition of the intellectual and the academic, whether they are and should be aloof, what constitutes their knowledge and whether they should be seen as valid in going beyond their own knowledge base. However, ultimately I am not making a plea to reclaim the intellectual, be they public or academic. I would agree with Bourdieu (1977) that there is a need for independent critique of government, its institutions, and simplistic binary public concepts such as immigrant/indigenous, deserving/undeserving etc. However I think there is inherent danger in this critique residing in any elite, as individuals can be bought off or silenced in other ways. The challenge is to develop these critical facilities in all, or at least many, and this seems to me to be part of the youth and community work project.

The impact of anti-intellectualism: the cult of the natural and the charismatic

The question arises as to how youth and community work's anti-intellectualism manifests and what its impact is. Smith (1989: 124) notes 'a cult of the natural and the emphasis on the charismatic'. In conversations with students, practitioners and colleagues I often encounter the aforementioned idea that youth workers are somehow born to it, not that their skills cannot be honed, but that there is a level where you can either intrinsically do it or not. This seems to be an aspect of this 'cult of the natural', the charismatic element meaning that youth work is about personalities and that much of the work is instinctual. While I have some sympathies with the view, I also see dangers in it in a number of ways. Firstly it can lead to unsolvable conflict when two workers who both claim to be working instinctually have no ways of resolving differences of approach. A number of years ago I conducted a piece of research into inter-colleague conflict in youth and community work setting. An interesting characteristic of the conflict, particularly more entrenched conflict, was that workers made claims to just 'know' the needs of their young people, echoing this instinctual view. In the research, to have the best interests of the young people at heart was a common claim of both parties involved in disputes. Workers seem to be resorting to the magical, in that they somehow, through experience or intuition, embody the needs and desires of young people and possess the appropriate methods of actualising them.

As Smith (1989) says, 'within informal education there is a tendency for personality, individual skills and motivation to be emphasised and for other elements to be overlooked'. There is traditionally a lot of emphasis placed on values in this work, which is good, but the important thing is how these values are mediated. Smith (2001) notes that many informal educators do not like to have criteria for good practice in their work, seeing it as restricting. Historically practitioners have resisted things like the development of occupational standards or codes of conduct. I do not think this necessarily a tactic of avoidance, or even a manifestation of anti-intellectualism, but a philosophical standpoint avoiding some of the tendencies of some care professions to try to pin down, quantify, and hence restrict practice (Everitt, 1995), embodied in debates around evidence based practice (Trinder, 2000). In the absence of some common criteria for what constitutes good practice, and to avoid falling into individualism and relativism, practitioners have often turned to the idea of reflective practice (Schon, 1987) as a tool for examining their practice:

> *Practice is developed through sustained and critical reflection upon intervention. This, in turn, contributes to the building and maintenance of a body of theory consistent with informed action and analysis of practice.*
>
> Jeffs and Smith, 1990

However, reflective practice is not without its critics, as we shall explore in greater depth in the chapter on conversation. Eraut (2007) questions the relationship between reflection in and on action, asking whether we can really cognitively distil and recall our previous reflections, almost instantaneously. Similarly Richardson (1990) talks of practitioners that are all reflection and no action, questioning whether reflection actually helps you work out what you need to get done, or whether they are separate processes. Wenger (1999) feels reflection is over rational; for him we engage in communities of practice where we can articulate and rationalise everything we do, and instead he believes in a longer process of a worker becoming en-cultured into a community of practice's 'ways' of doing things.

Youth workers can embrace this, but in a negative sense, with the common phrase that other professions do not 'get' us, but that you can 'always tell another youth worker' who somehow does. However the emphasis on the charismatic and instinctual is different from, and more dangerous than, Wenger's idea of a community of practice. For him professionals serve an apprenticeship where we learn our communities' practices, and everyone has the potential to do this. For youth work, that apprenticeship is instantaneous: you are in or you are out. You may be able to hone your skills, but you either fundamentally get it or you don't. In this context our over-, and sometimes sole, reliance on reflective practice is a bit of a chimera. What it certainly does not do is give us a steer when there is a dispute over practice, apart from a naive view that if the practitioners keep reflecting long enough they will somehow reach a compromise. Compounded with a cult of the charismatic, an emphasis on instinct, and in the absence of any common criteria, practitioners only have faith in themselves to fall back on. If you are wrong then your identity as a youth worker becomes threatened. In this context reflection can become a dangerous thing. There are other dangers to such a construction. In our research some workers, holding the conviction that they embodied the view of young people, were willing to be potentially unethical to achieve young people's interests. Some were prepared to use the methodology of informal education negatively to convince others of this:

> I will try to win them around to my point of view and make them see the way it should be done rather then me say 'listen I have worked in these places for years and I am telling you what is going to happen'.

Such charismatic management can also be autocratic, undemocratic, and even manipulative. One worker in the research stopped using their manager because, as above, when they went into a meeting with them, even when they were very sure of their point, they were persuaded in the moment, but then later, outside that person's influence, thought they were right after all. Ironically, where management is not charismatic, it can be seen as somehow lacking. One newly appointed manager in the research said:

> There is an expectation of the manager, they have to be very assertive, powerful whatever. I don't think I fit the image that they expected.

Doyle and Smith (1999) in their book *Born or Bred* talk about the dangers of charismatic leadership. They do not deny its usefulness, that in times of crisis or pain, we look to leaders who are 'strong' and can alleviate this pain (Gerth and Mills, 1991: 51–5). Ultimately, however, it is a deficit model: we ask such leaders to take responsibility when we cannot do this for ourselves. This then sets up a dynamic whereby they need us to not take responsibility, and remain dependant on them, to maintain their leadership. Interestingly they also talk about how ultimately we always turn against such leaders. I would ask practitioners to think about the projects they have worked with, and known, which have been run by such a charismatic leader, who has done well and had the loyalty of the workers, right up until the point where they do not. I have written elsewhere about the contradictory views workers have about what constitutes an effective manager (Seal, 2009). However, I think it stems from the instinctual model we have of workers – we need to change our cult of the natural and instinctual.

Youth workers: the organic intellectuals?

A second worry I have in seeing the work as instinctual, and being anti-intellectual, is that it underestimates the critical facilities we need to be effective youth workers. It says that to challenge, and question, received wisdom only comes naturally to a select few, and by instinct feels somehow wrong and elitist, and it underestimates the analytical skill that needs to be brought to the fore. Gilmore calls into question the idea of instinct:

> *What we label as 'natural' or 'intuitive' is frequently nothing of the sort; rather, it is the interaction, at a largely non-conscious level, of our critical faculties with the environments and behaviours we encounter. Effective interventions and actions arise from well-developed understanding and analysis.*
>
> Gilmore, 1991

A useful concept to introduce here is Gramsci's concept of 'hegemony'. He built on, and to a degree challenged, Marx's idea of class conflict. He tried to answer why Italian rural peasants voted fascist and conservative – against their class interests. For him any state cannot rely on coercion alone – it needs to persuade and 'manufacture consent' (Herman and Chomsky, 1988) as much as it uses raw power. Certain values, attitudes, beliefs and morality needed to be perpetuated, through culture, education, media and even industrial relations that support the status quo, and the interests of the ruling class. This view of society, and how things work, are portrayed as normal, obvious and common sense. As Boggs (1976: 36) puts it 'this prevailing consciousness is internalised by the population. It becomes part of what is generally called "common sense" '. The philosophy, culture and morality of the ruling elite comes to appear as the natural order of things. To challenge this common sense, following Gramsci, means unlearning a lot of what we 'know', and almost by definition will not come 'naturally'. If challenging the 'norm' just came instinctually, and through common sense, by definition hegemony would not be working well – which it is. Gilmore argues that youth work policy, youth workers' understandings of the work, and even young people, are socially constructed within an ideological context and we have a duty to develop and challenge our understandings as youth workers. We are complicit, and 'unless we investigate and interrogate it we are a part of maintaining that context'. Similarly in the United States, where there is no standard qualification for youth workers, Michael Baizerman (1989) makes a plea for training for workers, for the creation of a counter hegemonic space:

> *Directed at developing the skills necessary to pierce one's taken-for-granted, ordinary, mundane life so that one becomes aware of how the ordinary is*

constructed and how one is implicated in constructing one's own reality. Joining this skill to awareness of how one's biography pre-forms the present gives the youth worker the possibility of seeing in the moment its manifold possibilities, not simply what is there.

Baizerman, 1989: 3

For Baizerman then, the hegemony we are subject to extends to our own view of ourselves, our very identity and biographies. On our course, the first module we do, before we get people to look at youth works concepts and principles, is for people to interrogate their own value bases and senses of self, and this continues for the whole three years. This would concur with Baizerman's view, who thinks training for youth workers should focus on *unlearning* a wide variety of cultural, taken-for-granted, hence invisible, ways of seeing and thinking so as to be able to perceive the world in its 'uniqueness, similarity, normalcy and possibility' (Baizerman, 1989: 2). He is also quite clear that this is a necessary process: 'This type of unlearning is necessary before the youth worker can be an educator of youth' (ibid.: 2). To do this workers will need to see themselves as intellectuals, not neccesarily in an 'academic' sense, but in an 'organic' Gramscian sense, which he sees as a way of the oppressed challenging the hegemony to which they are subject. He has an interesting view on the 'intellectual':

All men are intellectuals, everyone carries on some form of intellectual activity, participates in a particular conception of the world, has a conscious line of moral conduct, and therefore contributes to sustain a conception of the world or to modify it, that is, to bring into being new modes of thought . . . but not all men have in society the function of intellectuals.

ibid.: 2

Similarly for Gramsci (1971), we are all intellectuals, or rather we all have the capacity for abstract conceptual thought. However, as Gramsci notes it is not a capacity we all cultivate 'while everyone at some time fries a couple of eggs or sews up a tear in a jacket, we do not necessarily say that everyone is a cook or a tailor' (Gramsci, 1971: 34). 'Organic intellectuals' are produced within a particular class, and are a strata that 'gives it meaning, that helps to bind it together and helps it function' (Burke, 1999, 2005). As such they represent those class interests, but also understand its needs and its culture. As Gramsci (1971) notes, such organic intellectuals do not simply describe social life in accordance with scientific rules, but rather articulate, through the language of culture, the feelings and experiences which the masses could not express for themselves. Gramsci also made a distinction between traditional and organic intellectuals. For him the 'traditional' intellectuals are the academics, the lecturers, the clergy, doctors etc, who have a claim on knowledge, and, echoing the earlier discussion about public intellectuals, also claim to be independent from the state and potentially critical of it. But, for Gramsci, they are inherently a part of it, reliant upon it, and, ultimately, serve its interests. While organic intellectuals from the ruling class will act to service and maintain a culture that sustains the status quo, those from the working class have the potential to develop a questioning counter hegemony.

Herein lies the potential for youth workers. Several authors make the plea for workers to see themselves as organic intellectuals (Spence, 2009; Dickson, 2005; Smith, 1988; Grattan & Morgan, 2008). Grattan and Morgan (2008), writing in the context of post conflict Northern Ireland felt youth workers were in a unique position 'to motivate their respective communities through their ability to understand and articulate the prevailing dominant 'commonsense philosophy' and world view'. Smith saw the organic intellectual as a concept and alternative to professionalism as a concept through which to define ourselves, a point of resistance. However, as Spence (2009) notes, it is easy to deceive oneself about what class we are representing and speaking for – it is easy to become colonised, especially in the mind. At the current moment the youth work base is being attacked physically by cuts and philosophically with the undermining of the principles of non targetting, voluntarism and an educational value base. The eternal debate rages about whether we should go or stay. Many choose to stay, to achieve the best one can for the young people, and this is a valid position, but when does it become collusion? On the other hand there is the danger of leaving and becoming a rhetorical radical (Alinsky, 1971) – principled, but ineffectual. As Alinsky says, 'he who sacrifices the mass good for his personal conscience has a peculiar conception of 'personal salvation'; he doesn't care enough for people to 'be corrupted' for them' (Alinsky, 1971: 25). Perhaps most insidious are the 'fifth columnists', the self styled radicals just waiting for their moment 'to bring things down from the inside', where each action against one's principles becomes constructed as one getting 'further inside', while the 'moment' acquires messianic qualities, receding into a myth of self deception, a beacon of false hope. I like Spence's (2009) notion that we need to constantly check each action to see if it still speaks for who we think it does. We need to constantly ask ourselves 'in whose interests is this piece of policy, this administrative task, this proposed practice etc . . .'

Perhaps a way through this is offered by Baizerman who offers another interesting justification for training and the developing of workers' intellectualism. He offers some interesting insights into what we might be trying to achieve in the moment with young people, something which is in itself under-theorised. To call our work instinctual rather than intellectual does not allow us to interrogate what, and how, we are actually trying to create in those moments of clarity with young people (on both sides), and instead mystifies it. What we are creating in those moments becomes undefinable, explained as just having 'known' you have got through to a young person. He sees those moments as developing organic intellectual capabilites in young people. He sees youth work as 'a facilitating process in which an individual penetrates this taken-for-granted reality and, by so doing, comes to understand how reality for her is constructed' (Baizerman, 1989: 1). As discussed before, he couches this in existential terms, seeing these moments as the ones where we have real choice and have true freedom. He is existentialist in the sense that he views that humans, through their own consciousness and will, create their own values and determine a meaning in their lives. He sees it as our duty to help people separate their perceptions, apperceptions, historicism and biography to 'perceive the world in its uniqueness, similarity, normalcy and possibility'. There are similarities here to Freire's notion of conscientization.

Conclusion: developing an intellectual alliance

Interestingly though, Baizerman also argues that it is unfair to expect youth workers to develop theory, as 'they are too busy working', and to blame them is again a social construction that serves to undervalue youth and community workers. For her, this absence of grounded theory is where anti-intellectualism stems from:

The whole process of theory development often ensures that those theories to be used in practice are developed by experts who in turn have separated their processes from those of the practitioner, hence the valid concern that they do not serve those whom they were designed to assist.

Ledwith, 2007: 9

In my view we need training for workers, to create a space, which a degree course has the potential to do, to develop a counter hegemony, but also to develop an alliance between workers and youth work academics, so that we can create the theory that matches the realities, or potential realities of workers and young people. For too long research has been seen as something that other academics do – we need to do it ourselves. One of the things I have found heartening about moving to a degree qualification is that honours students have to engage in 'real' research. Many start off seeing this as irrelevant, but go on to see that it is a vital part of our work, or building our community of practice, and that what they have to say is to be shared, rather than just seen by a few tutors. Most importantly we need to involve practitioners, and young people, and help them see that knowledge creation is something we can, and should, all engage in:

If we fail to generate theory in action, and move towards a unity of praxis where theory and practice are synthesised, we give way to anti-intellectual times which emphasise 'doing' at the expense of 'thinking'; we react to the symptoms rather than root causes of injustice – and leave the structures of discrimination intact.

Ledwith, 2007: 10

Furthermore it is one of our essential roles to encourage this in others, to see academia as something for all, and to develop the next generation of organic intellectuals. A friend of mine is active in community philosophy, which works with communities, using philosophy, to help them debate and engage in issues of common concern to them. I will leave you with its aims, as I think it challenges workers to embrace philosophy, and rigorous thinking, as essential tools in their work. Community Philosophy aims are:

- *To support the practice of Community Philosophy through developing self-determining and self-sustaining democratic communities of philosophical enquiry and action.*
- *To help individuals and communities develop philosophical enquiry as a practical tool for engagement and action in community and cultural life.*
- *To promote the creative, collaborative and caring aspects of philosophical enquiry, whilst developing critical, independent and reflective thinking.*
- *To make philosophy an accessible, purposeful and pleasurable means to the promotion of personal and community well-being.*

                                          http://www.sapere.org.uk/Default.aspx?tabid=102

SECTION ONE

CHAPTER 2

'We Should All Learn to Accept Each Other'

Simon Frost

This chapter is primarily concerned with the idea of tolerance. Its Latin root actually means 'to suffer', which at first glance doesn't sound that attractive. However as we start to explore the paradoxes and tensions about the idea of tolerance in a practice sense we should begin to see how this contested virtue adds value to our understanding about the way as professional youth workers we relate to others.

To begin this chapter we will attempt to understand the concept of tolerance whilst considering the conditions necessary for tolerance to exist. As we unravel the concept of tolerance we will look further at such questions as how far should we tolerate the intolerant, or whether there are things which should never be tolerated. Whilst initially we will focus on the attitude of youth workers towards young people, the significance of tolerance in youth work is not limited to this set of relationships. The way in which young people relate to one another individually and in groups also provides a useful context in which to think about tolerance. As well as in our work with young people, tolerance can help us to understand the way we relate as practitioners to our peers. By the end of this chapter I hope to demystify the idea that youth workers have some special gift that means they just accept young people for who they are. I want to use this chapter to suggest that the way youth workers think and feel about young people is hinged less on the principle of acceptance and more on the principle of tolerance. What do you think?

Acceptance

Before I start to talk about tolerance I would like to give a little bit of space to the idea of acceptance. There are many reasons for acceptance. What we like, how something makes us feel, a sense of connectedness or appreciation are all good reasons for acceptance. Acceptance is the relationship between what we think and how we feel about a particular state of affairs. Let's apply this idea to young people. One way or another young people you are working with present a particular state of affairs. It could be that they are happy, they have a sense of purpose, they are progressing happily through life. The way we feel about this state of affairs is likely to positive. We might then say that we are able to accept this particular state of affairs. In contrast a young person might be unhappy, rude, aggressive or violent. This would be a harder state of affairs to accept. Based on values of human dignity, flourishing and well-being, it would be difficult to wish this state of affairs on anybody.

The difficulty with the idea that we should accept young people for who they are is that in reality young people are often a range of things, happy, sad, up, down, enthused, demotivated and so on. On the premise that young people represent a range of states, the idea that we should accept young people for who they are implies that regardless of the state of affairs young people find themselves in, they need to be accepted.

One way of understanding what it is that is being accepted or not is to make a distinction between the young person as a human being and their state of affairs. For example we could say we do not accept the situation the young person finds themselves in but we accept the young person anyway. What we see here is an attempt to separate out the young person from their state of affairs, an abstraction that in some way provides us with a pure individual isolated from social influence (Downie and Telfer, 1969). Is who we are then, or indeed who young people are in terms of their feelings, identity and experiences in some way separate from the true young person? You may be familiar with the Christian doctrine, 'love the sinner, not the sin'. It's a similar principle of abstraction; it is the person that is to be valued, rather than their behaviour.

In my experience of working with youth and community workers there is a voice of advocacy that wants to encourage young people, not vilify them. We know that the period of adolescence is one of change and challenges, in terms of physical, cognitive, spiritual, cultural and emotional development. This in itself can create tensions both for the young person within themselves and those they interact with. The constant challenging of authority, apathy, moods, constant vying for status, dissidence and rebellion are just some of the behaviours that many adults find challenging about young people. Yet as youth workers we say we accept young people.

Herein we need to consider both the things we accept about young people and the things we don't accept about young people. To do this though we have to think about the young person as a whole, not as someone who can be abstracted from their state of affairs so that they can be accepted. As unsettling as it might seem I want you to consider the argument that youth workers tolerate young people more than they accept young people. You might not agree with me here, after all how often do you hear a youth worker saying we just need to tolerate young people? This is fair point, however under closer scrutiny the concept of tolerance requires us to be able to accept and at the same time reject or challenge someone without having to necessarily separate out the individual from their state of affairs.

What is tolerance?

In talking about tolerance we are admitting that there are things about ourselves and others that we do not like, we do not accept, we do not appreciate; otherwise there would be no need to tolerate.

There are those who would argue that tolerance is not the right approach. In many lists of virtues tolerance does not appear. There are also those who argue that love or compassion is more important. Try typing in the words tolerance and virtue into the search engine on your computer and see just how many internet sites are dedicated to discussing whether or not tolerance is a desirable trait or character. For now I want us to give space to the idea of tolerance as a virtue; that is a good characteristic or trait. Aristotle talked about virtues as being the means between the excess of our desires. For example the virtue of courage is somewhere between being cowardly and foolish. The mean is somewhere between the two, in this case a sort of reasoned bravery that prevents you from acting recklessly but at the same time means you shouldn't run away, you need to do something. The same principle can be applied to tolerance. At one extreme is the attitude of indifference, not caring and at the other end is the idea of non-acceptance, single mindedness. Somewhere in between is the point of tolerance where the willingness to suffer for positive reasons starts to outweigh reasons for not being prepared to suffer.

The word *tolerance* itself is derived from the Latin word *tolerare* which means to suffer or to put up with. If we think about the idea a bit more we might say that there are certain conditions that need to be fulfilled for tolerance to exist. Firstly in the absence of any objection we do not need to tolerate. The reason for tolerance is that we object to something that is bad or wrong in some way (Forst, 2012). Objection needs to be balanced by acceptance. This is the point where the reasons for accepting the person are more important than for objecting to the person, for example with the subject of religious belief we might say that respect for human beings and the right to choose is more important than their religious beliefs (Forst, 2012). There is however a point at which it is not possible to tolerate another. Again the example of religious belief is helpful here. Firstly we may choose to tolerate a belief that is different from our own out of respect for an individual to choose, but if that religion includes acts of violence and abuse we would probably say that the reasons for rejection are now stronger than the reasons for acceptance (Forst, 2012).

The importance of tolerance

There is an argument that we should not force people to think in a particular way. The kernel of this perspective lies in an emphasis on freedom of thought. One such philosopher who believed we should not tell people what they must think was Spinoza (Forst, 2012). As a Jew living in Holland, Spinoza came into contact with free thinking faith perspectives in the form of Protestantism which finally led to his excommunication from the Jewish faith. Spinoza thought that it is not possible to stop people from thinking in a particular way or holding certain beliefs; moreover the state should focus on curtailing behaviour and actions rather than controlling thought; we have a natural right to freedom of thought (Forst, 2012). Similarly albeit in the context of religious belief Locke (Forst, 2012) believed that (religious) belief could not be coerced. If we accept the principle that we should not make people think in a certain way then there is a greater need for tolerance.

Let's imagine then a practice example. Imagine a young person is expressing racist views. What do you do? Should you tell the young person what they should think, or is the right to be able to think freely of greater value? It is one thing to say people are free to think what they like, but to say that they should also be able to express their views is another matter. In *On Liberty* (Mill, 1985), the philosopher Mill argues that both freedom of thought and freedom of expression are required in pursuit of truth. To stop people from expressing their views, however objectionable, is to prevent the pursuit of truth 'if any opinion is compelled to silence, that opinion may, for aught we can certainly know, be true. To deny this is to assume our own infallibility' (Mill, 1985: 115).

For Mill, to suppress freedom of expression assumes we are both right and infallible, however if we allow for freedom of expression we are in a position to justify and defend that which we find objectionable in the first place. In other words if we suppress the voice of young people we miss an opportunity to engage with and defend against the voice of young people when necessary.

Whilst philosophy attempts to justify tolerance as an important component of liberal society, there is another argument that we should reserve the right not to tolerate the intolerant. This is expressed in the writing of Popper when he states:

> *If we extend unlimited tolerance even to those who are intolerant, if we are not prepared to defend a tolerant society against the onslaught of the intolerant, then the tolerant will be destroyed, and tolerance with them.*

> Popper, 1966: 166

Popper was concerned that we should not tolerate the intolerable because eventually the intolerable would take over; moreover a society should have the right in the name of tolerance not to tolerate the intolerant.

In the previous example of working with the young person who expresses racist views you might decide that the young person needs to be warned about their behaviour, being told that their behaviour is not acceptable; there are no grounds for accepting this particular type of behaviour, thus exercising your right not to tolerate the intolerable. At this point work with the young person reaches a standstill. A clear boundary has been drawn in terms of what is acceptable and what isn't. In this case the worker or the agency is effectively saying that the reasons for banning or punishing the young person are more important than tolerating the young person – the limits of toleration have been reached.

We know that certain attitudes are underpinned by intolerance, for example racism. Popper, like Mill, argues that we should seek opportunities to reason with the intolerant, but he is also distinct from Mill when he argues that should the intolerant choose not to reason then force is permissible to suppress the intolerant. Practitioners should consider at what point they are no longer able to tolerate a young person, or would we never get to this point? Similarly we need to consider whether we only tolerate the objectionable views of others on the grounds that they are prepared to engage in reasoned discussion. Where does this leave us in working with racists, do we not have a duty to reason with those people you cannot tolerate?

Conditions of tolerance

As with philosophical ideas certain conditions apply and tolerance is no exception. Without meeting these conditions it is difficult to see how tolerance might exist. The first condition I would like to consider is freedom. It is not possible to force someone to be tolerant (Williams in Heyd, 1996), rather we would be forcing someone to simply suffer or endure something which they do not find acceptable. Imagine if you were made to work with a young person or colleague you found objectionable, you would not be tolerating that person, rather you would be forced to suffer that person. With this in mind the first criteria for evidence of tolerance should include a voluntary component. Furthermore we might say that if one has the choice to tolerate, one also has the choice not to tolerate. It is hard to imagine a situation when working with a young person where you are forced to suffer, that is you have no choice but to suffer.

Have you ever been in a situation where you are constantly working under duress because of the way a young person behaves towards you? If such circumstances existed we would have to say that as a practitioner you are effectively powerless.

If however for some greater purpose you can find a reason where you are choosing to put up with a young person then you are thought of as being tolerant insofar as it is your choice. Even though you do not have the power to change the views of the young person, even though you may find certain views held by some young people to be disturbing to the point that they cause you distress, in effect you still have the power to choose to tolerate or not to tolerate. The young person, despite their views, is not in a position to deny you your choice. That isn't to say that there is no cost to you, the person working with the young person. In this respect the demands placed on the worker to tolerate might vary. In one instance we might find it easier to tolerate than in another. For example a young person who loses their temper quickly might be easier to tolerate than an ardent racist.

The second condition of tolerance I would like us to consider is autonomy. Freedom to choose, and freedom to govern one's own choices, are considered by many to be the most important principles of a liberal state. We have seen already in the thinking of Mill and Popper the importance of giving space to people to express their own views, albeit up to a point. If we accept that people are different, with a capacity to govern their own lives, to think and determine the most appropriate course of action whilst at the same time considering the expectations of those around them then tolerance is needed. The point at which people are governed in such a way that choice is taken away is when tolerance is diminished. Here we see the value of autonomy playing its part. In accepting the 'other' we are forced to recognize that the way in which we see the world is not shared by everybody (Hampshire, 1983). What we know about the world is both subjective and relative to the context in which we lead our lives. Whilst there are certain absolute principles by which our lives are governed, not bullying for example, there is a much louder voice which is less certain – 'it depends'.

> *Not only value judgments have difficulties getting beyond the subjective. Consider knowledge itself. How can objective knowledge be possible? We may be able to rise above our individual viewpoints – but we are still locked within a specifically human viewpoint – and one that is rooted in a particular historical and social milieu.*
>
> Baggini & Fosl, 2003: 162

In response to such dilemmas ethics, particularly normative ethics, attempts to understand more carefully the relative/subjective judgments we make about how people should behave. The extent to which our views about what is acceptable or not is debatable. Knowing how we ought to behave requires careful deliberation which in turn can only exist in a state of tolerance.

The third condition of tolerance is not so straightforward. For want of a better term I would like to call this condition being virtuous. But before I get to that I want to consider the following paradox. Anyone can be tolerant, for example even a racist person. If we return to the earlier principle of acceptance versus objection then a racist person who objects to particular groups of people on the grounds of ethnicity but chooses to do nothing about it, in the main only sharing their views privately with people of a similar view, is in a literal sense being tolerant based on our conceptualisation so far.

Paradoxically the more extreme the racist views, the more the racist is demonstrating greater tolerance. But how can that be so? How can a person who has an irrational hatred of a particular group and who chooses not to act on that hatred be described as tolerant. Here the thinking of Aristotle provides us with an answer. For Aristotle, being virtuous (*eudaimonia*) is about human flourishing, well-being and happiness. From the perspective of the virtue ethicist a racist person is not being tolerant, because tolerance as a virtue requires people to act with good character and disposition – to want to see others flourish, not abused and victimised for no good reason. Another way of looking at this dichotomy of acting virtuously versus being virtuous is to think about the tolerance in both a strong and weak sense of the word (Horton, 1996). One might say the person who is morally virtuous in their choice to tolerate another is being tolerant in a strong way whereas the racist who is able to repress their attitude is being tolerant in a weak way. That said the idea of weak tolerance shouldn't be ridiculed if as a result of repressing their attitude the racist person starts to change their attitude (Raz, 1986).

Consider this scenario. How might you respond to young people who show weak tolerance or tolerance without virtue? What about the young people who are being weakly tolerated? Does their experience affect your interventions? Can you see weak tolerance as a stepping stone to strong tolerance; or put another way, tolerance in a literal sense as on the way to someone becoming tolerant as a virtuous person? If so how this might be encouraged?

By tolerating young people you are in a position where you could engage the young person. They have come to you, they are expressing their views. One way or another they are probably looking for a response. By questioning the logic and consistency of their views you are inviting the young person to apply reason to their thinking. By not agreeing with the views of the young person and by inviting the young person to question their views you are showing the limits of what you are prepared to tolerate. At no stage have you showed any empathy with or appreciation of the racist views of the young person. Herein lies the boundary of what you are prepared to tolerate. Before this condition can be met you will have to decide whether only virtuous people can be tolerant. Is there a difference between behaving in a tolerant way and being tolerant?

Tolerance and young people

Tolerance affects all types of relationships. For now I want to focus on the way in which young people relate to one another, both individually and in groups. One of the questions I want to ask is what impact tolerance has on these relationships; moreover, whether youth workers should encourage tolerance in relationships, particularly those that contain a degree of conflict.

The balance of power between groups and individuals plays an important part in identifying degrees of tolerance. The line of power in a relationship is not always equal. It is easy to think of relationships where one party has more power than the other. When someone with power tolerates someone who does not have power it is often described as permissive tolerance (Forst, 2012).

Permission

- *The least costly form of tolerance.*
- *The majority tolerate the minority.*
- *The minority cannot claim status over the majority.*
- *The minority has to accept the dominant authority of the majority.*
- *Toleration is granted on the premise that it keeps the civil peace.*

Forst, 2012

If we apply this idea of permission to practice we might think of a dominant group of young people who are prepared to tolerate a much smaller group within say a club setting. The size of the group and their presence means that although space might be given to the distinctly smaller group, it comes at no real cost. In the main the large group gets their own way most of the time. The dominant group is prepared to give space to the smaller; moreover this is allowed because the force of their voice and presence is more greatly felt.

Somehow this doesn't seem right given all that we have said about tolerance as a virtue. I think it would be hard to find a youth worker who would not prefer to have a state of mutual respect amongst those they work with, regardless of size, strength and authority. By allowing a smaller group to have their say are larger groups being tolerant? Similarly is a young person who is bigger, stronger, more articulate and less afraid being tolerant when they allow a smaller weaker young person to interrupt what they want to do? We might think of this type of behaviour as weak tolerance again. There isn't much by way of being virtuous in what we see here, but perhaps it could be the start of being more tolerant. At second best it is better to have a state of tolerance where the weak have a say providing there is an ongoing commitment to furthering a more virtuous response. If we value liberalism we want to get to a position where all are valued equally, where the weak are not subjugated to the power of another. As Scanlon describes, 'The tolerant person's attitude is: "Even though we disagree, they are as fully members of society as I am" ' (Scanlon, 2003: 193).

What we see here is a conflation of two principles, tolerance and equality. If we are to value equality we need to be more tolerant to accommodate difference. Such an attitude would require a shift in thinking on the part of the dominant group or individual who weakly tolerates. However not all relationships between young people reflect such power imbalance. Where we see a greater parity in the power between groups and or individuals the idea that one group permits the existence of another group suggests a state of coexistence.

Coexistence

- *Toleration of groups who have equal power.*
- *For the sake of social peace and the pursuit of their own interests mutual toleration is the best of all possible alternatives.*

- *The relation of tolerance is no longer vertical but horizontal: the subjects are at the same time the objects of toleration. This may not lead to a stable social situation in which trust can develop, for once the constellation of power changes, the more powerful group may no longer see any reasons for being tolerant.*

Forst, 2012

Here we see tolerance allowing different groups of equal size and power enabling a sort of coexistence. Perhaps this is something you can identify with where groups of young people have to come together side by side to share resources or space. We need to ask ourselves why we encourage young people to tolerate for the sake of coexistence and peace. Is it because we just don't want the aggravation of dealing with conflict all the time? Perhaps it is because young people aren't really bothered about what others do? Maybe young people do care what others do but they respect their right to do it anyway. Or it could be that although young people disagree, they are at the same time prepared to learn from those they see as different (Waltzer, 1997). The purpose of the group is also significant here. Whilst two groups who have different interests might be able to coexist, asking two rival groups to coexist by being more tolerant of each other is a less stable state of affairs. Ideally we don't want to see groups of young people fighting to defend a particular area or a belief. Neither would we be happy in the knowledge that at any time one group might no longer see any reason to remain tolerant and therefore conflict may be reignited. With this in mind, the coexistence model we see here is more dependent on the level of acceptance if stability is to be maintained, and this stability is then further reinforced by a level of appreciation between different groups.

What do you think about encouraging tolerance as a way of beginning to reconcile conflict across groups? Can we expect groups who have existed in a state of violence and conflict to simply reconcile their differences? Does tolerance have something to add to the value of bringing together groups in conflict? Does tolerance always help?

Hitherto we have been concerned with Forst's invitation to look at the notion of power in relationships in relation to tolerance. This is significant given the constant struggles and vying for position that drives young people to compete against one another. However, Forst's third and fourth concepts look at the significance of tolerance as part of more consensual and appreciative relationships as we think about the importance of tolerance in relation to esteem and respect.

Respect
- *People respect each other as political equals with a certain distinct ethical-cultural identity that needs to be respected and tolerated.*
- *Social and political equality and integration are thus seen to be compatible with cultural difference.*

Esteem

• *Being tolerant does not just mean respecting members of other cultural life-forms or religions as moral and political equals, it also means having some kind of ethical esteem for them, that is, taking them to be ethically valuable conceptions that – even though different from one's own – are in some way ethically attractive and held with good reasons.*

Forst, 2012

Whilst there may be elements of other groups we object to, our consideration here is whether it is possible to respect at the same time. This suggests more than just accepting. Having worked in a number of faith based contexts as a youth worker I would regularly encounter young people who objected to the faith element of the youth work practice they were accessing. That said many of the same young people also had a level of respect and appreciation for the workers and the projects themselves. Similarly I have worked with discussion groups which encourage the subjective relative voice of young people and students, coupled with the certainty of their beliefs and values. As a result of these types of discussions young people and students have recognised, even valued, the experiences of others even though they may see the world differently. In some ways tolerance gives permission for people to object without causing offence. In a multicultural, pluralist society it is helpful to have a mechanism that allows for difference, which encourages a respect for different values. In such situations tolerance still meets the principles of objection and acceptance; however the level of acceptance is informed by a sort of appreciation that means we can respect those we object to.

Perhaps a less obvious example is where you have two groups or individuals who have clear opposing views. If you have ever seen a debate between two academics, for example, you will be aware that there can be a great deal of disagreement, even shouting, often fuelled with reasoned argument and passion. Whatever you think about the motivation of academics and their pursuit of truth, just because they disagree, often strongly, does not necessarily make the other party their enemy. Despite strong criticism and accusation towards one another you can still identify acceptance, objection and respect.

The final suggestion here is that we can both object and hold others in high esteem at the same time. This is more than agreeing to disagree. If I think of my own experiences, I have a high regard for faith and religion and at the same time there is a great deal I object to, so that at times I find it hard to participate in acts of faith and religious ceremony. I imagine my comments here about faith and religion would be hard to accept. For someone who has a strong faith to be told that I tolerate their ideas and beliefs is likely to cause upset. When dealing with degrees of certainty someone who holds an unequivocal position on a particular subject will find it hard to accept someone who only tolerates their ideas. That said here is an example of being able to hold in high regard many of the tenets of faith and religion, for example the generous acts of compassion and love towards others that informs a great deal of theological doctrine. At the same time, the public judgment and condemnation of certain groups within a place of worship and the deficit model that underpins certain theological arguments I find to be highly objectionable to the extent that I cannot participate.

In the context of youth work there are similar layers of complexity that structure the way young people relate to others. Consider if you will the following example. Imagine a youth work project working with a marginalized group of young people. Within the group there is a young person who really values the support and opportunities that are afforded by being a member of the group and at the same time resents the idea that they need special provision because in some they are seen as different. In an ideal world, if the group were accepted rather than marginalised the young person in question would not feel tolerated, but simply accepted, and could in effect value the experience itself rather than having to challenge the deficit view others may hold. This raises another important issue around how we determine how people ought to be treated. Again we see some of the weak tolerance issues emerging again.

In effect though, both examples reflect the complex relationship we have with others. Whilst seemingly contradictory it is possible for the same person to have quite different feelings towards the same circumstances. Again tolerance provides a justification for such complex and to some extent inconsistent feelings. I find this idea quite liberating. To not have to have a clear view I think provides a truer representation of the way we all relate to others.

What do you think? Does the targeting of particular groups in our youth work perpetuate the need for tolerance towards the group when what is really wanted is acceptance? What is the alternative?

To conclude, I want to leave you with the idea that our ability to tolerate is being eroded, to the extent that for much of our modern existence tolerance is not necessary. We have a normative perception of the world about what is right and wrong, which has come about through various processes of socialization such as schooling and family life. It is possible now in modern society to exist with a fairly minimal amount of direct human interaction whilst at the same time maintaining some sort of position on what is right and wrong. The medium of technology such as electronic communication means that in many ways we are able to function at a distance from others. In such circumstances where interaction with others is diminished it is easier to ignore others, to separate ourselves under a veil of indifference and neutrality, what Marx would have called alienation and dehumanization. For some this may seem an attractive proposition; however for many, especially those who see the world in a state of conflict, it is wrong to accept such hegemonic ideals.

As Marcuse (1964) suggests, capitalism has reached a point where 'the people recognize themselves in their commodities; they find their soul in their automobile, hi-fi set, split-level home, kitchen equipment.' To exist in such a state suggests a weakening of consciousness which in Freirean terms allows for others to tell us what we think and need. If we would prefer a more deliberative state of affairs where people come together to debate and exchange views, tolerance is required as people learn about the opinions of others and acknowledge that people are different. As Spinoza (Rosenthal, 2010) reminds us, given our desire to preserve our own being in relation to external influences, we cannot agree with everything.

CHAPTER 3

'I Work in a Democratic Way!'

Simon Frost

Introduction

When you hear the word democracy what comes to mind? Voting perhaps or maybe government – if you work with young people and I assume you probably do (otherwise why are you reading a book about philosophy and youth work?) you might see democracy as a way of making decisions with young people. In addition to the way we experience democracy there are a number of values such as fairness, liberty, rights and so on which add value and meaning to the way we conceptualise democracy. In the field of youth work the term democracy itself is often used descriptively to imply a sense of value about the way in which young people and youth workers are able to work together. The National Youth Agency's introduction to valuing youth work (NYA, 2010), for example, talks about participating in democracy; seminal thinkers such as Jeffs (2005) emphasise the need for genuine participative democracy; and more recently those who have attempted to defend the purpose of youth work politically are quick to point out the significance of democratic practice, such as the *In Defence of Youth Work* campaign. Democracy itself would seem to be held by most to be a good thing; that is, where we see the word democracy we assume something of value is taking place. The purpose of this chapter is to consider the justification of democracy as a central value of youth work, and central to this consideration is the question of who, if any, should govern. Whilst supporters of democracy argue that rule by the people is both the fairest and most effective way of governing in terms of benefiting society there are ethical and philosophical arguments for other types of government as well; moreover the principles and values that provide the necessary conditions for democracy are not exclusive to democracy.

To think of democracy as a set of values that must be embraced suggests that those who benefit from and participate in democracy are in need of a system where people can live and work together in a safe and just way. By stating that people need democracy we are also making a value judgement about life without democracy. Whether it is through attempts to bring about peace and security in war torn nations or encouraging a group of young people to work together through deliberation and consensual decision making, democracy is used to justify a mechanism for fairness and consensus in what would otherwise be a state of potential conflict across a broad range of people groups. It is this justification that will provide the focus of our enquiry in this chapter.

What is democracy?

Literally, democracy is defined as *demos* – the people, *kratia* – governance; hence democracy is essentially rule by the people.

Participation and support

Whilst the definition of democracy appears to be straightforward there are two sets of conditions which affect the way in which we understand and practice democracy. The first set of conditions is to do with the variables of participation and support and the second set of conditions is concerned with those values widely associated with democracy. Let us now consider the first set of conditions.

Participation

Our concern with participation is to do with its significance and impact. Imagine a group of people where the authority of the decision taken is contained within the members of the group. For example a group of young people could work together to reach a decision which would affect the whole group of which they are a part. An important condition of this example is that the young people in the group are responsible for the decision that is taken. This we would call a form of direct democracy. It is the responsibility of the group to participate in the decision making process based on an appreciation of all contributions in the group, and ultimately the decision taken affects the whole group.

In a different set of circumstances a group might choose to defer responsibility to those in the group who were better informed. Here the idea of representation is used to reflect a less participative democracy. This we would call an indirect democracy. A more obvious example can be found in British politics where in theory the majority of ordinary citizens are expected to vote for a small group of people to reflect their interests in the governance of the country. Here I am linking the amount of energy, thinking and deliberation in measuring participation. As well as helping us to distinguish between direct and indirect forms of democracy, participation is also one of the values that are used to measure democracy. I will say more about that shortly but for now it is important to note that if people are not allowed to participate freely in governance either directly or indirectly any claims to working democratically or governing democratically are swiftly eroded.

Support

The second important variable of democracy is to do with the amount of support needed for a decision to be binding on the group. At one end there are conditions where we might say a decision requires unanimous support whereas in other situations the majority will is sufficient to justify decisions. Unanimity requires everyone to agree, whereas a majority means the choice with the most support is upheld. The more options there are the less a majority would need to be. For example, if a hundred people voted according to three options the majority would only need 34% of the overall vote. The issue of majority versus unanimity brings us to two linked questions. First, do decisions that are made within a democracy require majority support or unanimous support, and is this the support of the representatives or of the people themselves? Second, if decisions are not unanimous, what happens to the liberty of the minority, which is subject to the will of the majority?

Let us take the decision to go to war. What should the level of support be for a country to go to war, and who should have a voice, the public or only their representatives? Should the support be unanimous, 90% or even 51%? If we decide on a simple majority, what about the voice of the 49% who might be opposed? Now consider a different sort of decision with less grave consequences, for example a group of young people choosing to spend some money. Again should the support be unanimous, 90% or even 51%? Again if we decide on a simple majority, what about the voice of the 49% who might be opposed?

At one extreme, the freedom for all to self-determination will only be realised if every democratic decision has unanimous support. In reality this is never the case, yet decisions still have to made. The debate continues as to how much support is required before a decision can be said to be made democratically. One way of including the public, as well as their elected representatives, in a decision is through referenda. Governments differ considerably on how important a decision needs to be before they will offer voters this opportunity. In Britain, referenda tend to be used only to seek approval for a major constitutional change, such as the decision to join the European Community or to accept the European Union's proposed new constitution. Some American states and local governments use referenda very liberally, to approve a tax levy for a particular purpose, for example. Beetham (1999) in his work on democracy and human rights, cites the Swiss federal constitution, in which all legislation that is passed by the Swiss parliament is subject to a potential referendum if there is enough public support. What we have here is a decision-making process that is first subject to majority support among the representatives in parliament; however the decisions that are taken there are not necessarily final. Perhaps this idea, that democratic decisions cannot and should not be viewed as categorical, encourages us to look at democracy as a process. When decisions are made, it could be on the premise that they might have to change.

It's also worth considering that the requirement for majority support forces us to gauge the level of approval for a democratic decision; however, it does not provide any indication as to whether a democratic decision is a moral decision.

Hitherto what appears a relatively straightforward idea has managed to generate a range of pertinent questions which affect the way we understand democracy:

- *When should decision-making be deferred to a small body of representatives?*
- *When should everyone be directly involved in making decisions?*
- *Should the decisions taken by those elected to represent be subject to the scrutiny and validation of those affected?*
- *What constitutes a majority and how is this determined?*
- *Do all decisions taken need the same amount of support?*

Democracy can be used to determine a range of processes many of which can be applied to youth work practice. For now though I would like you to reflect on all areas of your practice, for example face to face work, programme management, decision making processes, organisational structures and anything else you can think of. How do these questions around participation and support relate to your practice? Here are a few ideas to get you started:

- *When young people are called upon to make a choice as a group on a matter that will affect them, do you go with the majority decision? What if the majority are wrong?*
- *Should youth workers intervene when a group is going to make a decision that will have a negative impact or should the value of direct majoritarian democracy take precedence?*
- *Would you ever encourage a group to defer decision making to a small number within their group?*
- *What would happen if the group of young people who were voluntarily accessing your youth work agency decided they were unhappy with the decisions of your management committee to introduce a new focus in their provision – is it reasonable to think that the young people should expect a management committee to reconsider?*
- *Should young people be expected to deliberate all decisions or is it right to think they should be happy to pass over decision making to those perhaps better qualified?*

Values of democracy

Before I talk about the value base of democracy I would like to briefly mention the significance of authority. There are many situations where as human beings we are subject to authority, i.e. as students, as employees, as citizens and so on. There are also certain conditions where we are not subject to authority, for example those groups in which we voluntarily participate, for example a club, a community group or a youth project. Whilst there may be an expectation of conformity around values, purpose and boundaries, any authority resides within the group itself; the group's authority is not given from a higher authority outside of the group.

One way in which we might differentiate here is to think of an autonomous group, responsible for its own governance and a group who is expected to participate in democratic processes to varying degrees whilst subject to authority. The former could be a local group of people who share a particular interest. The group meets, deliberates and collectively shares responsibility for its own decisions. An example of the latter might be a school where young people are in certain circumstances expected to work together to make a decision that will affect everyone, for example a consultation on a new school uniform. Whilst young people may be encouraged to participate in democratic processes to decide on the uniform the ultimate decision resides with the school management. If the young people in the school did not participate the decision would return to the authority position of the school. Keen eyes may note a parallel here with the sovereignty of parliament and UK citizens.

With the differentiation I have attempted here, there is an inference that autonomous groups are more democratic in their nature than those groups subject to the authority of others. To help us explore this distinction we need a set of criteria for democracy. Dahl's (1989) criteria listed below provides us with a useful set of conditions which in theory need to be fully exercised before the title democracy can be legitimately used:

Effective participation (Equal opportunity to participate). Here Dahl is concerned that everyone has an opportunity to have their say before a decision is taken.

Voting equality at the decisive stage. Equal opportunity to express a choice that will be counted as equal in weight to the choice expressed by any other citizen. Only those choices may be taken into account otherwise they become unrepresentative. If we stand by the idea of rule by the people as opposed to say rule by the best, or rule by the strongest, then a provision is required to ensure that all people have an opportunity to influence political decisions. This provision is best fulfilled by voting equality.

Enlightened understanding. Each individual should have equal opportunities for discovering and validating the choice on the matter to be decided. Here Dahl provides a set of standards which encourage an opportunity for all to make an informed contribution, which in turn validates the decisions taken, for example by providing accountability through the use of a public referendum.

Control of the agenda. The demos (i.e. people, citizens) must have the exclusive opportunity to decide how matters are placed on the agenda of matters that are to be decided by means of the democratic process. Where there is little accountability, for example in a state of authority, it is easier to select which areas are represented on an agenda. To withhold certain issues from political decisions may create an advantage in seeking support from particular sections of an electorate. Where there is greater accountability the agenda is more likely to be determined by the people.

Inclusion. The demos should include all adults subject to the binding collective decisions. The issue of inclusion is closely linked to the subject of boundaries. Essentially the challenge before us is to decide who decides on the boundary. Should it be an all-embracing boundary such as the borders of a country, or is it okay for a small autonomous group to draw a boundary by definition of its activities and purpose.

Dahl, 1989: 109–18

Based on the values of effective participation, voting equality, enlightened understanding, control of the agenda and inclusion, is democracy more likely to flourish in an autonomous group, a group which is subject to the authority of another, neither or both?

Alternative perspectives

To say we need democracy is something of a normative assumption (a sort of claim about how we ought to be). By saying that we value democracy we are at the same time saying that it is not right for people to arbitrarily govern through force and coercion; rather we do need to work collectively for the good of all and this is more likely if we have a system of fair governance like democracy. Hume (1960) suggests that there comes a point when our own self-interests take precedence over others to the extent that our passions override our ability to comply with one another, therefore we need some sort of fair structure, hence the need for government to enforce what is right and good. Essentially Hume is saying governance is required because we aren't capable of getting on without being governed. Democracy as we know it then is a way of making decisions in the interest of the whole rather than the needs and wants of individuals.

What if Hume is wrong? What if we were able to coexist voluntarily through negotiation without a governing structure? Were this the case we might not need democracy. There are other political structures which provide the necessary principles to encourage individuals to work both autonomously and collectively, for example anarchy. For some political philosophers this is an important issue, as Wolff suggests:

> *If autonomy and authority are genuinely incompatible, only two courses are open to us. Either we must embrace philosophical anarchism and treat all governments as non-legitimate bodies whose commands must be judged and evaluated in each instance before they are obeyed; or else, we must give up as quixotic the pursuit of autonomy in the political realm and submit ourselves (by an implicit promise) to whatever form of government appears most just and beneficent at the moment.*

Wolff, 1970: 47

Whilst anarchy is often regarded as having nihilistic traits, for the purposes of this philosophical enquiry I am suggesting that anarchy can be distinguished as a peaceful movement, different from the destructive impulses of nihilism. We need to be wary of this prejudice against anarchy, or anarchism, as necessarily seeing it as violent and aggressive. Some conclude that anarchy is built on a strong ethical premise that seeks to empower the individual against coercion and manipulation. Moreover, such empowerment need not be through violence (Frost, 2003).

In his seminal defence of anarchy, Wolff (1970) argues from the Kantian perspective that we are metaphysically free and capable of choosing how we ought to behave; moreover because we are capable of determining for ourselves, we are obliged out of moral duty to determine how we should act. Herein Wolff identifies a tension between the authority of those who believe they have the right to rule and the autonomous person who refuses to be ruled. The assumption that we need to be governed collectively rather than being morally autonomous is challenged. The idea that we need to be governed depends then on the idea that we are not capable of being good and acting in the best interest of ourselves and others all the time. Where we see communities of good will and a genuine commitment to the good of all, we do not need to be governed by those who claim authority.

In response to this anarchist ideal Dahl argues:

> But we do not live in a perfect society, and we are not likely to. We are likely to go on living in an imperfect world inhabited by imperfect human beings, that is, human beings. Therefore, unless and until your society comes into existence, the best possible society would have the best possible state. In my view, the best possible state would minimize coercion and maximize consent, within the limits set by historical conditions and the pursuit of other values, including happiness, freedom, and justice. Judged by ends like these, the best state, I believe, would be a democratic state.

Dahl, 1989: 51

Dahl's response seems to appreciate the value of anarchy in an ideal world, similarly Wolff goes to great lengths to explore the circumstances in which authority and autonomy can be resolved by democracy. With this in mind we see a shared appreciation of a society comprising autonomous people able to self-determine and at the same time able to work with others to reap the benefits of working consensually.

At the other end of the political participation spectrum there are those who think that strong government is needed which in turn reduces the need for political participation from ordinary people; moreover it is argued that not everyone is qualified to govern therefore the responsibility for governing should be left to those who are best suited for the job. This is sometimes described as meritocracy or guardianship.

Dahl provides us with a clear working definition of guardianship. Guardians, such as those who rule in Plato's ideal Republic, are a small group of selected people 'who are specifically qualified to govern by reason of their superior knowledge and virtue'.

> *A perennial alternative to democracy is government by guardians. In this view, the notion that ordinary people can be counted on to understand and defend their own interests – much less the interests of the larger society – is prepos- terous. Ordinary people, these critics insist, are clearly not qualified to govern themselves. The assumption by democrats that ordinary people are qualified, they say, ought to be replaced by the opposing proposition that rulership should be entrusted to a minority of persons who are specifically qualified to govern by reason of their superior knowledge and virtue.*
>
> Dahl, 1989: 52

Note well the emphasis on virtue as much as knowledge in Plato's criteria for guardian- ship. It was Plato's belief that citizens would recognise the benevolence and integrity of such rulers and therefore citizens would be prepared to be subordinate within such a hierarchy to those who would have possessed no self-interest other than the good of the people (Plato, 1987). Here we see an example of authority which is not bound by desires of power, control and wealth. There is almost something servitudinal about the idea of the guardian we see here. You may want to reflect on your own experi- ences of authority and leadership or maybe the experiences of young people. Would you respond differently to an authority which is only committed to what is right and true, with nothing to gain other than the good of the people? The argument for meritocracy is further justified by the idea that not all are capable of governing. There are many who argue that young children do not possess the capacity to reason in deliberative situations. Mills' thoughts on what constitutes competence force us to consider a number of harsh possibilities. For example, in Mills' mind, should people who are dependent on others be entitled to govern?

> *At a minimum . . . to demonstrate that persons are qualified to engage in gov- erning requires a showing that they have acquired the commonest and most essential requisites for taking care of themselves, for pursuing intelligently their own interests and those of the persons most nearly allied to them.*
>
> Mill, 1958: 131

While we might agree that young children might find it difficult to participate thoughtfully in national politics, this does not necessarily hold true in other situa- tions, such as decision-making within a family. Indeed, since citizenship has been made part of the national curriculum, it seems that the present Government is very much concerned with the idea of children and young people developing skills to become actively involved as citizens. Therefore it seems logical that in certain situations young people should be given an opportunity to have some influence over decisions that affect their lives. In many instances, social policy research prides itself on drawing out the views, through a process of research and analysis, of those groups it seeks to represent. One might argue that in this way young people are contributing towards a democratic process, even if they aren't the final 'decision makers'. We could say that, through representation by professionals, there is an opportunity for all to contribute to political debate.

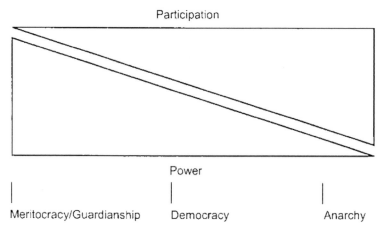

Figure 3.1

To summarise, we have three models, two reflecting a form of government and the third a form of non-government. There is a variable balance of power and participation in all three examples given here. Essentially the less power people have the less they are able to participate in the act of governance and vice versa.

Stop for a moment to consider the balance of power and participation in your practice. You might find yourself thinking about the relationship between you and the young people you work with, you might choose to reflect on the governance structure within your agency and the involvement of young people, or maybe you find yourself pondering the way in which groups of young people make decisions. Youth work practice has many layers which require decision making processes. From what you have read so far, are you able to identify democratic principles in all areas or only some? Is democracy always the best principle for making decisions? The following questions might prove helpful:

- *Do we require direct leadership? Then we will favour meritocracy or guardianship.*
- *Is it up to the individual to be autonomous, while striving for voluntary association? Then we will choose anarchy.*
- *Should we try to work together? Then we will opt for democracy.*

Whatever the scale of governance whether it be a youth committee, the state, a vote taken in a youth club, the varying levels of power and participation can be applied.

Democracy, deliberation and youth work

We have seen that participation can vary according to scale and levels of representation. Youth workers have an important opportunity to foster participation with young people in various ways. These might include contributing in management committees or taking part in debates. Such experiences offer obvious correlations between democracy for young people and political activity. However, what about the less obvious processes of democracy in youth work, for example the practice of deliberation?

Deliberation as a social process is distinguished from other kinds of communication in that deliberators are amenable to changing their judgements, preferences and views during the course of their interactions, which involve persuasion rather than coercion or manipulation in the pursuit of truth and understanding. The deliberative turn represents a renewed concern with the authenticity of democracy; the degree to which democratic control is substantive rather than symbolic, and engaged by competent citizens (Dryzek, 2000).

Deliberative democracy is a move away from making sovereign decisions in favour of a more reasoned approach to moral thinking that is flexible and open. Here we might argue that democracy provides a framework for moral philosophy. Youth workers who use the process of deliberation in their work are asking young people to debate what is right and wrong across a range of issues, including their development, behaviour and education. Through this deliberation with others, they are provided with a framework for moral reasoning. Habermas (Pusey, 1987) would argue that collective action is essential to the discovery of truth; moreover through informal adolescent networks we have a natural forum for such deliberation. It is the process of democracy that allows this to happen. A useful model here is Habermas' ideal speech situation, where the dynamics of the relationship change so that any claim can be defended or questioned, where there are no constraints made by the role of those engaging in the dialogue and where there is commitment towards discovering truth.

Given the importance that is placed on dialogue in youth work, deliberation has a natural ground within its practice. However, as youth workers involved in fostering democracy, we might want to consider the following issues, identified by Dryzek. My comments/examples are in italics:

* Should deliberation be restricted to rational argument, or admit other kinds of communication (emotional, or rhetorical, for example)? *Should a young person*

be listened to if they have strong feelings on an issue which they cannot substantiate with a reasoned argument?
- Are there some kinds of communication (perhaps prejudiced, racist or sectarian) that should be ruled out in advance? *How do you work with dissident views in young people, such as racism or sexism? Should such views be automatically excluded, or do they are have a place in democratic deliberation?*
- Must acceptable argument be couched in terms of public interest, common to all, or are more particular and partial interests admissible? *If the latter can enter, do we allow deliberation to coexist with bargaining? How do you encourage a 'closed' group of young people to consider the needs of others beyond their own friends?*
- Should deliberation be orientated to consensus, or is it just a prelude to voting? Is youth work a means to an end or an open process? *What are the strengths and weaknesses of forcing a group to make a decision?*
- Might existing representative institutions prove inhospitable to effective deliberation, such that alternative locations should be sought? *What effect does adult intervention have on the deliberations of young people? Are you encouraging young people to reach their own conclusions or forcing a professional agenda?*
- Should deliberation be constrained by constitutional specifications that rule out in advance particular outcomes of deliberation? *How do you work democratically with a group of young people who have different views or ideas from the organisation they are a part of?*
- Is political equality central to the deliberative ideal, and if so how much deviation from that ideal will be tolerated? *What if anything is to be done about unequal individual capacities to deliberate? Do all young people want to be heard? Are there such groupings as natural leaders and followers?*
- Is deliberation to be confined to members of a predefined community, or can it occur effectively across community boundaries, or when no established community is present? *Should young people who are not members of a group, whether the group has formal or informal boundaries, be allowed to have a say?*

Dryzek, 2000

Perhaps deliberation as a form of democracy is simply another concept or model, in that deliberation is the process by which a democracy might function. Putting this idea to one side for a moment, it is also worth considering the intrinsic value of deliberative democracy as a way of encouraging reasoned dialogue. While at times the responses we get from young people as they seek to express their views might make for a messy process, still something is happening; people are talking, drawing conclusions, questioning, and making judgements, striving for understanding and possibly justice. Given all that has been said about the restrictions on political participation, it is worth considering how the practice of youth workers can foster what might be called a democratic disposition in the people they work with.

Conclusion

Our reflections on the justification of democracy have led us to consider issues about scale, participation and power and the different models of democracy that may result when these vary. Whilst I have focused mainly on the political sphere, and on questions of governance, many of the arguments transfer directly to youth work, given the inherent role of dialogue and deliberation we find in practice. We have seen that the concept of democracy can be applied to a wide range of practices. Moreover, as a concept, democracy seeks to redress the ills of a people who cannot work consensually without a fair system of control. The issue of authority remains a tension. Where we are subject to the authority/will of others we are not free to work together collectively to determine as a group what is right. This tension is slightly tempered by the idea of rules and laws that are given by the people to the people (Wolff, 1970). Similarly democracy attempts to bring together autonomous people in an act of collective government. In modern representative democracies the issue of scale stretches the link between autonomy and democracy to breaking point. In youth work the issue of scale and representation has the potential to be much less of an issue as youth workers encourage a morally autonomous disposition that is capable of working together with others. What do you think?

CHAPTER 4

'It's Not Fair . . .'

Simon Frost

Introduction

The overarching theme for this chapter is fairness, particularly the fair treatment of young people. Young people often use the idea of fairness when they feel they have been wronged in some way. In response to this commonly held concern by young people, two questions must be answered. First, what do we mean by fair treatment? And second, what can be done, if anything, to ensure young people are treated fairly?

In brief, to treat people fairly or indeed unfairly is an ability that most of us possess. The ability to treat people (un)fairly is closely linked to our capacity to distribute and control those things we are able to give to others. Here I am mindful of my youngest son who, at 8 years of age, has the power to enact fairness. For example, he may choose to share his sweets with both myself and my wife, but not his 12 year old sister. In this instance my daughter would probably argue that she is not being treated the same as her mum and dad, in other words she is being treated *unequally*, and is therefore, by her way of thinking, not being treated fairly. She might also argue that as a member of the family she *deserves* to be treated the same when it comes to sharing out sweets. If we are in a position to distribute something to others, we are in a position to treat people fairly or unfairly. Similarly if we are in a position where we are able to give someone what they *deserve* or treat someone according to their *entitlement* we are able to enact fairness also.

Furthermore, the ability to treat people fairly doesn't necessarily refer to the way we distribute things such as possessions or money: it could be about giving someone more time, or showing more interest or enthusiasm towards a particular individual or group. Similarly treating fairly is not the reserve of personal relationships. There is currently a great deal of unrest surrounding the size of Britain's welfare budget and whether cuts in welfare spending are a way of treating people fairly or not. Fairness or unfairness is not limited by scale. Individuals, groups, communities even nations are all susceptible to unfair treatment. For now though it is important to recognise that fairness is an issue that we are all affected by; moreover to be fair is an ability most of us possess.

Equality

I think I could say quite confidently that every young person I have worked with at some point has suggested that they have been treated unfairly. Whether it be as a result of a judgement I have made as a youth worker, or whether it is in response to the intervention of another adult, such as a teacher or a carer, the phrase 'it's not fair' is a common theme amongst adolescents as they attempt to establish their place in the world. But what do young people mean when they say they have been treated unfairly? There are a number of conditions on which fairness is based of which equality, or rather lack of it, is the one most often utilised. However, equality should not be considered alone as the sole basis of fair treatment. Entitlement and desert are equally important.

Fairness and equality

If we pause to think about those situations where young people claim they have been treated unfairly it is normally as a result of what is seen as unequal treatment.

Fairness is primarily a matter of distribution, for example slicing up a cake or giving of your time or money. However to be treated fairly is not simply a matter of making sure everyone gets the same share of the pie. Maybe there are conditions such as working hard which make people more deserving of the pie that is being shared. For those who haven't worked as hard, we could argue they are less deserving.

A second criterion that is often used in matters of distribution is entitlement. Some people might already have already eaten their own pie and therefore have less need of the pie that is being shared. However because of certain conditions the same people find themselves entitled to more pie. Let me give you an example. Due to a number of circumstances, there are parents who earn reasonable salaries. Under current legislation these same parents are entitled to receive Child Benefit. If we compare their circumstances to a family living in poverty we might say that the family in poverty are more deserving of Child Benefit. To be entitled to something does not necessarily mean we are deserving of that thing also.

When considerations of desert and entitlement are juxtaposed with the idea of equality, claims of unfair treatment are strengthened. To demonstrate this point let us consider a set of circumstances where young people claim to be treated unfairly. In the first set of examples we will look at inequality as the basis of unfair treatment and the second time round we will include entitlement and desert as well.

Firstly here are some fairly typical types of occasions where a young person solely uses inequality as evidence of unfair treatment:

1. If a young person feels that others are treated with more respect.
2. When a young person perceives other young people receiving preferential treatment by virtue of their wealth or cultural background.
3. Where a young person feels they are being marginalised because of their beliefs and values.

Can you think of any other occasions?

In this approach we see some strong claims for being treated equally. For example why is one person's dignity any less important than another person's? Why if a young person works hard should they not receive the same rewards as others? Why shouldn't a young person's beliefs be afforded the same respect as others? By comparing the way they are treated to others, young people are able to make a crude calculation using equality to measure their experiences with those they perceive to be treated more favourably. However, if we extend their argument to include desert and entitlement as well, their arguments for fairer treatment are strengthened.

(a) Young people are more likely to think they have been treated fairly if they think they are getting the level of respect they deserve.
We might use the Kantian argument that we should treat all people as ends in themselves; not to be exploited for the gain of others (O'Neill, 1993). By virtue of a shared humanity young people are both deserving of and entitled to dignity and respect in equal measure.

(b) Young people are able to justify their status when they are able to show what they have is what they deserve. Conversely if young people do not get what they deserve they have not been treated fairly.
Given that so much of what we have is determined by things beyond our control, this makes arguments for deserved wealth and status hard to justify, particularly when there are those young people with whom we work with who suffer in poverty and disadvantage, often for reasons beyond their control.

To be able to argue that disproportionate wealth and status is permitted insofar as the less well-off are more likely to benefit is a popular argument for free market economics. However when the level of unequal wealth distribution is disproportionate to need (Locke, 1689) the desert claims of the wealthy are harder to justify ethically, especially when those who deserve more do not have enough to survive, let alone flourish.

(c) Young people are treated fairly when their beliefs and values are accorded the level of respect they deserve.
Whether all values and beliefs are deserving of respect is difficult to determine. The certainty of values and beliefs are easily deconstructed using a range of intellectual arguments, for example relativism and subjectivism, or perhaps something more sociological like post structuralism or post modernism. What is important for many liberal thinkers is that we all have the right to think and express ourselves. However much we might object to the views of young people we should value the higher

principles of free thinking and freedom of expression. As youth workers we can always debate and if necessary challenge the views and beliefs of young people: but, out of respect, young people deserve to be heard, more so at a time when their ideas and values are being shaped by the world around them.

Equality of capability

Is it fair that some people are free to choose the life they desire and value and others are not? There is much about us that we are responsible for, how hard we work, and how we treat other people for example. At the same time there is also a great deal about us that we do not have control over.

> *Of course the extent to which life can be made fair is limited to the extent that we have no control over the way some things are distributed, for example illness and intelligence – though note the things we do control, like pollution and education, affect these.*
>
> Baggini & Fosl, 2003: 170

We do not choose our parents. We do not choose the community into which we are born. We do not choose the values and beliefs that are used to shape our lives. Similarly we have little say in how our natural dispositions are encouraged, particularly in the formative years of our lives; moreover our dispositions are rarely the same. Yet all of these factors are significant when it comes to finding our way in life. Given such levels of 'untouched natural disadvantage' and 'inborn disadvantage' (Swift, 2005: 100) what if anything can be done to ensure young people are treated fairly? Is it enough to legislate that all are given an equal opportunity in life or is something more radical required?

In other words is it fair to receive less simply because of the natural conditions young people are born into? How do we determine young people get what they deserve? Why, for example, is a young person born into a privileged background thought to deserve more than a child born into a disadvantaged background?

Arguably we are all free to choose what we want; however, there are many conditions as free, rational human beings which mean we are unable to fulfil our needs and wants. Whilst on the one hand we have *formal* freedom, we do not necessarily have *effective* freedom (Swift, 2005). For example, formally I am free to go and buy a new car – there is no law that says I cannot by a new car. However there is the small matter of not having the money needed, and therefore effectively I am not free to buy a new car (ibid.). There are many situations where we could apply the principle of *formal* and *effective* freedom to the lives of young people. For example, *formally* there are no laws which prevent someone from a disadvantaged background from going to university. Providing you get the grades you need relevant to your chosen subject area and you are able to secure the finance required, you are able to go to university. Now let's consider the potential lack of *effective* freedom. Not growing up in a culture which expects a young person to go to university, attending a school where the probability of going to university is relatively low, and being educated in a class where there is lots of disruption and low aspiration amongst peers and so on are all conditions which are likely to restrict *effective* freedom.

Where we see people unable to choose those things they value we also see a difference in people's capacity to choose effectively, often as a result of matters beyond their control. In thinking about the young people one works with, a practitioner needs to ask: what are the circumstances and conditions that restrict the effective freedom of young people to choose? In developing freedom to choose the life we value, Sen (1999) argues that we should be concerned with who we are and what we are capable of so that we are able to choose the life we desire. He states that if capability is encouraged and developed more people would have more choice to do the things they value. Central to the idea of capability is what Sen describes as 'functionings' and 'capability':

> The concept of 'functionings' reflects the various things a person may value doing or being. The valued functionings may vary from elementary ones, such as being adequately nourished and being free from avoidable disease, to complex activities or personal states, such as being able to take part in the life of the community and having self-respect.
>
> A person's 'capability' refers to the alternative combinations of functions that are feasible for her to achieve. Capability is thus a kind of freedom to achieve alternative functioning combinations, (or less formerly put, the freedom to achieve various lifestyles). For example, an affluent person who fasts may have the same functioning achievement as a destitute person who is forced to starve, but the first person does have a different 'capability set' than the second (the first person can choose to eat well and be well nourished in a way the second cannot).
>
> Sen, 1999: 71

In summary Sen (ibid.) encourages us to carefully identify those conditions which affect our capability to choose and then develop capabilities so that we are able to function in a way we value. But perhaps more significant in light of our overall focus is what can be achieved through the Capabilities Approach. If we are all equal in our capability to function in a way we value, we become responsible for the choices we make. Hitherto any concerns that young people have been treated unfairly are diminished (Robeyns, 2011). Questions a practitioner should ask themselves include: would equality of capability ameliorate tensions caused by inequality? Where all are seen to have the same capability to effectively choose the life they value is unfairness eradicated? In what way does your practice affect the capability of young people to develop as autonomous, self-determining adults?

Equality of what?

It is important to recognise that it is normally those things we value where we desire equality, for example, wealth, quality of relationships, time etc. In contrast there are many examples where people are treated equally unfairly, for example a group of people who are collectively oppressed in some way. Oppressed groups do not deserve to be treated equally badly; neither is oppression something groups are entitled to or deserving of. Equal treatment therefore does not necessarily equate to fairness. This leads us to the question *equality of what?*

There are values and principles which most would agree apply to all in equal measure. For example, we could say that everyone deserves to be treated with respect, to live free from oppression, to be able to make one's own choices, to be treated with kindness and compassion, and so on. If you are looking for a moral compass to determine how people should be treated you may want to look at the UN Declaration of Human Rights (UNDHR), and supporting legislation such as the Human Rights Act. Here you will find a list of universalisable articles which are committed to the dignity and equal value of all human beings. It is this type of equality which should be applied to everybody.

> *A morally sensitive person will respect the basic moral rights of other persons as equal to her own, not just because they are alive and sentient, but also because she can reasonably hope and demand that they will show her the same respect.*
>
> Warren, 2007: 310

Herein we are invited to distinguish between equality of what we value versus undesirable equality of those things we do not value – for example oppression. That said, we risk by oversimplifying saying we should only be treated equally in those things we desire. This is because what we desire is not always worthy. I might say I want to live in an enormous house with luxuries and space beyond my needs. As seen previously in our earlier discussion on entitlement and desert it is hard to argue that I am either entitled to or deserving of such riches. When we talk about what we desire as being of value we should also be seeking some kind of ethical justification. Normatively this requires us to think about our duty to one another, being a good person and committing to the maximum happiness for the greatest number. Questions that arise from this that a worker should consider include: when is it fair to treat young people equally and when is it fair to differentiate in the way you treat young people? And what criteria do you use to determine what it is young people deserve?

Equality of opportunity

As youth workers committed to justice and fairness we should be concerned by the unfair treatment of young people. Our response as practitioners is likely to be informed by our professional frame of reference which should draw on our own attitudes, values and beliefs and also the legislative frameworks which regulate our practice. It is important that we recognise the significance of legislation and how it affects the way we work with young people. In response to claims of unfair treatment we have seen a rise in legislation through the 20th Century aimed at ensuring that people are not discriminated against. An obvious example of this is equal opportunity policy, designed to ensure all are entitled to the same treatment in terms of opportunity. To discriminate against someone on the grounds of race, ethnicity, gender, sexuality, faith and so on is unfair.

At a minimum, equal opportunity is easy to apply. Providing there is no evidence of preferential treatment, equal opportunity can be seen to exist. However there is an argument that equality of opportunity requires more effort. Swift (2005) suggests that there are three levels of equality of opportunity, minimal, conventional and radical:

- *Minimal.* A person's race, religion or gender should not prevent them from getting a job, an education, obtaining access etc.
- *Conventional.* The minimal is not enough, people's prospects in life should depend on ability and effort, not on social background. Coming from a poor family should not be relevant in terms of getting a good job or going to university.
- *Radical.* More than social background, natural ability should not restrict opportunity. Regardless of ability we should all have the same opportunity of getting the same rewards.

Minimum equal opportunity should be commonplace in most organisations today, with very few exceptions. If you work in the voluntary sector or public sector I am confident you would have been made aware of your organisation's equal opportunity policy at some stage in your employment. Such policies and procedures are used to ensure no one is discriminated against in the services and opportunities that are on offer. Very little intervention is required. However, whilst from a legislative perspective equal opportunity provides a useful monitoring framework for procedures around recruitment and admissions, it is weak in the face of natural inequality and social stratification.

> *This latter goal of positive equality will not be realized since equal opportunity combined with unequal ability and luck produce unequal results.*
>
> Honderich, 1991: 248

In the *conventional* model there is a suggestion that preferential treatment is needed. For example, widening access to university as seen in the previous government's education policy (DfES, 2006) would be an obvious example whereby extra support and encouragement is given to those who, for reasons other than ability, would not access higher education. Educational interventions such as Gifted and Talented (ibid.), is another example of attempting to ensure those with ability, regardless of socio-economic background, will go on to university study.

In the *radical* approach we start to enter the realms of a different sort of political discourse, one which places greater emphasis on neutralising difference. More socialist in its perspective, radical equal opportunity is more concerned that all receive equal reward regardless of ability and social background. To engineer such an approach would undoubtedly affect individual freedom (Swift, 2005).

How far we should go in preventing inequality in natural talent/ability from creating barriers is a contested debate. In applying Swift's concepts of equal opportunity to a practice scenario we are able to add some useful context to this discussion.

Imagine the following scenario: you are working with a group of young people who decide they want to have a talent contest.

- At a *minimum* all young people are invited and receive the same encouragement, no one is discriminated against; the offer is open to all, regardless of talent or ability. No further intervention is required.
- A more *conventional* approach might require you to provide extra support for those young people who do not have the same resources needed to participate in the contest, maybe you provide some technical equipment, thus removing social and or economic disadvantage.
- In the *radical model*, it is natural ability as well as social disadvantage that needs to be neutralised. In this scenario a lack of talent would not prevent a young person from receiving the same rewards as those more talented.

In the radical model we see the contest element of the talent show effectively cancelled out. However there are other scenarios where the radical concept of equal opportunity could be applied. Where young people's activities are accredited in some way you could reward all equally regardless of ability. Those in support of a more radical approach to equal opportunity would argue that natural ability should not prevent you from receiving the same rewards as those with greater ability. Thus in the radical approach for fairness to exist, other things need to be rewarded such as effort and enthusiasm, not just ability. A question that arises from this is whether there are any circumstances when it is appropriate to neutralise different ability to ensure all are rewarded equally. Similarly under what circumstances should ability and performance be reflected in the level of reward young people receive?

Fair society

As much as we are able to reflect on our interventions as youth workers it is also helpful to consider the wider societal context in which we practice. Youth work does not exist in a vacuum. Whether we like it or not, youth work is part of a political discourse which is primarily concerned with ensuring young people are equipped and willing to fully participate and contribute in all areas of society as active citizens.

Here we are presented with a dilemma. Whilst it is reasonable to think that those who benefit from society should contribute to society as well (Hume, 1985), how do we respond to those who argue they have not chosen to benefit from society? One response would be that in benefiting from society we have given tacit consent to be governed by society. A second response would be that we have a duty to support that which we have benefited from (Hart, 1958).

With these responses in mind let us assume that as members of society we accept and appreciate the benefits of living in a modern democracy, i.e. free education, health care, security, welfare, public services and so on. A society that is able to offer all of these things through the redistribution of wealth via taxation is, therefore, working to ensure that despite inequality, all are able to have what they need in order to survive.

Does this mean that a society which is committed to redressing social and economic disadvantage is also acting out of a sense of fairness? One way of answering this question is to consider the veil of ignorance that arises in Rawls' text *Justice as Fairness* (1999). Essentially the question that Rawls asks is this: what type of society would you choose if you knew nothing of your own status? Rawls suggests that it is unlikely that a basic system would exclude or disadvantage, on the grounds that one is not aware of one's social and economic standing from behind the veil of ignorance.

When Rawls developed the 'veil of ignorance' he was talking about a total system where from the original position all would be committed to ensuring fairness. Rawls also argues that inequality is justified as long as it can show that it is improving the position of the least favoured; moreover people are prepared to accept inequality providing they can see that the difference principle is working to minimise their position of social and economic disadvantage (Swift, 2005). Those with the most would have to be committed to helping those with the least.

Rawls goes to great lengths to articulate the importance of acknowledging those with fewer 'native assets', and the importance of redress, whilst also offering a word of caution for those who believe themselves naturally entitled to more than others:

> *Those who have been favoured by nature, whoever they are, may gain from their good fortune only on terms that improve the situation of those who have lost out. The naturally advantaged are not to gain merely because they are*

more gifted, but only to cover the extra costs of training and education and for using their endowment in ways that help the less fortunate as well. No one deserves their greater natural capacity, nor merits a more favourable starting point in life.

Rawls, 1999: 87

As much as Rawls' veil of ignorance would be impossible to apply, it does provide an interesting thought experiment which allows us to consider what a fair society should look like. The extent to which all are committed remains doubtful given concerns that, under capitalist free markets, employers are more concerned with profit which in turn results in the objectification of the worker rather than recognising the worker as an intelligent creative human being (Marx, 1992). At risk of getting drawn into a debate on planned economies versus free market capitalism, Rawls (1999) provides something of a challenge to those who find themselves in positions of social and economic advantage. As much as those with wealth have the resources to enjoy *formal* and *effective* freedom and power (Swift, 2005), the same people also have an opportunity under the 'strains of commitment' (Rawls, 1999) to use their wealth to benefit the least advantaged.

On a broader scale Rawls' ideas have a resonance with regards to practice, especially given the widening gap between rich and poor. Moral arguments for increased wealth and prosperity for the few are hard to justify, and claims for a fairer society ring aloud as we speak. On a micro level those skilled in youth work will recognise the need to work with a range of abilities and resources. Here Rawls' thinking about redistribution provides us with a just and fair approach to working with inequality. To work to this model we must accept that inequality is acceptable as long as those with more are committed to helping those without. We also would need to embrace inequality in a positive way, seeing its benefits. Or should people be free to do as they want with the wealth?

Conclusion

Hitherto our response to the unfair treatment of young people has emphasised the importance of fair conditions in which young people might flourish. We have come to see that many of the conditions that prevent young people from flourishing are in the first instance a matter of chance when it comes to the conditions we are born into. We have also seen that whilst legislation and policy emphasises the importance of valuing people equally, this does not always mean people are treated fairly. As much as we can legislate for fair treatment, it is important to recognise the need for a more altruistic attitude from those who find themselves in positions of advantage as well. Acting fairly is not simply a matter of ensuring that fair procedures are duly followed, rather it is a matter of being fair. How we respond to matters of fairness varies from one situation to the next. However if we value young people and want to ensure they all have an opportunity to develop as autonomous adults, rich in human agency, then a more egalitarian approach is needed.

So to conclude, how will you respond the next time a young person claims they have been treated unfairly?

SECTION TWO

CHAPTER 5

'Young People Need to Respect Themselves and Others'

Mike Seal

When (young people) feel cared for and respected by their peers, teachers and staff, they are significantly less likely to use alcohol and other drugs, engage in violence, depression or suicide and initiate early sexual activity.

King, 2010

The extent to which we respect ourselves is intimately connected with our idea of our worth, with our self-confidence, and with our sense of competence and control of our lives.

Beneditt, 2008: 487

How can you expect young people to respect society when society has not respected them for years?

Blog in response to the riots of August 2011

Does respect matter? The first two authors quoted above see it as vital in terms of young people's self-belief, confidence, sense of control and not needing to engage in 'risky' behaviours, although the nuances, and pros and cons of the latter are another debate. Other researchers have found respect an important element of developing and maintaining cultural identity (DeCremer, 2002; Jetten et al. 2005) self-esteem (Ellemers et al., 2004) gender identity (Jackson, Esses, & Burris, 2001) positive personal relationships, satisfaction (Frei & Shaver, 2002) communication (McCann et al., 2005) a sense of social justice (DeCremer & Tyler, 2005) relations with authority (Tyler & Lind, 1992) and general quality of life (Sung, 2004).

It is perhaps the third quote above that is most pertinent. As I am writing this there is rioting across the UK with politicians of all hues labelling the young people who have engaged in them as 'mindless', 'having no respect' and no reason for rioting apart from selfish acquisition; and therefore deserving no respect back. At the same time young people counter this with social networking, saying on Youtube they feel betrayed by consumerism's false promises; that the opportunities they were promised have not come to fruition; that the recession has left them behind; and that they are demonised for this, denied job opportunities and the material things that go along with them. Some talked about the powerful feeling, even for a few nights, of taking those things that are denied to them, including the streets that they have been excluded from through ASBOs, curfews, stop and search policies etc. It feels odd to be writing about philosophy in the heat of such a debate and it will be interesting to see how history has remembered these riots by the time this book is completed.

As well as being current, the concept of respect, and what we mean by it, seems crucial for a youth and community worker to consider. As a worker I sought it from young people, pilloried other agencies who seemed not to be giving it to them, and encouraged young people to give it to others, and particularly, themselves. Yet, as we will see, it is a remarkably contested term, and has a multiplicity of meanings that need to be unpacked. To these ends I want to examine several aspects of respect. First, I will ask what it is; making a distinction between the respect we give to all, and that which is earned, and show why this is an important distinction. By extension I will look at what respect we should give to institutions, and try and balance this with the respect that these institutions need to earn. Finally I think the word respect has currency with young people. I remember working with one young man who had attacked another quite seriously, and when I asked why, he said the other young man was not showing him respect. After further discussion a tangled web emerged of things that the other young man had done, talking about him behind his back, chatting up his girlfriend, selling drugs on his patch. It had got to a point where he had felt compelled to act, reluctantly he said, so as to not lose face, and more insidiously, so as not to be seen as soft and a potential target to others, who were watching for his reactions. We need to work with young people on what respect means in their lived lives.

I make a distinction between three close, but distinct, concepts: Reverentia – awe, a religious view of respect; Respekt (Feinberg: 1970) which is akin to inspiring or feeling fear, a type of respect that some young people I have worked with have sought, but which does not, ultimately, live up to expectations; and respect as normally understood. This confusion is not unique to young people as I will argue that current measures against those involved in the riots will at best invoke Respekt, not respect. Importantly I will argue that to give respect – true respect – is both a subjective and an objective process and, as such, we can work with young people on defining it for themselves. Finally I will examine self-respect, arguing it to be the bedrock of respect from which respect for others stems. It is, however, a slippery concept, and easily confused with pride and self-esteem, which can have unfortunate consequences for the individual and us all.

What is respect?

I will start by looking at some other definitions. Feinberg (1970) distinguishes three ways that the concept of respect has been used. First ther is *Respeckt*, which has elements of fear and warriness, as in how you should respect power tools, or the sea, or the local gang, particularly its leader. *Observantia* is respect for another's autonomy, or their rights, and is an intrinsic respect we should have for all, as distinct from *Respectia*, which can be earned, or lost, a distinction I shall return to. I would argue that a practical usage of respect, with young people at least, needs narrowing, otherwise we would say that fear, based on a rational appraisal of another's danger, and awe in the presence of something divine (which Feinberg sees as beyond the rational), are the same as actively deciding to honour the autonomy of another, regardless of one's own views and desires. I would like to argue that it is *Observantia* that is a practical usage of respect, and the one to work towards with young people, and I will spend this chapter examining the ramifications of working towards such a view. I think it is particularly important to contest the idea of Respeckt, as it is this concept of respect that is held by young people I have worked with who are in gangs (or attracted by the idea of being in them) – although not in a consistent way, which gives the worker a chance to challenge.

However, in order to do this consistently ourselves, another distinction needs to be made: aside from the respect we should give to all, there is respect that people earn, and lose. To these ends Darwall (1977) distinguishes between recognition respect and appraisal respect. The former we would give to, say, the law or people in general, and the latter to individuals for things that earn or lose respect. Recognition respect is not comparative, unlike appraisal respect which is. Appraisal respect is also relative, whereas recognition respect tends towards the absolute. We can appraise someone as being worthy of respect from their teaching ability, but not for what they say, or in their personal life. We do however recognise their intrinsic worth as a human being, as indeed we do with everyone.

I think this distinction is important because, for us as workers, it differentiates between telling young people that we should recognise everyone as a human being, and therefore deserving of respect, or other forms of recognition respect such as respecting elders, and appraisal respect which has to be earned. Some would argue that the aforementioned respect for elders should not be given, but appraised. More importantly as workers we can be conceptually confused. Looking back on my practice I was often talking about recognition respect, when the young people were talking about appraisal respect. For example, when I challenged young people's bullying or attacking of another young person, or group of young people, I challenged them for not intrinsically respecting them as people, whereas they were working through an appraisal construct of respect: and they had appraised them of not being worthy of it.

We can have both elements of respect towards the same object. For example, we can have recognition respect for a political or religious perspective's right to exist, but 'appraise' one of them as being less worthy of respect than the other. Looking back at the example of the young people not respecting and bullying other young people, I could first say that the bullies needed to give respect to them as human beings, challenging the act of bullying, and second challenge the basis on which they have appraised them as not being worthy of respect beyond this, expecting debatable criteria and consistency in their assessment. However there are assumptions we need to challenge here, not least that we need to be consistent and transparent in our challenging of appraisal respect.

Who deserves respect: appraisal respect

We have a chance to challenge if we accept that appraisal respect must be governed by reason (Cranor, 1975; Dillon, 2010; Raz, 1986). As Dillon says, we need a criteria to respect something or someone: it cannot be for 'just any old reason or for no reason at all' (Dillon, 2010: 2). But does this mean that we need objective appraisal criteria for the reason we should apply? To do so falls into the dangers of essentialism and begs the question of what these criteria would be. At the same time if we descend into relativism, and say that the individual is the sole determinant of their reasons to respect, and even that their criteria need to be rational, there are few grounds to challenge young people. Dillon (1997, 2003, 2010), in searching for a definition of respect, goes back to the Latin *respicere*, which means 'to look back at' or 'to look again'. He says that:

> The idea of paying heed or giving proper attention to the object which is central to respect often means trying to see the object clearly, as it really is in its own right, and not seeing it solely through the filter of one's own desires and fears or likes and dislikes.

Interestingly, in Dillon's conceptualisation of respect, there are both subjective and objective elements. It is subjective as in it is the young person's judgment of the other and based on the young person's criteria. However it is objective; or at least inter-subjective in that, by Dillon's definition, it needs to be judged with the perspective and reality of the other person taken into account, or at least some reference point outside of the respecter. Dillon also says that in judging something as deserving respect we are making a universalised statement, in that if we respect another, we believe that this respect should be afforded to them by others.

As we are claiming that respect is not dependant on or stemming from our feelings, desires, and interests, we are making a claim that something deserves respect independently of us. Dillon (2010) also says that respect is naturally universalising in that, if we respect something for having certain subjective characteristics, we imply that, if something else had the same characteristics, we would also respect this. Thus 'subjectivity defers to objectivity'. This universalising tendency will become important when we return to making a distinction between respect and Respeckt. Raz (1986) would also argue that an individual's respect can be inappropriate or unwarranted, for the object may not have the characteristics they think it has, although he does not go on to say what these criteria should be.

For me, the view that giving or withholding appraisal respect needs some subjective/objective rationality on behalf of the young person offers a youth worker the chance to challenge their rationale for respecting, or not respecting, something or someone. This challenge will need to be rooted in that young person's own understanding and frameworks, but there will need to be some logic to it, and some reference to the other person's or object's own perspectives and rationales. Looking again at my earlier example, they may appraise those young people as not warranting respect, but they will need to explain, and be challenged, on why they did or did not give this respect, including reference to the perspectives of others, including those other young people, and other young people to whom they do afford respect. We are also not saying that young people should just give total respect to anyone, or any institution, that they should just unquestioningly 'respect their elders', apart from to give them the respect they should to any human being.

Returning to the respect/Respeckt debate, Dillon distinguishes respect from fear of others or Respeckt, saying we do not respect those we fear as we do not respect the person enough to get to know them in their own right, but only in so far as we need to allay the fear of what they might do to us. Similarly we may not respect the natural world for itself, only what it could do to us. Otherwise we could not distinguish between a hunter and a conservationist's respect for nature. A hunter may not respect an animal in its own right, but only its ability to kill – the danger it represents. Interestingly, Dillon (2010) feels that respect, as opposed to fear or Respekt, is something that the respecter gives independent of the respectee's desires or wants for it. We cannot force someone to respect us, only fear us, perhaps make them say they respect us. Fear is also not universalising, it is conditional on the circumstances that make that fear arise in us; and we would not want others to respect that person, only fear them in certain circumstances, which we might advise them of. These distinctions may seem semantic, but they could have important implications when working with someone who wants to join a gang, and/or engage in illegal activities to get 'respect'. We can also not deny that for many young people Respeckt is how they see and live the concept of respect (Langdon, 2007) and we need to engage with it thoughtfully.

I recently worked with a group of young people who had been caught up in the dynamics of gangs and illegal activities. We had an interesting discussion about respect that echoed some of Dillon's thoughts on the distinctions between respect, Repeckt and fear. They talked about how they, and young people they knew, engaged in such activities seeking respect. However they were not respected in Dillon's terms as people in their own right, only in terms of what they could do for those in the gang, or the threat of what they could inflict on people.

Looking at another distinction, Beneditt (2008) and Frank (2007) say respect is important because we want to live in a predictable world where we have some guarantees about how we will be received and treated, especially by others who do not know us. Fear or Respeckt does not give us this. The group of young people talked, ironically, about the fear that remained for many at the top of gangs, and how they could never leave their own organisations. This was because any decline in the characteristics that had made them feared, such as being perceived as getting old or 'soft', made them vulnerable, both from outside and inside, to being replaced by those who wanted their power, or those who wanted revenge for how that power had been obtained and maintained.

On another level the young people's discussions showed a real recognition of the distinction and difference in value of respect and Respeckt. In their activities they were not getting 'real' respect, only fear, and this felt lesser to them. Some talked about knowing that the elders in their community did not really respect them, even when they said they did, it was actually only fear, concealing private distain. One young person memorably said that the motivating factors for them giving up this life was that his mother could not talk to people about what he did – she, and they, did not respect what he did. This similarly applied to the group dynamics of the 'gang'. They talked about the wannabes' or runners' desire to be respected by those higher up in the gang, when in fact they were often being used to do the dangerous jobs, and were expendable. Those on the next rung up were respected if they could get things done, but those who were too competent might be seen as a threat by those at the top who, as said before, knew that their underlings' loyalty was limited to their own interests, and if their interests were better served by taking over or being disloyal, they would. This was not to say that real respect was not present in the gangs, and some talked about getting it there for perhaps the first time in their lives, something else we will return to. However, this mix of respect and Respeckt certainly did not make for feelings of stability and security.

However misconceived, we can see that appraisal respect, the need to be considered good at something, and in some cases to be considered better than others, is very important to young people. Frank (2007) contends that we tend to admire or respect people for something that is not only distinct, but something that we ourselves desire. Such a view is highly contested, and easily draws us into a debate about what is innate, a part of human nature, and what is socially constructed. I do not wish to go into that debate here. However, whether innate or socially constructed, the need for status is common in the way in which many of the young people I have worked with see the world, and gaining it was one of the other reasons the young people I worked with gave for going into gangs and organised criminal activity. Frank (2007) notes that this status can be defined by such things as material wealth (power), as we saw in the cases of the young people, but could also be defined as 'higher' values such as selflessness, benevolence etc. In this way he feels the desire for status is there, but it is flexible in what it can be attuned to. This again gives us scope with young people to work on what, if they need it, they need status in terms of, and why they are constructing it in a particular way. Also, as Frank conflates status with respect, it reminds us that certain ways of getting it are in fact not going to satisfy the young person, as this status, as in this kind of Respeckt, will be permanently vulnerable.

Recognition respect: what or who should we respect innately?

Recognition respect is that idea that people or things deserve a degree of unconditional respect. It is not something to be earned. *Observantia* is that respect we give one another regardless of our own views and desires. Such a formulation is derived from Kant who argues that all people are intrinsically deserving of respect, as people or humans. Following from Dillon (2010), people must be treated as worthy of respect in their own right, and not as a means to fulfilling our own desires or wants. One formulation of Kant's categorical imperative, for him the fundamental supreme principle that determines morality, shows that we must act with respect for the inherent worth of a person: 'act in such a way that you treat humanity, whether in your own person or the person of any other, never simply as a means but always at the same time as an end' (*Kant, 1948*). Even if we accept this as our premise (and we will come back to those who do not), we are still left with several questions to answer:

- First, on what grounds is this premise true? What is it about humans that they deserve respect, and is this not true of other animals or even objects?
- Second, do we really mean everyone, even those who do not respect others as humans or are not capable of doing so?
- Third, even if everyone is due respect, what is the nature of this respect we owe them.

Looking at the first question, as Dillon (2010) says, for humans to deserve respect there needs to be something that all humans have in common, and it must be a quality deserving of respect. He notes that philosophers have claimed many things to be common to all humans, such as the ability to be moved by considerations of moral obligation, the ability to value appropriately, the ability to reason, and the ability to engage in reciprocal relationships. Yet can we say this is true of everyone? Some would argue that certain animals are capable of such abilities, and that we should therefore afford them equal respect (which we certainly do not). Even if we could find something that all humans uniquely had in common, and could agree that it was something of value, it does not necessarily follow that this would afford them respect. Some authors argue that this link is historical rather than logical and borne out of a desire for a coherent guiding moral philosophy (Buss, 1999; Gibbard, 1990).

Kant answers both this and the second concern about who deserves respect, in terms of humans being rational agents. Kant says that the very definition of a person is a rational being that is an end in themselves. The term 'person' means a being whose rational nature 'already marks them out as ends in themselves. . .and an object of respect' (Dillon, 2010: 428). While this may seem to be a tautology, or obvious, at the time it was a radical claim that countered the prevailing aristocratic view (Hobbes, 1994) that saw respect only in terms of appraisal respect, akin to honour, and was based on a person's achievement, standing, status etc. Kant, conversely, saw the dignity of persons, and our obligation to respect this dignity, as an 'absolute, unconditional, objective and independent of any other aspects of them'. Such a position, as Dillon notes, has several implications. First it means that only a rational agent can be a person, and some humans therefore might not count as people. Second it opens up the idea that other non-humans, who may be rational agents, could be people. Finally, the respect owed us is for our potential for rational free autonomous action, it is independent of what we actually do, even if we never act morally, or commit actions that many would consider abhorrent such as willful murder or child rape. In Kant's view, such actions do not diminish a person's right to respect.

Looking at the first implication, this could mean that those who do not yet have the capacity to be a free rational agent are not yet people. This might include young people, who even in UK law cannot be seen as fully morally responsible persons until they are ten, and in many other countries the age of responsibility is a lot higher. As Stojanov (2010) says, part of the rationale of school education is precisely to aid young people in becoming such persons: the notion of citizenship education is an echo of this. Curren (2007: 470) suggests the concept of 'prospective respect', which might be helpful in order to overcome this difficulty. While young people cannot be taken to be fully capable of reason yet, adults such as teachers and parents should recognise them as having the potential to become rational and have moral autonomy. Indeed, for Stojanov the recognition of this should be understood as a 'central norm of pedagogical action.'

A more complicated example might be people with severe enough learning disabilities or mental health issues that they could never become such 'free rational moral' agents. While I would rather not debate the nuances of personhood and what constitutes such 'agents' here, it opens up the potential that some humans would not be considered people. Dillon (2010) says that we can exchange sentience for rational autonomy as what deserves unconditional respect. However, the link to why humans deserve respect becomes broken in such an argument, as a sentient being has no obligation to give respect to another in the way that a rational autonomous being does. Or perhaps we can look for another basis for the argument that humans deserve respect. Traditionally Utilitarianism is seen as in opposition to Kantian perspectives (Benn, 1988; Brody, 1982) in that it cannot accommodate respect for persons, because situations may arise when not honouring the autonomy of the individual is for the greater good.

However some supporters of Utilitarianism argue in different ways that it can accommodate the idea of respect for persons (Cummiskey, 2008; Downie and Telfer, 1969; Gruzalski, 1982; Landesman, 1982; Pettit, 1989) One argument is that the bad created by disrespecting the individual cannot be outweighed by any greater good, particularly if it creates a dynamic where anyone could be that disrespected person. The fear caused by such Respeckt would severely damage utility. Others, such as Downie and Telfer (1969) argue that Utilitarianism is actually derived from the principle of respect for persons, and is thus synonymous with it. Again, the rest of the chapter could look at the traditional Utilitarian/Kant debate, and I would rather not do that. Suffice to say that some formations of Utilitarianism may provide a better grounding for the duty to respect persons, as they can rely on sentience alone as grounds for respect (Pettit, 1989). All of these things provide a point for debate with young people. In my experience the debate about respecting animals, including which animals, is often heated. As ever in philosophy, however, final agreement is unlikely to be reached.

Respect for institutions

Finally, Hudson (1986) identifies an aspect of recognition respect he calls institutional respect. It is to give deference to institutions, which could be the things that an institution does, which are not necessarily predictable beforehand, but we respect them to do the 'right thing'. This could include say institutions such as school, or the law, or individuals in institutional roles such as doctors, teachers, but also parents. I think for young people this is an interesting one. Kant was generally in favour of this kind of institutional reverence, particularly for the law and the church – however this could be seen as blind obedience (Dillon, 2001) and I would find it problematic, and probably not possible to work with young people towards a blanket respect for institutions.

The question seems to be how much should institutional respect be recognised or appraised. One view of this, and the one I would subscribe to, would be that we sometimes need to give enough recognition to an institution to be able to appraise it fairly. Taking school as an example, if I am not educated, or have a restricted view of education, I need to go through a level of education to be able to recognise and appraise it properly. At the last college I worked in, our study days were very experiential. There would be no set agendas, the students would be expected to develop one, and the role of the tutor was to facilitate learning, not to teach in the sense of imparting knowledge. Some tutors would not even announce themselves as tutors until asked. Interestingly students often reject this model before going on to embrace it. It took them out of their comfort zone not to have the teachers at the front, and for their own role not to be a passive one.

Conversely institutions may not have this liberatory agenda, and do not encourage, or see it as their role, to help people develop these appraisal skills. I went to a traditional grammar school and, in my by now informed opinion, received a poor education. However, while still at school I had only an inkling of this, and lacked the vocabulary, or critical ability, to say that with authority. It is only now, as an educator myself, that I can know for sure that I received a poor education. It is here that the youth worker's role becomes apparent. We can help young people develop the critical facility to meaningfully appraise, which may initially include some recognition respect. This may be difficult if their experience of an institution, school, the justice system or the care system is entirely negative. We are helping them make sense of their experiences, rather than simply rejecting them outright, even if it is rejection that they ultimately return to.

What does it mean to respect someone?

Even if some consensus is reached with young people as to who deserves respect, it still needs to be debated as to what this respect will look like. What does it mean we should still do in our behaviour that is respectful, say, to a war criminal or a paedophile? Interestingly Kant originally framed these as strictly negative duties, in that we should refrain from treating others as means, showing contempt for them thereby denying that they have worth, treating them with arrogance, publicly exposing their faults, and ridiculing or mocking them. He also said we have a duty to ourselves to control our own desire to think well of ourselves as for him this is the main cause of disrespect. These do seem hard to stick to as individuals, let alone as society, and it is interesting to think about them in the context of the current riots. Judges have been explicitly instructed to 'give high sentences' and praised when they do, as this gives out the 'right message to others', including giving two people four years each for their postings on social networking sites. Is this not treating people as means? As for mocking them, exposing their faults and treating them with arrogance, I think the media coverage speaks for itself (with headlines like 'British Youth are "the Most Unpleasant and Violent in the World" ' (*Daily Mail*, 10 August 2011), 'Flaming Morons' (*Daily Express*, 11 August 2011)). This is an example of the kind of discussion that could be had with young people, both about how they are treated, but also in how they treat others.

Other authors (Gaus, 1998; Lysaught, 2004; Norman, 1989) have tried to look at more positive formations of these duties, in particular the idea that, in order to respect a person, we need to nurture and develop their autonomy. These authors have seen the notion of autonomy as particularly important in the medical field, observing some quite radical shifts in how medical staff view patient autonomy, including in the diagnostic process. It would be an interesting point to see if young people have experience of being afforded the same degree of autonomy by other professionals. Simon covers the notion of autonomy in greater detail elsewhere; suffice to say that some Utilitarians question its privileging, saying that it should be balanced against community interests, not that the two are exclusive. An alternate view of positive duty is about equality. As we noted before it is our standing as free rational beings, as Kant says, 'by which we exact or demand respect from one another' (*Kant, 1948*). Darwall says this puts the individual in the position of being 'an equal (with) the authority to make claims and demands on one another as free and rational agents' and to hold each other accountable for complying with these commands (Darwall, 2004: 43–4). A Marxist interpretation of this would be to ensure the other has enough material standing to make this freedom possible, to enable us to exercise our autonomy, rather than just subsist.

These are, again, all points for debate with young people. A study in the States, (King, 2010), looking at what respect meant in schools, found students saw it as having four elements:

1. *Treating others the way that you would like to be treated (The Golden Rule).*
2. *Listening to others when they are talking.*
3. *Honouring others' property and personal space.*
4. *Refraining from talking negatively about other students when they are not present.*

I think that would be a good starting point for young people, or perhaps it should be applied to the youth club, or even the street.

Self-respect

As Dillon says, while the concept of respect and its relative importance is quite hotly debated, most commentators agree on the importance of individuals having self-respect, both for their own sake and for that of society (Buss, 1999; Dillon, 2010; Thomas, 2001). Kant argues that it is a similar duty to the one we have to others, to respect their freedom and autonomy, in fact it is the primary duty, because if we cannot do this for ourselves then we cannot do it for others. Self-respect, again, has both appraisal and recognition aspects. Dillon (2010) however sees self-respect as qualitatively different from respect from others. He sees it as more akin to a disposition, as it is something we hold all the time, while respect for others, or other things, often only comes into play during our encounters with them, be it directly or indirectly.

Several commentators (Buss, 1999; Dillon, 2010; Thomas, 2001) talk about a base level of self-respect that is needed before we can even engage with the other forms of respect, or even life itself. These authors see this bottom line variably in spiritual (Buss, 1999) psychological (Thomas, 2001) and political (Dillon, 2010) terms, but share the same pessimism about possibilities when it is absent. Unfortunately, there are numerous accounts about how such a base level of self-respect is forcedly broken, such as with slaves (Du Bois, 1903), in concentration camps (Levi, 1947), or in general with political groups that regimes seek to subjugate (Orwell, 1949). On a more individual level I have worked with people who have been on the edge of such despair, and while some have come back from it, once over the edge, when people lose the will to live, I personally have not been able to do much. However, unless it is at this extreme, oppression can be overcome, and can even be a catalyst in communities developing and fighting for self-respect and autonomy in the face of oppression (Freire, 1972).

Dillon sees three aspects of self-respect, which he sees as an aspect of recognition respect. The first is recognition of our status as rational free agents, and therefore deserving of respect. Internally this can give us a duty, again, to respect others, but also specifically a duty to present ourselves to others in keeping with self-respect (Boxill, 1976; Hill, 1973) We should not be servile (believing others to be better than us) but we should also not be arrogant (believing that we are better than others). We should not put up with being disrespected, although our reactions to not being respected should remain respectful. A second form of recognition self-respect that follows from this, means that we must behave as we believe a free moral agent, who respects themselves and others, would. What such behaviours would be is contestable, but could include not being 'shameless, uncontrolled, weak-willed, self-consciously sycophantic, chronically irresponsible, slothfully dependent, self-destructive, or unconcerned with the shape and direction of their lives' (Dillon, 2010: 4).

Again, these are all areas where we, as youth workers, engage with young people, including challenging them when they assume such traits exist in others. I have found the concept of not being self-destructive or unconcerned with the shape of their lives to be effective in my discussion with young people, particularly with the aforementioned young people involved in gang and criminal activities. It could be said that their perusal of these 'careers' is a mark of self-respect, especially in the face of denied opportunities. Indeed the young people I have worked with would not consider themselves uncontrolled, weak willed or even irresponsible. However, as we have discussed before, their paths are ultimately self-destructive, even, or especially, at the top of 'gangs', and will not give them the control over the shape and direction of their lives that they think it will. Hill (1973) extends this, saying that self-respecting people will judge themselves according to whether they are living up to their ideals, including their interpretations of their life goals and guiding moral principles that stem from them. In youth work terms we often call this 'authenticity'

(Smith, 2002) and see it as one of the yardsticks by which workers should measure themselves, and encourage others to do so.

Self-respect, self-esteem and pride

However, are judgements about what kind of life stems from what values, and what constitutes honouring them or degrading them, subjective or objective? Kant, and Dillon again, argue that it needs to be both, as self-respect is by definition inter-subjective, as is all respect, as one person's actions can impact on the autonomy of others. To help us in this some authors make the useful distinction between self-respect, self-esteem (Darwall, 1977) and pride (Dillon, 2010). Darwall (1977) sees the distinction in terms of morality: self-respect is by definition related to one's moral sense, while self-esteem is not necessarily so, and can be based on achievements such as job promotion or acquisition of wealth. However, we can have self-esteem and not respect ourselves, or even be in a situation where our way of getting self-esteem undermines our self-respect.

To give an example: as a trainer I often encountered people who previously had jobs that were more financially rewarding, such as working in the City, but they were aware that their actions actually made many people's lives worse, and this was not compatible with their own view of themselves. They often willingly took a large pay cut to do something more worthy and 'fitting'. I find this interplay between self-respect, self-esteem and pride fascinating, and am coming to think that they are a hierarchy, starting with pride, building through self-esteem and culminating with self-respect, somewhat akin to Maslow (1968). In my experience as a trainer, the person who gave me the most to reflect on was someone who said that his self-esteem had been so low in his upbringing that he continually needed to prove himself, and did this through wealth acquisition, which eventually proved to be a chimera. Most tellingly he did not think that he could have seen this unless he had tried to achieve self-respect through wealth, so low was his self-esteem and pride in himself. I am reminded of a previous piece of research I conducted with homeless people (Seal, 2008) where some long term homeless people, particularly those who used drugs, felt that their experience, or survival as they put it, had made them self-ish. This in turn made them run from themselves because they did not want to face this selfishness. They also made a distinction between pride and self-respect that echoes Dillon (2010), seeing that pride can be a form of arrogance, or simply false, and therefore needing a degree of objective criticism to become self-respect. The specific example talked about was the danger of pride in not asking for help. For those involved in the riots it could be pride that resulted in looting things that they felt they 'deserved' but could not access.

This need for some objectivity brings me back to me the dangers of overemphasising autonomy in regards to, and making it synonymous with, respect. I have written elsewhere about the difficulty in recognising that you cannot help yourself and need the intervention of others (Seal, 2005). It was the desire for autonomy in homeless people, seen here in terms of pride, that stopped people asking for the assistance they would need to develop self-respect, and indeed 'true' autonomy, which includes an admission of needing others. It was a false pride that the research recommended other homeless people challenge in themselves. It is a false pride that those who looted in the riots need to reflect on, in terms of their actions, what they think they deserve in life, and what they have to do to get it. In turn those who demonised those who looted as inhuman and deserving of severe prison sentences need to examine their own false pride that society has no responsibility here, and their certainties that the looters had the complete autonomy that such condemnation needs. The relationship is complex, and one well worth working through for both workers, and in turn with young people. On reflection, as a worker I was often conceptually confused in my work with young people, blending self-esteem, self-respect, and pride into one, and then asking them to be autonomous, but also responsible for others – I think I must have confused others as well as myself.

Ironically it is perhaps this recognition that self-respect is socially constructed (Moody-Adams, 1992) which shatters the binary of subjective and objective, and gives us the potential to rescue, or restructure, autonomy. The traditional, and Kantian, view of respect is as an obligation on the individual, which then universalises to society. For Rawls (1999) this does not tackle the idea of justice satisfactorily, particularly where a society is structured in a way that respect for individuals is not embedded in its institutions or cultures, and people are not encouraged to develop autonomy. For him, social institutions need to be designed in such a way that supports and nurtures self-respect. Other authors have concentrated on the ways that individuals and groups have developed a sense of self-respect in the face of, and as a counter to, their oppression within society (Freire, 1972) Youth workers should perhaps remember their wider role in countering such injustices; which stop people from being able to develop self-respect; and their role in enabling them to develop self autonomy and respect despite oppression.

Conclusion

I would briefly like to return to the concept of Respekt, as I think it is a relevant concept in examining how young people have been treated by many adults, and society, and in turn how young people have responded. Much of UK policy aimed at young people, particularly criminal justice measures, has been in the name of Respeckt, at best, of young people, and certainly not respect. In turn these same policies have engendered Respekt, not respect in young people towards adults and their institutions. These policies have not given young people respect for their rationality or autonomy. Their perspectives are rarely sought (remember 'understand a little less and condemn a little more'). Measures are intended to deter and instil fear; CCTV shows that young people cannot be trusted, and also a lack of trust that the community can deal with them. ASBOs exacerbate relations with the rest of the community, rather than develop mutual respect. Then, like the underlings in gangs, when young people see an opportunity, or a moment of weakness in those above, to challenge those who control them, they will take it, because they have been instilled with Respeckt, or fear, not true respect. Then what is the response? To label them mindless, further denying their personhood, to propose using water cannons, and to increase police powers and presence. This will create, at best, a vulnerable peace, until the next opportunity arises for young people to cast aside the fear instilled in them.

CHAPTER 6

'I Like to Think Young People Can Trust Me'

Mike Seal

Trust is the truly mysterious, barely known entity that holds society and ourselves together, the 'dark matter' of the soul.

Bowman and Spicer, 2007: 1

The desire for trust in relationships is commonplace amongst youth workers; we wish to have others trust us, and get to a point where we can place trust in them. The notion of relationship is a thing many authors consider essential to youth work and the helping professions (Duck, 1999; Goetschius & Tash., 1967; Perlman, 1979; Rogers, 1967; Smith, 2001). These same authors often see trust as one of the essential elements of that relationship. This is equally true of practitioners. When students discuss practice in class, trust features heavily when they look at the components of an effective relationship. Yet what do we mean by trust? Is it a rational or even useful thing? And if it is, what are its parameters, limits and dangers?

I will make the argument that is vital to youth and community workers, as we base our interactions around relationships, which need trust as a basis for them. Positively, I will also argue that one of the unique aspects of youth work relationships is that they allow for trust to flourish, and in its most powerful form, mutual trust. I think that this has been eroded in many care professions in the name of professional boundaries and, through a mechanised view of safeguarding, is in danger of happening in youth and community work, and we need to make a claim for it. We also need to think carefully about trust because it is a slippery concept that is not always used precisely, or even ethically. Reflecting on my own practice I asked people to trust me when I could not really explain the reasons for what I was doing in relation to them, and really just wanted them to stop asking for an explanation. Conversely, I made implicit threats in telling people that I trusted them – not to exercise their own judgement, but to do as I would do – the threat being one of rejection if they 'betrayed' me.

McLeod (2011) identifies five dimensions of trust in interpersonal relationships that I have adapted and re-interpreted into five questions about trust for practitioners to ask themselves in their everyday practice. There are also other types of trust apart from an inter-relational one, such as trust in institutions (Hardin, 2002) or self trust, but McLeod sees interpersonal trust as the central concept from which these others stem. For the purposes of this chapter I will take the same approach, mainly because it seems to be the most common way that practitioners discuss the trust between themselves and another, and because I considered the self and institutions when considering respect (Chapter 5). My five questions are:

- *What is the nature of trust?* How it is distinct from other concepts and phenomena, such as reliance? Within this is the question of what we mean when we ask someone to trust us, or we say we trust them, the expectations on both sides, and how this can be negotiated.
- *What is it to be considered trustworthy?* What are the conditions of us trusting others, and for others to be able to trust us? When we say we trust a colleague, are we saying their actions are reliable or predictable, or is it an assumption of goodwill towards us in their actions, regardless of whether we can predict, or agree with, what they do? Other debates concern whether trustworthiness is a virtue we seek to cultivate, or if it is always contingent on circumstances.
- *Is it reasonable, or a good idea, to trust others?* McCleod terms this the epistemology of trust. Is it a good idea to trust others, is the world a trustworthy place? In asking this we need to look at a person's disposition towards trust, whether they tend to trust or not, and what the right balance should be in our society. The central question here is whether one ought to trust others or not, and under what circumstances.
- *What is the value of trust?* In other words, is it important or useful to trust others, and if so, why? McLeod argues that to trust others provides 'opportunities for cooperative activity, knowledge, autonomy, self-respect, and overall moral maturity'. These opportunities seem akin to the values and overall project of youth work, but are they justified?
- *How do we cultivate trust?* McLeod calls this the will to trust. She examines this particularly in the context of those who, for whatever reason, do not trust people, or have learned not to trust others. This seems a very pertinent question for youth workers as it explores how we can build trust and how can we work with people on the issue.

What are the nature and limits of trust?

Mayer et al. (1995) view trust as our willingness 'to rely on the actions of another party' with a 'reasonable expectation' that they will act in our interests. However trust also entails that we should not have control over this, and we therefore risk that the other party will not act in our interests. (Mayer et al., 1995: 710). Similarly McLeod (2011) says that trusting requires that we can:

1. *Be vulnerable to others (vulnerable to betrayal in particular).*
2. *Think well of others, at least in certain domains.*
3. *Be optimistic that they are, or at least will be, competent in certain respects.*

There are important implications from both these accounts.

Vulnerability

Mayer, McLeod, and other authors (Becker, 1996) are saying that in order to trust another, we need to make ourselves vulnerable to that other person and that there is the potential to have this vulnerability betrayed, but we think, or at least hope, that they will not do this. These conceptualisations have big implications for youth workers. Take the idea of vulnerability: do we expect young people and colleagues to open up their vulnerabilities to us, and does this necessitate the potential that we could betray them? As McLeod (2011) and Becker (1996) say, if it were guaranteed that the other person would not betray us, or that there would be no consequences for us if they did, then there would be no need to trust them. We may just respect their ideas etc. Maybe we do not want, or need trust in our relationships with young people. The question for me is, what advantage is there for a young person to make themselves vulnerable and open to potential betrayal? It may be enough that they value our relationship. We will explore in this section the merits of young people placing trust in us, and thus exposing their vulnerability to us. We could, for example, decide that we are mutually better off with Baier's (1986) lesser notion of reliance, which does not necessarily entail vulnerability and its risk of betrayal, just the lesser ill of disappointment. If, for now, we accept that it may be worthwhile, as youthworkers, to have trust as a part of our relationship, we need to ask ourselves if this vulnerability is reciprocal, and whether we should open up our own vulnerabilities to young people and colleagues. If we do not, we are not reciprocating their trust and the question then arises as to whether this matters.

It would seem pertinent to investigate what we mean by vulnerability and betrayal – concepts in themselves. Vulnerability is often defined in terms of being subject to harm, physically or emotionally. Common usages might include not feeling safe or protected, and being subject to ridicule. This is akin to sociological definitions which tend to see vulnerability in terms of safety, risk and being unable to protect oneself (Davies, 2005; Harden et al., 2000). I do not imagine we would want young people or colleagues to be subject to ridicule but in my experience, young people and colleagues will tell me things they are uncertain about, and sometimes feel a degree of shame about. They were also fearful that they would come to harm if I revealed what they had said to others, or more generally that what they had done was somehow wrong. This seemed to be rooted in uncertainty about the basis of their actions, which is again a form of vulnerability. Assuming, for now, that this vulnerability or feeling of uncertainty has some value, there are still other questions about its nature.

Mutuality

I want firstly to consider whether trust needs to be mutual. For me the question is whether we should expose our vulnerabilities to the young people and colleagues who place trust in us, allowing them to hold our trust, or even if we should place our trust in them first. Perhaps the starting point for this is the notion of reciprocity, which is cited by youth work authors (Ledwith, 2007; Putnam, 2000; Smith, 2004; Young, 2010) and government alike as an essential aspect of our relationships with young people, and sometimes even as what distinguishes us from other professions (Smith, 2004; Young, 2010). If we do value reciprocity, then there is a danger of a power imbalance. Talking from a supervision perspective, but one that I think could be applied to our relationships with young people, Page and Wosket note that:

> *The supervisee is regularly exposing his shortcomings and difficulties in a way which the supervisor is not required to do. This difference in degree of vulnerability, along with the authority within the supervisor's role, lead to a natural imbalance of experienced power within the relationship. . .There are also likely to be imbalances resulting from the personal material.*
>
> Page and Wosket, 1994: 11

Game theory also points towards the fact that while mutual or reciprocal trust is not essential for a trusting relationship, it certainly fosters and deepens it (Birk, 2000; Falcone & Castelfranchi, 2001). Perhaps part of the fear of not allowing ourselves to trust others, even when we encourage them to trust us or others, has roots in negative constructions of vulnerability. Some of the fears or vulnerabilities of colleagues that I hold as a manager are uncertainties about their practice or themselves as academics. Habermas said that to have an 'ideal speech situation', whereby we can have coercion-free and democratic dialogue, 'depends on vulnerable forms of innovation-bearing, reciprocal and un-forcedly egalitarian everyday communication' (1985: 82). We need uncertainty, or we are just rehearsing or repeating already run arguments. Wolfe and Richardson (2001) talk about how true conversation, and learning in conversation, happens not when we are within our boundaries, understandings, or knowledge, but where we are on the edge of them, in the realms of uncertainty and vulnerability. Perhaps I should therefore share my own vulnerabilities and uncertainties with those I supervise. We have then already established at least one value for trust: it is essential for learning.

This may be true in terms of developing shared conceptual knowledge, but does it apply to practice? The question of whether I should share my vulnerabilities and uncertainties about my practice with the young person, student or supervisee, who is subject to that practice, seems pertinent. I have heard practitioners say that if we admitted our uncertainties then young people would not have confidence in us. An alternative view is that if we share our own uncertainties and vulnerabilities, it validates and normalises the uncertainties that young people feel. I remember as a worker hearing the phrase 'ambiguity is normal' (Milner and Rollnick, 2003) and feeling very empowered by it, as I had self-labelled my own indecisiveness as pathological.

Smith (2002) in exploring the concept of authenticity in youth work said a key is 'accepting that vulnerability within the work is necessary and inevitably can go some way in keeping a level of realness in our interaction with people'. She looks at authenticity in the context of Palmer's (1998) work on teachers' inner lives, which suggests that 'people who engage in something they care about and bring themselves to it, become vulnerable' (1998: 17). It is this fear, of being vulnerable, and of a live encounter where we may hear, or say, something we do not want to (1998: 36–7) that pushes them to create an (un)professional distancing (Illich, 1977) from themselves, the young people and their practice. This is compounded by a fear of criticism of their work, which in turn, because of its closeness, becomes criticism of the self, a vulnerability that consolidates this distancing. Yet, as Palmer says, 'this fear of losing identity, through a conflict of ideas can also help workers to grow and develop both as practitioners and as people' (1998: 18).

A colleague of mine recently took a risk, and made himself vulnerable, both with a young person and with his colleagues. He had a deteriorating relationship with a student, albeit one that had started well. He had often defended this student to other colleagues. However, this student did not like various challenges my colleague had made, and marks he had received from him. Eventually this student dressed down my colleague in front of other students and subsequently implied he was going to bring a grievance against him. My colleague continued to be professional in his dealing with the student, despite the hurt, while the student got more unreasonable in his reactions, to the point where he was becoming 'vulnerable' to being formally disciplined. The risk my colleague took was in dropping his professionalism and being very honest about his feelings about the situation, his personal humiliation and his own feelings of betrayal. This was to the point where my colleague's reaction could have added to the grievance case the student had threatened. Interestingly it was at this point in the relationship that the student felt there had been a breakthrough, and that he had a 'real' relationship with my colleague again. They were both now vulnerable to each other.

A relative concept

Thus far, trust seems to be an all or nothing proposition. However most authors (McLeod, 2011; Dasgupta, 1988) recognise it as a relative concept. The truster may reduce their risk and vulnerability by having parameters to their trust, or monitoring the behaviour of the trusted. Yet, as Dasgupta (1988) and McLeod (2011) note, the more we monitor and constrain the areas of trust we allow someone, the less we trust that person: 'a refusal to be vulnerable tends to undermine trust or prevents it from occurring at all' (McLeod, 2011: 12). We must again remember that trust breeds trust, and distrust distrust (Birk, 2000; Falcone & Castelfranchi, 2001). Another qualification that could be made is that we may trust people, even without monitoring, but only in certain aspects. Most authors concede (Hardin, 2002;

McLeod, 2011) that we rarely, if ever, trust people in every respect . For example a friend of mine said of her husband recently that she trusted him in terms of practical things like driving, and looking after their children, but not in terms of his fidelity.

We also need to challenge two other common usages of the word trust (Hardin, 2002; McLeod, 2011) which I do not think qualify as trust. The first is where the truster 'trusts' the trusted to carry out certain actions, and if they do not take these actions, the truster has had their trust betrayed. An example seems pertinent. A friend of mine acted up for his manager, who on appointing him said it was because he could be 'trusted'. By this the manager meant that my friend could be trusted to act as the head would do. My friend did not feel this was trust, merely an expectation of certain behaviours. My friend also experienced anxiety because what these actions would be was not always possible to know, but he felt that departure from actions that would be defined retrospectively would be seen by the manager as betrayal. I do not think these kind of expectations are a fair use of the word trust. I cannot see where the vulnerability is for the truster, apart from anger if the trusted does not follow, or anticipate, precisely the actions the truster would do. Conversely, the trusted is very vulnerable. My friend felt paralysed to act, and certainly not trusted. Trust seems to be a substitute here for an expectation of compliance at best, and obedience to undefined, and unpredictable, actions at worst.

A softer line would be to see trust as being where the trusted acts in the truster's interests. The truster may not have done the same actions as the trusted would have done, but the truster can understand those actions, or come to understand them, even if they do not necessarily agree with them. However, this may take time. When I worked with homeless people, one of my clients brought his children, whom his partner had left with him for the weekend, to the day centre where I worked, for food. I knew that social services, because of his drinking, did not allow the children to stay with him, and I felt I had to tell social services about the situation. My client felt betrayed and angry and I had certainly lost his trust at that point. However, some months later, after some other incidents, he came back and said that he now understood my actions. He also felt, as a consequence, he could trust me again.

An interesting question here is whether my client could have trusted me even if he could never have understood my actions. I think this would have been hard in my client's case, and is the second example of a misuse of the word trust. We need to ask ourselves what the potentially trusted is asking of the truster in such a position. Can we ever expect someone to unconditionally trust us, perhaps more than we do ourselves, and can we call this trust? While this may feel extreme, looking back on my practice, it was something I would frequently ask of clients and young people, even quite early on in the relationship. In doing this the potentially trusted is still invoking the notion of vulnerability, but this vulnerability is not being conceptualised as we have done so far, as something the truster sees in themselves. It was something the potentially trusted had assumed in the truster, and sometimes even got assent to this from them (perhaps expressed by them saying 'I'm too confused, you tell me what to do'). The potentially trusted assumed that the truster is too vulnerable, or immature, to be able to make a decision in their own best interests. They have to 'trust' the trusted to be able to make such a decision. Trust seems akin to faith in this context, and can we really ask for this level of trust from the truster? For me, where this construction of trust falls down is that I cannot see where the potential for betrayal on behalf of the truster is, the other condition for trust. If the truster could never understand the action the trusted takes, how could they feel betrayed? Without the potential for betrayal this is not trust, the trusted is just asking the truster to surrender to them. Vulnerability in trust needs to be present for both the trusted and the truster, at least in some measure, and the truster needs to have the potential to feel betrayed by the trusted, and the trusted to the hurt or rejection of the truster. The question then becomes what level of vulnerability each party has in the relationship.

What is it to be considered trustworthy?

The previous discussion leads us neatly into our next consideration: what it is to be considered trustworthy. From the outset it is probably worth establishing where we think the assessment of trustworthiness lies. Is it something for the truster to assess and ascribe to the trusted (a relational view) or is it something that lies within the trusted, that the truster may or may not recognise (an objectivist view)? Different schools of thought have different views on this and I will make reference to them as they are discussed.

Several authors (Govier, 1997; Jones, 1996; McLeod, 2011) take the view that trustworthiness is something for the truster to give, akin to the idea that we earn another person's trust. They note the importance of optimism on the part of the truster that the trusted will act in their interests in a way that is understandable to them (as per the discussion above). Whether this optimism on behalf of the truster is a generally good thing to have as a disposition is something I will come back to in the fourth section of this chapter. McLeod (2011) breaks truster optimism down into three components. It is optimism that the potentially trusted is competent; that they have the necessary skills to look after our interests; and that they have the commitment and/or the motivation to do so. I would imagine that most youth workers would like to think that young people think we have all these qualities, but it begs the question of how the trusted earns such belief from young people.

Social contracts

Another school of thought, broadly labelled a Social Contract approach (Dasgupta, 1988; Hardin, 2002; Mullin, 2005; Jones, 1999; O'Neill, 2002) says that the truster does not necessarily have to think that the trusted necessarily has the right motivation, but that social contracts (in our case what is expected in terms of youth worker behaviour) will make the trusted behave in a young person's interest. My worry with this approach is twofold. Firstly I wonder what these social contracts are. Several authors (Brookfield, 1994; Christian & Kitto, 1987) have talked about the autonomy of youth workers, and how we are answerable, primarily, to ourselves. In such a context, where are the social contracts? The Social Contract is in danger of implying that all youth workers are trustworthy, or they would suffer socially if they are not. Secondly the model does not ring true with my experience. I have known several youth workers that some young people would not trust, even those considered worthy of trust by colleagues or in their community. Perhaps these people have just got away with it, but the social contract approach assumes that self regulation works, whereas it may break down. It can also break down with whole institutions. Have we not heard young people say things like they do not trust teachers, social workers (and even youth workers!) or more specifically saying they do not trust people from a particular agency? Social contracts can break down.

Encapsulated interest

An alternative approach is what Hardin (2002) calls the 'encapsulated interest' view. This is again relational, but with the emphasis on the trusted's motivation. In this view the trusted (i.e. the workers) 'encapsulate' the truster's (i.e. the young people) interests because the trusted has an interest in maintaining a relationship with them. This just seems back to front; surely we maintain a relationship with a young person because we have their interests at heart, rather than the other way around? I think it is not the case that workers 'need' these relationships. In fact many workers have talked to me about 'people saturation' (Seal, 2005) whereby they do not need any new relationships in their life, as their job is having relationships with people: they do it because it is how we can care for others. Also in such a conceptualisation we would not have to encapsulate all the person's interests – only enough to maintain the relationship, which seems partial and shallow and certainly not trustworthy.

Goodwill

The dominant alternative relational model is the 'goodwill' model, whereby the trusted is trustworthy if they are motivated by goodwill towards the truster, which of course, can be a value in itself. (Baier, 1986; Jones, 1998; McLeod, 2011). However, it is unclear in this model whether this goodwill is assessed by the truster, or the trusted. If it is the truster two points arise. First, how does the truster come to assume goodwill in the trusted, and can they be wrong about this. Second, how does it explain when we trust people who are relative strangers, as we may well in situations such as when we are lost, and have to trust their directions. The first point is acknowledged by Baier, who cites the example of the confidence trickster.

On the second point, Nickel (2007) and McLeod (2002) see a solution in an adapted version of the social contract model as a more generalised assumption of moral integrity on the part of strangers, a common decency, not through social pressure, but through values we may hold in common. However, this begs the question of what these values are, and whether they are held in common. Positively though, this seems attractive for youth workers in how they build their relationship, especially the emphasis in the youth work literature on holding and being explicit about certain values (Spence and Devaney, 2006; Young, 1999). Again, however, it falls to the same issue of regulation as the general social contract model. A youth worker can espouse these values, but how can the truster be assured that they live by them? Perhaps we should not trust strangers, or such actions should not be considered trusting, but merely risk taking. However, this again does not ring true. To say we trust no one until we are assured of their goodwill towards us seems overly pessimistic; although it is certainly the world view that some people have.

The alternate view, that the goodwill is something for the trusted to assess about themselves, is again problematic. First, it again leaves the truster vulnerable to tricksters and those deliberately appearing trustworthy. Second, in my experience, the best manipulators believe they are acting in others' interests, that they have the young person's interests at heart: sometimes the best way to sustain a lie is to first convince ourselves. The worker may also be permanently self-deceptive, but good at convincing themselves and others that they are trustworthy. Jeffs and Smith (1996) talk about the dangers of charismatic leadership in youth work. I have written elsewhere about the dangers of reflective practice in such hands, where it is used as a tool of (often retrospective) self-justification (Seal, 2009) rather than development.

Virtue

A final objectivist view is that trustworthiness is a virtue (Potter: 2002; Hardin: 2002), something Potter calls 'full trustworthiness'. We are trustworthy in every situation, rather than the specific trustworthiness most of us enjoy. Mcleod (2002, 2011) critiques Potter, asking whether this means we can be trustworthy for someone who has committed an immoral act, or where someone extends trust beyond what is reasonable or wanted from the trusted. Potter qualifies her view of trustworthiness saying it is contextual: one responds to situations of trust in an appropriate way, given the context of the truster and the other qualities the trusted has such as compassion, justice etc. However, such an argument is susceptible to the general criticisms of virtue ethics: that actions are not predictable (Pincoffs, 1971; McDowell,1979), that what is acceptable varies between communities as well as within them (Solomon, 1998), and that it does not account for any dilemmas, since as a virtuous person you will do the right thing (Hursthouse, 1991). It also does not help us discern who decides whether a person is trustworthy, or who has, and does not, have this 'virtue'.

Negotiation

Ultimately I think that who decides a person is trustworthy is relational and a nego-tiation: even if a worker is 'objectively' trustworthy, unless the young person comes to believe this, then they are not going to trust that worker. Also, if the truster is not a part of the assessment of trustworthiness, then should they trust everyone who tells them they have assessed themselves as trustworthy, or even that others have? This again does not seem to reflect how trust operates. The assessment of trustworthiness seems to necessitate a joint enterprise, and perhaps a combination of all of these perspectives. If you work on generally being considered trustworthy by others, are clear about your values, demonstrate to yourself and others your commitment to their goodwill, open yourself up to criticism around your trustwor-thiness, or the potential for it, from young people and colleagues, and still recognise that you will need to earn the trust of each individual you encounter, then perhaps you could consider yourself trustworthy, and expect others to start doing so.

Is it reasonable to trust?

This would seem to be a huge question for us all, both as workers and human beings. If, as Hobbes and Glaucon would have it, we are naturally amoral and self-ish and are only kept in check by others and the state, then unless others are in fear of reprisal we should not trust them. On the other hand, if we view human nature as naturally benevolent (Hume, 1960) then trust in others should be our default position, learning only the circumstances where we should not. Such views are described by McLeod as externalist, that is to say we need to assess whether the external conditions justify and influence our orientation towards trusting others.

The internalist view

However, before we consider an externalist view of whether to trust is reasonable we need to look at the internalist view i.e. whether a decision to trust is internally valid, often based on rationality. As a youth worker this was probably my major intervention with young people, helping them assess whether they should trust a person or not, normally with references to honing their reasoning. However, several authors would contend that trust is not wholly rational, or is in fact its opposite (Baier, 1986; Baker, 1987; Coady, 1992; Fricker, 1995; Jones, 1996; Webb, 1993). Indeed some human biologists believe humans have a natural disposition to trust, and to judge trustworthiness, that can be traced to the neurobiological structure and activity of a human brain (Kosfield et al., 2005) and that drugs such as oxytocin can increase our capacity to trust. They would see it not as a rational thing, but a chemical one.

Baier (1986) would argue that we rely daily on irrational trust all the time, in the form of untested knowledge from the testimony of others, e.g. the world is flat, the hospital will treat my illnesses. We have not verified this and it is therefore not rational. Similarly we trust individuals to take actions such as driving the bus, marking assignments, without having had this trust verified personally. Baker (1987) and de Sousa (1987) talk about different forms of rationality, saying that Baier's view is a truth-orientated version that is not sustainable in all situations. They talk about goal orientated and strategic rationality. Using the example of being treated in hospital, one could rationalise that we may not be able to trust their treatment of us completely, but by doing so we will remain calm in a situation over which we have little control; or that we trust young people because it enables us to have a rounded relationship. However, such a view is unclear on the relationship between the strategic goal and the person we are trusting; even in the case given it could be seen as arbitrary. Are we really trusting them, or going along with them for another reason?

McLeod would go as far as arguing that rationality and trust are in conflict: 'since trust inherently involves risk, any attempt to eliminate the risk through rational reflection could eliminate the trust at the same time' (McLeod, 2011: 3). Similarly McGeer (2008) believes that trust is more substantial or pure when the available evidence does *not* support it. Authors such as Baker (1987) and Jones (1996) see trust as making us blinkered towards rationality. We resist evidence that contradicts our trust and optimism about the trusted. For example, many mothers, or fathers, trust their children not to harm anyone, and therefore resist seeing and accepting any evidence to the contrary. If we seek out evidence to rationalise our trust we may be placing that trust in jeopardy. The question seems to come back to the centricity of vulnerability; if our trust is based on rational reflection then where is the uncertainty and potential betrayal?

However, in an attempt to avoid complete subjectivism and irrationality, other authors (de Sousa, 1987; Calhoun, 1984; Lahno, 2001) see the internal judgement to trust as less irrational, and more akin to an emotional response. This would fit in more with the selectivity of how we see facts about those we trust as mentioned above by McGreer (2008) and McLeod (2011). Jones (1996) notes how emotions narrow our perception to certain 'fields of evidence' (ibid.: 11) that support the emotion, i.e. we look for the evidence that supports our emotion and minimise or ignore the evidence that counters it. However, emotional responses can eventually change in response to evidence and internal discussion.

The externalist view
Understandably to avoid such difficulties some authors believe that the reason to trust must lie, at least in part, in external conditions or criteria for trust (Goldman, 1992; McLeod, 2002; Webb, 1993). This would again seem to fit into my practice as a youth worker: my second biggest set of interventions around trust were in the form of challenging people's rationality, or judgement to trust, often with reference

to external criteria. This often takes the form of a list of common 'justifiers' for trust (Goldman, 1999). The lists vary, and thus fall foul of the essentialist critique of whether such a common list is achievable or desirable. They often include factors such as the relative role of the trusted and truster, the context in which the trust occurs, the history of reliability of the truster's assessment, and of the trusted of being trusted, and the social or political climate in which the trust occurs (Govier, 1998; Jones, 1996). I do not have the space to elaborate on all of these here, and some of them have already been covered to some degree. In keeping with the opening context I gave for whether it is reasonable to trust, we should perhaps examine the last of these, the socio-political climate, as it will also lead us on to the next discussion, of whether being able to trust is of any use to us.

As we have discussed before, if we live in a society where there is a common morality that we can trust one another then trust and trustworthiness tends to increase (Baier, 2004; McLeod, 2011). However the question of which political system engenders more trust is highly contested. There is often an assumption, in the west, that democracy is the society where we can trust each other most (McLeod, 2011) yet there is often evidence that trust is higher in non-democratic countries (Uslaner, 1999). In liberal democracies, in Britain only 17% of people believe that official figures are produced without political interference and only 14% say the government uses official figures honestly (Goddard, 2005). In the USA just 42% say they have a great deal or fair amount of trust in the executive branch. Linked to this is a debate about the socio-political system that underpins the political system, whether democratic or not. Some would say that capitalism needs trust to function, and therefore encourages it, while other would say it is essentially de-humanising and competitive, engendering the opposite (Guevara, 1989). As an example, some would say countries like Cuba are totalitarian, where there is little trust, and instead fear, of government and fellow citizens who may report you as a dissident (Gonsalez, 2004). Others see it as a country where there is much trust, of both one another and government, as you can trust that you will be materially looked after (Darusenkov, 1975).

It therefore seems difficult to assess whether we should trust. External factors seem to be too contested and internal factors too unreliable and not as dependant on rationality as we might imagine. Perhaps, though, this is not a bad position to adopt. We may need to apply rationality, both external and internal, to our decisions to trust another or not, but we should not ignore our instincts. Rather we should recognise that instincts are, if they are seen in terms of motivations and drives (Maslow, 1968), cultivated or cultivatable and to some extent socially determined and constructed. Perhaps though, before trying to build our trust in others, as this seems one of the biggest determinants of trust and trustworthiness in society, we should ask whether it is worth doing – how does trusting others benefit oneself?

What is the value of trust?

Do we need trust to function as individuals and as a society? Baier claims that trust is 'the very basis of morality' (2004: 180). If we take a social contract view, that is a tautology. We need to trust in others, at least to have some moral basis for their actions, to make any kind of social contract possible. For others, such as Hardin, trust is one of the essentials of being human, or trying to be transcendent of a purely instinctual or instrumental existence, even if trust has irrational elements. In assessing the value of trust we need to look at three dimensions. First whether there is any intrinsic value to trust, second how trust benefits the truster, and third how it benefits the trusted.

Intrinsic value

Several authors (Hardwig, 1991; Hardin, 2002; Gambetta, 1988; Jones, 1999) argue that knowledge (which as educators, most youth worker's would see as having intrinsic value) requires trust, as we are largely relying on the testimony of others. However, we still may need to test the knowledge that we receive, or we would believe anything. In addition, as discussed before, we probably do not have the time to check out all information, which therefore begs the question of what information we should check out. If I am working with a young person, I will work with someone on their critical ability, but they will still need to discern. I remember saying that young people should always question things, and seek to back up their assertions, and ask others to back up theirs. Am I therefore asking them to be less trusting about information? I seemed to be taking a stance of saying that they should be less trusting of knowledge than of relationships. Perhaps this is no bad thing but it is a stance nonetheless. If I can still live with this. Did I always help them discern what knowledge they should take on trust and that which they should interrogate? Looking back, my work was often to help them subject their knowledge to rational scrutiny, to assess evidence etc. I was falling back into a positivist stance, and ignoring the irrational, emotive side of trust, and indeed knowledge. Mussolini famously said that fascism was 10% fact and 90% emotion. Gramsci also recognised that when Italian agricultural workers sided with the fascist, against, he argued, their rational interests, they preferred the mythical romantic, non material appeal of fascism instead of the material appeal of scientific Marxism.

Many authors have talked about a similar irrational appeal of racism. I have had many conversations with young people, for example over the facts about asylum seekers, which are useful to rationally dispel many of the myths about them, but this was not necessarily effective. Young people trusted, in so far as trust can involve holding a belief in spite of facts, their belief to the contrary (McGeer, 2008). Perhaps, as stated in the previous section we need to engage with people's irrationality on issues such as racism. Burton (1990) has always provided a starting point for me. Writing in the context of entrenched conflict, he found that many of the deep roots for the racism, conflict and the creation of enmity of the other were in denied human needs, such as for identity, security, meaning etc. However, the conflict is not articulated like this, rather it will focus on particular issues or instances, such as asylum seekers taking our jobs, or not integrating enough (two of many endlessly circular arguments I have engaged in). The danger is trying to rationally solve, or resolve, the particular issues, which are rarely rational and are rooted in these greater denied needs. It is in these that we should try and find common ground. This is recognised by some fascist groups. It is no accident that the BNP has changed the name of its monthly journal to *Identity* – they see the connection.

Benefiting the truster

Going back to trust, Gambetta (1988) and Jones (1999) relate the benefits of trusting to those of co-operative engagement. They argue that trusting others allows us not only to reap the benefits of co-operation, but increases our opportunities for co-operation. We get to know people and become seen as trustworthy ourselves. Several authors argue that trust is not needed for co-operation (Cook et al., 2005; Skyrms, 2008) but Luhmann (1979) counters that trust makes co-operation easier and enhances it, as it removes the need to check up on the others. Interestingly some feminist writers such as Mackenzie and Stoljar (2000) view autonomy as being dependant on trust. Autonomy, ironically, or at least the cultivation of it, is necessarily relational. To develop opinions, to have the knowledge required to make decisions and to have the safety that allows us to act autonomously, necessitates a social context that encourages this. Lehrer (1997) and Foley (2005) claim that the internal aspect of evaluating whether we should trust or not involves self-trust. It seems autonomy needs trust and trust needs autonomy.

Benefiting the trusted

One aspect of trust that is particularly relevant to the issues of autonomy in the context of the instrumental benefits of trust to the trusted is 'therapeutic trust' (Horsburgh, 1960; McGeer, 2008). This is where we trust others, knowing that they may well betray that trust, in the belief that giving such trust will eventually elicit more trustworthy behaviour. For youth workers this is the idea of 'giving people a chance', in the hope that in doing so they will honour that trust. Interestingly therapeutic trust also taps into the irrational side of trust, on the side of the trusted, but hopefully in a benevolent way. As McLeod says, 'therapeutic trust leaps ahead of the evidence, which means that it is hard to justify epistemically' (McLeod, 2011: 15). It is an act of faith, which we hope will become justified, and be seen as rational, in time, but it is not rational in the moment.

For workers, a point of reflection could be who we extended this trust to, and who we do not, because for me it has certainly not been an open invitation. On reflection, my personal construction was to place this trust when the young person had never been trusted, in the belief that this would evoke a positive response, and develop trustworthiness and autonomy. But on reflection was this fair? Expecting people to respond in a way that was outside of their norms and culture – for what reason would they do this? Was it to honour me because I was special, or had touched something in them that warranted such a leap? It seems narcissistic in retrospect.

Yet it seems to be a narcissism that is all too common. When I have discussed the topic with colleagues about who we would place such trust in, it starts off very rational, we would do it for everyone, or we make a judgement on rational criteria such the probability of a result, balanced against not setting people up to fail etc. But this does not answer the nuances of the situation: for how long will we proffer this trust? How many chances do people get? Or more to the point, who gets the chances, and repeat ones, and who does not? Who do we keep having empathy for even when they have betrayed us? It is at this point that discussions become more irrational, and narcissistic. It is more about who touches us, or reminds us of what we see as injustices in the world, or more simply who reminds us of ourselves, particularly if we have had periods when we were not trusted, or felt we could not place trust in others. As I say, it is a point of reflection for us all.

How do we cultivate trust?

If we believe that trust has some value, even on a base level, then we need to look at how we, as youth workers, can cultivate it in others. We have mentioned two dimensions – first that placing some trust in others, even making ourselves vulnerable to them, can engender trust. Also that to trust others, even when we think they may betray us, can have the effect of making them more trustworthy. As McLeod (2011) says, this is particularly important for people who have gone through experiences, such as abuse, rape or witnessing atrocities, that makes them consider the world as not a generally safe place, or make a judgement that they should never make themselves vulnerable to someone else again.

Baier (1986) takes the view that we cannot simply will ourselves to trust, even if we want to. I am reminded of the phrase I have heard from some young people that 'I would like to trust you (them etc.), but I just can't'. Similarly the worker phrase of 'you have to trust me' is missing the nature of trust for Baier. But in terms of potential impact, if we were to look at the aforementioned idea of trust as an emotion, or, as Hardin (1996, 2002) and Jones (1996) do, see it as an attitude, then it could be cultivated. If we encourage others to look for trustworthiness in others, and cultivate what they see in them, then they could reap the benefits of trust. On a wider scale we can try and work on some of these wider conditions for trust. If being able to trust is about being able to be vulnerable to betrayal, but not a victim of it, we need to tackle some of the reasons for that betrayal happening, asking why people feel unsafe. Is this possible in a society that only partly condemns rape and simultaneously portrays women as sexual objects, that continues to allow children to be abused, or rather bureaucratises the processes that are meant to protect children to the point where workers are simply protecting themselves?

This last point needs expanding upon as the development of current practice in safeguarding is an interesting one in terms of trust. The direction of safeguarding practices in the last twenty years has been an understandable reaction to a system that has neglected individuals and betrayed them. Yet in an attempt to rectify this, we have tried to eliminate trust, in the sense of being vulnerable to particular workers' judgements. This development of highly systematised procedures and protocols has, understandably, tried to eliminate human error and subjectivity, yet in doing so has eliminated the conditions of trust. We do not need to trust individuals – in fact this was seen as one of the problems of the old system. Sadly this has not, to date, resulted in a failsafe system of detecting and reporting abuse, and at the same time has encouraged a loss of trust in workers. The recent Monro report has called for the cultivation of professional judgement and a retreat from a reliance on protocols and policy. This would require more than trust in a worker's judgement.

Conclusion

To conclude, there is value in trust, especially when one party may never have been trusted before. At its most powerful it involves mutual vulnerability and the potential to be betrayed, but the giving of it is not always a rational act, including whom we as workers extend it to – and whom we do not. As such, we cannot really assess whether the world is intrinsically trustworthy, and this does not really matter because trust breeds trust.

However, workers need to examine what we mean when we ask people to trust us, as sometimes we are actually asking people to surrender to us, to stop asking questions. Sometimes when we say we trust young people and communities, we are really saying that we expect them to behave in a certain way, and will feel betrayed if they do not.

Youth and community workers perhaps need to trust more the people in whose name they work, to allow ourselves to be vulnerable to young people and their communities. I have heard people say that if you admit your uncertainties, and show your vulnerabilities, people will use it against you. This seems to be a pretty damning construction of young people's motivations. It also misses an opportunity. A student once said that I had made her think when she had shared her concerns about revealing herself. Apparently I said (though I am ashamed to say that I cannot remember saying it) that if you allow people to see your vulnerabilities they cannot hold them against you. What she took from this was that if someone wanted to use something against you, it is the things that you do not reveal, that you want to hide, that have the most power. Honesty can be very disarming.

I said at the beginning that I believe youth and community workers can foster meaningful trust so let me finish with an example of this. I was away recently with an international group of young people for a research project I am doing around violence. One group had brought along two workers, a senior worker and a relatively young new worker, as well as five young people. On the first night the senior worker fell ill and had to take to his bed. This left the relatively inexperienced worker on his own. Late into the night, when this worker was occupied with something else, the young people had an altercation with another group of young women that got quite heated. Other workers from other projects stepped in and diffused the situation. The discussion they then had with the young people initially centred on trust, not their behaviour, which they defended. The workers spoke about how the young men knew that the senior worker was ill and that they took advantage of this. Discussion was then around what this meant for the trust that had built up with the senior worker, who had been vulnerable, and how they had taken advantage of this vulnerability. The young people discussed other adults who had betrayed their trust and how it had felt having their vulnerability taken advantage of, saying how they valued that others did not do this. They then discussed how they could rebuild things with both workers, the less experienced one also feeling vulnerable that he had done wrong, and rebuild the trust they valued. They then trusted these new workers enough to drop their bravado, and admit that their behaviour with the young women had been out of order, but they had been unsure what to do about it (showing vulnerability) and wanted to discuss how they could make amends. I suspect other professions, and indeed other youth workers, might have taken a very different approach.

CHAPTER 7

'It's All About the Conversation'

Mike Seal and Peter Harris

Informal education is driven by conversation and being with others. It develops through spending time with people – sharing in their lives – and listening and talking.

Jeffs & Smith, 1997, 2005, 2011

Education: facilitating the process by which an individual penetrates his taken-for-granted reality and, by so doing, comes to understand how reality for him is constructed. Thus are extended the possibilities of finding moments of/for choice, and, in this, for extending and living his freedom.

Baizerman, 1989: 1

The first quote is probably the most familiar quote we encounter in students' assignments. Unfortunately, its presence rarely signals a good assignment, in fact it is normally the opposite. Students who are struggling, particularly to articulate what they do, latch on to it presumably thinking along the lines of 'oh, that's what I do, we talk to people, we have a conversation, that's OK then'. Unfortunately, it is not enough, and this is what we wish to explore in this chapter. The second quote is probably where we want to end up. Baizerman defines the aims for what he terms an 'educational encounter', and what in our context is a youth work conversation. There are several dimensions of conversations we wish to explore before we get there. First, what the nature of the youth work conversation is and what the difference is between a 'good' youth work conversation and one where an adult gives a young person 'a good talking to'. Secondly we wish to highlight the spontaneous nature of that conversation, and why we privilege that. Lastly we wish to explore how the youth worker achieves this spontaneous conversation in practice as opposed to a reliance on stock responses.

The nature of conversation

Dialogue is the encounter between men, mediated by the world, in order to name the world.

Freire, 1972: 2

Before we look at what we are trying to create in conversations, we need to look at the nature of conversation, or in Freire's terms, dialogue. We think there are two or three strands of thought on this, one of which goes back to Socrates, by way of the Enlightenment, and incorporating Marxist and post-Marxist thinkers such as Freire. This perspective seeks ways that a conversation can rationally interrogate the world, and how the parties to the conversations are positioned within it. Another strand, with debts to post-modern feminist and existential thinking, traditionally thought of as oppositional to this, but which we think could be more compatible than at first appears, critiques this way of thinking as being 'logocentric', i.e. privileging the logical, rational side of arguments, at the expense of their emotional dimensions, and not acknowledging the importance of the relationship between the two parties. A third linked strand (Marxist again) says that we cannot ignore issues of power between protagonists, and their positions in the outside world, and that the conversations we have are always interrupted by other factors.

Interrogating the world

Socratic dialogue or method, later adopted by Freire (1972) examines the words and concepts that people actually use in reference to a given topic, seeking to critically analyse and de-construct them, testing them for logical rationality and compatibility with other linked concepts and beliefs held by those in the dialogue. The facilitator, possibly the youth worker, facilitates, builds on and interrogates people's thinking, but importantly through the other person or group's own words, rather than imposing the facilitator's own world view. This is not always an easy or welcomed process. A friend of mine uses such techniques in 'Community Philosophy' sessions and often encounters initial antagonism. In class, student contributions are often initially in the form of making a statement or opinion, quickly followed by a statement like 'and that's just what I think', which is an interesting double-edged comment. Such statements are diminishing, in that they are not making any claims beyond themselves, more through lack of confidence than conviction, and defensive, in that, particularly if challenged, students will say that they have a 'right' to that opinion. One often responds by saying that they might be surprised by how many people share this view, or even if they do not, its expression may be enlightening. At the same time, in this space, you do not have a right to an unqualified opinion. It has to be defended and be open to challenge and change, as is anything I, as the lecturer, say, which often causes the most surprise. Such is the nature of education.

Gadamer saw knowledge as not being a static thing, but as something that arises out of interaction and the process of conversations. He saw the most important aspect of these conversations being that people understand each other; and from this, new knowledge will flow. To achieve this understanding he thought conversation needed to have certain characteristics, and needed to be distinguished from arguments, persuasion etc. These characteristics included that:

> . . . each opens himself to the other person, truly accepts his point of view as worthy of consideration and gets inside the other to such an extent that he understands not a particular individual, but what he says. The thing that has to

*be grasped is the objective rightness or otherwise of his opinion, so that they
can agree with each other on a subject.*

Gadamer, 1979: 347

He places great emphasis, in conversations, in our trying to understand the perspective of the other. Otherwise he thought we are limited by the 'horizons our own understanding'. In examining and truly trying to understand the perspective of the other, the understandings we bring from the past are tested in encounters with the present, and form what is taken into the future (Louden, 1991: 106). The aim, in Gadamer's terms, is to create a 'fusion of horizons'. We find this particularly important when being a facilitator in a dialogue between two people who disagree with each other. Rather than trying to arbitrate who is right, as they have often wanted me to do, I keep emphasising the importance of understanding the other's perspective – often there is then no need for a resolution, as a compromise becomes obvious. As often as not, in the process of understanding each other's perspectives, unexpected commonalities are found, meaning a compromise was not even necessary.

I remember a friend of mine describing bringing together some Asian young men with some white young men from a BNP voting community. At first they had little in common and just argued. It was only when the Asian young men grasped the difficulties that the white young men had faced from their own community in even coming to the meeting, because of their own families' opposition, something the Asian young men had also faced, that understanding started to happen. Baizerman (1989), whose work we will look at in more detail later, sees this wish to understand, at least on behalf of the workers, as vital in allowing young people to develop a sense of themselves and to flourish. He also saw the desire to understand the other as being one of the defining differences between youth work and other care professionals in young people's lives:

> *Youthwork education and training must focus on how to learn about youth from youth in their terms, so that the youthworker can struggle with accepting them on their terms. This is a basic youthwork value and set of skills. It is also suggestive of the basic youthwork orientation – an anthropology of youth in everyday life.*

Baizerman, 1989: 2

Emotional relationships

Gadamer and Baizerman's thinking, for us, is an important bridge to the second strand of thought on conversations in that they saw the importance of the relationship between the parties to the dialogue, and that a 'good' relationship aids both sides' conceptual sharing. Using an old groupwork metaphor, we need to look at maintenance of the group, as well as the group task, or the task itself starts failing. Jeffs and Smith throughout their work, as well as privileging conversation, place a strong emphasis on relationship, seeing them as integral to each other. For there to be dialogue 'entails a particular kind of relationship and interaction' (Jeffs and Smith, 1996) and 'certain virtues, emotions and commitments to each other'. At different times they stress the importance or giving space for each other's emotions and feelings, a commitment to not trying to change the other's perspective, but to exploring it, and being open to changing one's own opinion. There are several versions of what these characteristics should be and we will not attempt to cover them all. There are some of particular interest that we will highlight here. Burbules (1993) lists some of the virtues we need to have towards the other party as:

- *Concern.* A recognition that there is more going on than talk about the overt topic. That we have an interest in, and a commitment to, the other.
- *Trust.* We have to take what others are saying on faith – and there can be some risk in this, as we have explored elsewhere.
- *Respect.* This is often expressed as mutual regard. This involves the idea that everyone has value in some basic way and entails a commitment to being fair-minded, opposing degradation and rejecting exploitation.
- *Appreciation.* Linked to respect, this entails valuing the unique qualities that others bring.
- *Affection.* Conversation involves a feeling for our partners.
- *Hope.* We engage in conversation in the belief that it holds possibility. While it is not clear what we will gain or learn, there is faith in the inherent value of education.

Some of these are the subjects of other chapters, as how they relate to young people, and they to them, needs greater exploration. On a practical level, arguments such as these remind us that we need to give attention to both the logical content of debate, but also to the relationship that fosters it. We concur with feminist thinkers such as Braaten (1991) whose criticism of logic and rationality's claim to supremacy asserts that, 'sympathy, and affection have at least as much claim to this status'. Even Community Philosophy, which is in the Socratic tradition, is self-consciously influenced by the idea of 'community enquiry', which has as its four guiding 'C's, 'critical, creative, caring and collaborative thinking' – an interesting synthesis of the two traditions.

On a philosophical level, whether all discourse needs to be rational and logical is a huge question and one of the primary concerns of Twentieth Century philosophy. Wittgenstein (1922) sought to purify language of its irrational and illogical elements but ultimately found it an impossible task which highlights that conversation is not purely logical and rational, particularly when dealing with metaphysical questions concerned with ideas like justice, ethics and morality. Logic and rationality in this context become much looser ideas, and one of many 'language games' we can enter into. Indeed placing an emphasis on scientific and logical reasoning has been used to justify many abhorrent regimes and practices throughout history. Government policies will regularly make reference to a number of 'scientific studies', used in particular ways.

Paradoxically, it is for these very reasons that we would be wary of abandoning logical and rational argument, suggesting working instead with young people to be aware of how rational argument, and irrational argument, are used. One of the most fascinating subjects I studied in my own philosophy degree was a module on rhetoric, or as Aristotle put it, the art of persuasion. The Greeks saw it as an essential part of any young person's education, as did Muslim scholars later. Enoch Powell's 'Rivers of Blood' speech is a fascinating study in rhetoric. Looking at it through an Aristotelian lens, he first establishes *ethos* (that the speaker is a good solid honest character, to be trusted) by speaking not as himself, but through mystical constituents – the solidly working class people he met who were worried about immigration. This is backed up with the use of strong historical and emotional metaphors, such as 'Rivers of Blood' establishing *pathos* (using emotive language and images that gives the audience resonance and sympathy with the speaker). For us, racism always works on such an emotional level, meaning that youth workers cannot counter it by logic alone. Young people need to be enabled to see why the argument is working on them and others. It also explains why the BNP has fought for years to establish *ethos*, to be seen as reasonable and respectable. Finally Powell uses selective 'facts' (*logos*), building a 'logical', 'objective' argument.

I have also found awareness of rhetoric very useful to distinguish and identify the dangerous 'charismatic' youth workers I have mentioned before. Their heady combinations of *ethos* (which establishes that they are a good character, one to be trusted) and *pathos* (the uses of emotive language and images that people will have sympathy for) means people will be ready to listen to their argument. By beginning with these, their *logos*, the rational argument they create, will be ready to be listened to, or more worryingly, people will be more ready to follow partial and half logical statements.

On a much smaller scale and as an example of a half logical argument, I remember seeing a TV evangelist talking. He argued that there are only three ways of seeing Jesus, either he was a fraud, he was mad or perhaps (carefully phrased as the least likely, to appear reasonable) he was as he claimed, the Son of God. He carefully and dispassionately showed how Jesus was unlikely to have been a charlatan, dying for his cause, turning down chances to escape etc. He then showed how Jesus was unlikely to have been mad, going through the signs of madness and how Jesus did not meet them. He then said that, given that the first two arguments were not true, we can only really conclude that he was who he said he was. There are, of course many other options, but he closed this down early on and concentrated on the logic of the three options he presented.

Power differentials

Looking at the third strand, concerning power, Freire (1972) thought a part of developing relationships was to examine the understandings of knowledge of all parties to the conversation. He thought that much of what was called education was a banking model, whereby the educator conveyed 'knowledge' which the student 'banked'. In such a model for education there is no 'concientization', or mutual learning, and the social situation and its hegemonic construction of knowledge is not challenged, something covered in this book's chapter on common sense. Marxists such as Habermas (1984) were critical of Gadamer and others, saying that they did not take account of the massive power differentials in conversation, and that we need to develop an 'ideal speech situation', to do this. The conditions of such speech included that every subject with the competence to speak and act is allowed to take part in a discourse; everyone is allowed to question any assertion whatever; everyone is allowed to introduce any assertion whatever into the discourse; everyone is allowed to express his attitudes, desires and needs; and no speaker may be prevented, by internal or external coercion, from exercising his rights as laid down in the first two conditions. In meeting these conditions, all parties needed to operate on several levels, recognising that if we are in conversation with those with power over us we will be cautious, but also that the very language we will use will not be neutral, and will be imbued with the hegemonic assumptions of the powerful.

Habermas later recognised that such an ideal speech situation had to be in the context of a wholesale moral and political shift. For these reasons, he thought dialogue cannot occur 'between those who want to name the world, and those who do not want this naming'; or 'between those who have been denied the right to speak, and those who have denied them the right'. (Freire, 1972: 61). Perhaps the role for youth workers becomes one of the 'organic intellectual' speaking for, but from the perspective of, the young people we work with to those who have power over them – a theme I explored in the chapter on common sense and anti-intellectualism.

The privileging of spontaneous conversation

The greater part of one's education is acquired, not at school, but in life.

Tolstoy, 1967: 24

Given this observation by Tolstoy, how can a youth worker effectively engage, and be a positive force, in this education, this lived life. We (and many youth work authors) argue that to engage in life's educational opportunities workers need to be able to think creatively and spontaneously 'on their feet', to create and seize upon learning opportunities as they evolve. Such a skill could arguably be identified as a key feature of professional practice and expertise (Fook et al., 2000). As Jeffs and Smith (1997, 2005, 2011: 1) say in their opening description of informal education, 'informal education tends to be unpredictable – we do not know where it might lead – and spontaneous.' We may create activities and programmes, but this is with an aim for the spontaneous conversations to be able to arise, where we know the greatest learning occurs.

Reasons for privileging
We can see three groups of reasons for this privileging of such spontaneous organic education: instrumental reasons, philosophical pedagogic reasons, and arguments around authenticity and what is unique and potentially transformative about these spontaneous moments and conversations. Youth work happens in youth clubs, on the street, in public space, and in young people's 'free' time which means that opportunities for learning are necessarily negotiated, often occur during real time, and need to be drawn from the immediate environment, in the moment. Youth workers often cannot know who they will meet and under what circumstances. Groups can be transient and particularly susceptible to random events (Harris, 2005: 59–60). Often the work occurs in environments where tension is high with young people who have previously rejected structured, formal education and may be involved in activities or behaviour that can be challenging to deal with. Therefore, workers often need to be able to rapidly recognise aspects of young people's eve-ryday life, within their immediate environment (events, images, and conversations etc.) as potential stimuli for educative dialogue, rather than relying on structured lesson plans or preconceived programmes of activity.

But beyond these reasons of necessity, or simply because it works better, we as youth workers have often fought to keep such practice. Therefore we have ideo-logically, value driven reasons of *purpose* too – a purpose that is centred around notions of the common good and social justice. Through adopting an educative process that begins with their immediate, concrete reality, youth work has argued that young people are then more intrinsically motivated to examine how they are positioned within their social world. Engaging with young people in this way allows for both seemingly trivial or significant aspects of their life to be first discovered and named, and then imbued with meaning. In turn this enables them to act more autonomously and in ways that enable their personal development or change within their social reality.

A third reason links to what we are trying to create in those moments. Neeland, looking at the use of drama and particularly improvisatory drama, sees something more genuine about those moments, both in our own authenticity as workers, but also in a conversation's ability to allow all parties to transcend social constraints, i.e. to show that we have agency:

> To be spontaneous requires the [youth worker] to imagine and respond to the immediate in ways that are authentic and existential. It is a crucible for the creative exploration of the centrality of the social context in determining human agency and capacity. To be authentic, [youth workers] must bring what they collectively know about human behaviour to a newly created situation which requires their verbal and physical responses. These responses, shaped by prior experience, must be truthful to the situation – to the social and cultural conventions and codes that determine the context. Improvisation flexes the muscles of a [youth worker's] potential to act on and within the constraints or structure of the imagined situation. It provides the direct lived experience of the tension between social and cultural structures and the capacity for human action. The given circumstances of the improvisation determine the authenticity of what can be said and done.
>
> Neeland, 2011: 171

Acheiving agency

Here we see a vision of youth work practice that begins to hint at how its immediacy and spontaneity can carry an added intrinsic value in terms of greater authenticity and a stress on human agency. This links to what are we trying to achieve in these conversations, in so far as we have an agenda. We think we have two drivers. When we ask workers what they are trying to achieve in their conversations, we tend to get two types of responses. The first is that they are trying to get young people to understand the situations they are in, following Freire, or to understand and think about a particular thing or idea they are grappling with. The second is that they are trying to help the young person see their own potential, and their possible actions. These seem to be the essential components of youth workers being agents for social change rather than control (Belton, 2010): we help people understand (conscientization), and then take action (agency). As agents of social change, youth workers seek to promote Freirean moments not simply to re-engage young people in the mainstream (social control), stopping them being NEET, or whatever the current aim is for youth workers to do to young people, but as the means by which they enable young people to gain an insight into their limited circumstances and challenge how they are marginalised within society too (social action). Accordingly, youth workers are not just interested in doing something to solve 'problems' but are also keen to problematise social issues, i.e. ask, 'whose interests does solving the problem serve?' and 'what has produced the 'problem' in the first place?'. Freire's notion of dialogical practice is therefore both practically and ideologically wedded to youth worker's professional identity.

However, in recent research we conducted into how detached workers work with violence, we found that many youth workers tend, in reality, in their conversations and action, to operate predominantly on only one of these aspects of social action, or both, but separately. In fact, with regards to action at a structural level, there was a lot of pessimism. Workers explored with young people the structural forces people were subject to, but there was a pessimistic view of what could be done about them. Workers therefore retreated into a solely person centred approach, seeking to raise self-esteem, and explore young people's identities. Workers focused on getting people back into education or training or employment, as the action element of their work. What seemed to be lacking was looking at any political agency, at what people can actually do about the structural forces they were subject to. This seemed to stem from workers' own structural pessimism.

Unfortunately, we also encountered, perhaps most challengingly, a sense of hopelessness in young people, a loss of agency, particularly in the current economic climate, sometimes as a result of worker interventions. As a result of youth workers highlighting structural oppression, young people now had a 'knowing' hopelessness, an informed sense of powerlessness, not one borne of ignorance of their potential or chances, but one that stemmed from knowledge of the limited nature of them. In the absence of a sense of agency they had nowhere to go. To give a couple of examples. I remember a young person saying to me that as a result of youth work they had gone and got an education, perhaps even a degree in business studies, but were still working minimum wage in their dad's shop – why? Because, according to a structural analysis, they were still Asian and working class and they were therefore unlikely to get the few jobs that were available. In these circumstances why not engage in criminal gang activity? What had they to lose?

I remember talking to one young woman who was doing a hairdressing apprenticeship, earning £2 an hour in London, knowing she could never get her own home, even a council flat, or move out of her parents' house. She also knew that criminal activity could earn her ten times what she was earning, as her friends and family had chosen to do. She also knew that a mile down the road, in the city, people were earning a hundred or a thousand times that an hour, but, for various structural reasons, that was an opportunity that was not open to her, nor would she want it. I also felt she knew that a return to crime was highly probable, but she was hanging on to her pride in doing what she found meaningful, but by a thread. We asked them to create a collage about their lives in London and she wrote the sentence 'I am not everything you think I am' in shit. It kind of stayed with me.

Constructing meaning

So can we instil a sense of agency in young people? Would we want to, and is conversation the best tool for it? Baizerman places himself firmly in the existentialist camp. In agreement with Freire he thinks that our primary concern as youth workers should be about getting people to understand the ways they are socially constructed, but also to help them to find ways to construct their own meanings in life. No matter how limited those choices are, they are still freedoms to be nurtured.

> Youthwork is a form of education, i.e. a facilitating process in which an individual penetrates his taken-for-granted reality and, by so doing, comes to understand how reality for her is constructed. Thus are extended the possibilities of finding moments of (for) choice and, in this, for extending and living her freedom. Youthwork is a process of creating the opportunities for a youth to choose more often about more things in her everyday life and in this way more thoroughly construct herself. Choice is a freedom-in-action.
>
> Baizerman, 1989: 1

In creating this project he has some interesting priorities for the worker. One is on how the young person and the worker understand themselves in conversation, or 'encounters', as he frames it. He talks about the importance of uncoupling perception (how we see the immediate), apperception (how this perception relates to our past) and biography (how we make sense of our past), or at least that we understand how we tend to join and conflate them. He also emphasises the need to stop looking at the chronology of our lives, and begin to look at it as a series of experiences in, but also outside of, time. It is the meaning that we put on it that is important, not necessarily that, or even if, it happened, as that is something we do not have control over. He thinks this is particularly important with young people, as 'adolescence is understood as time, a span of (linear) time, as is development . . . (but) neither is "life lived" '. He buys into Gadamer's idea that a conversation needs us to recognise and understand the other, but takes it much further. He talks about 'confirmation' whereby the youth worker 'induces this other's inmost self-becoming' (Friedman, 1981). We cannot assume it is there, as many people, including ourselves, are fragmented and partial. He thinks this is very important, particularly with young people who have been pathologised and are used to dealing with 'professionals' who see them as a collection of problems of symptoms. He echoes Illich (1974) in seeing this as one of the unique features of youth workers, to be able to see and cultivate the human uniqueness.

> Youthwork is orientated away from the explanatory and towards understanding, away from diagnosis and the medical model within which it resides, and toward the youth at that moment in her concreteness and uniqueness. Away from notions of 'personality' or 'character' or the like and toward this kid, now, as she is now: 'Why?' does not matter; what is and what emerges does. Life

is forward and is to be lived together, worker and youth, from 'right now' to 'next minute'.

Baizerman, 1989: 1

In my work with homeless people I came to see the most important thing I could do was to treat people as human, in a very dehumanising process, to give them some sense of dignity, and that they had some sense of 'self' to give worth to. Similarly, I remember working with some 'dockers' wives' in Liverpool, as that is how they thought of themselves, dockers' wives. They did not often see themselves as having independent ideas until they were brought out in them. Baizerman also has a belief in spontaneous moments being the places that induce this becoming, precisely because they are personal, unplanned, non-linear and the process of two human beings coming together. These things also have to happen in the ordinary and everyday, as that is what we are trying to understand.

Training in youthwork as herein conceived is directed at developing the skills necessary to pierce one's taken-for-granted, ordinary, mundane life so that one becomes aware of how the ordinary is constructed and how one is impli-cated in constructing one's own reality. Joining this skill to awareness of how one's biography pre-forms the present gives the youthworker the possibility of seeing in the moment its manifold possibilities, not simply what is there. Done well, all of this slows down the instantaneous process of seeing and making meaning. Once slowed, the youthworker (and young person) can 'control' how she makes sense, and, in this way, come to be accountable to herself.

Baizerman, 1989: 1

Celebration

He also has some powerful things to say about the idea of normalcy, and what we as youth workers have to de-construct about it in the conversations we have with young people. For him we have a 'powerful belief in normalcy and in the transitory nature of personal trouble and problems'. I think again this is powerful in our work with young people, to help them see that they are not their problems, their prob-lems do not define them. However, he goes further than this, saying that we then need to challenge this idea of normal. For him the normalcy assumption must be treated as a failed hypothesis. I am reminded of those young people I have worked with who say they just want to be normal, or the homeless who say they just want a house, with a wife/husband, a job, loving family etc., not realising that this situa-tion is largely a myth, both in its existence, and where it does exist, is no guarantee of happiness.

All of this has power in terms of developing people's appreciation of self, agency and sense of possibility, but does it achieve agency? The temptation when developing agency is that unless we 'achieve' something, i.e. structural change happens, then we have failed. In the context of youth work we can see where there the pessimism comes in, with legislation that has systematically demonised young people being enacted for the last 20 years. This is not a call to give up trying to 'affect' real change, it is a call to value the small achievements as well. The acts of resistance, even the symbolic ones, should be celebrated. Otherwise we encourage the aforementioned sense of hopelessness in young people. In the research we are conducting we have seen agencies achieve real change in terms of public space, with governments in Austria passing bills to say that young people have a right to be in public spaces. These achievements may turn out to be symbolic achievements, but should none the less be celebrated. Within them are the seeds of wider change. In this context the young woman's reaction, writing that phrase in shit, should not be seen as wholly negative, it showed a sense of agency and defiance that needs to be celebrated, which the reaction of going into crime, as everyone expected, does not. As a final word I think the ideas of celebration and positivity need to be cultivated and developed from the conversations we have with young people, particularly where they are done in the context of challenging structural oppression:

> The English language is more exact in the negative than in the positive, with the result that the language of hurt, pain and conflict are more easily articulated than the experiences or ways of being of health, joy and peace.
>
> Baizerman, 1989: 1

In Graz, in Austria, they took action against the planned banning of young people from public space by holding a festival of youth culture in front of the Opera House (high, adult culture!) with graffiti artists, rapping, face painting, etc. going on all day. They invited people to comment on the idea of taking young people out of public space, but also to enjoy young people's culture and positivity. The event certainly was not spontaneous, but the conversations, with young people and old, certainly were, and they achieved human connection and hopefully developed a sense of agency for all.

How workers are responding in those, by definition, unpredictable conversations

Youth work's academic and professional community has employed interchangeable terminology in its struggle to define and defend how we act in those spontaneous moments, and how, and when, we allow the conversation to arise and develop. Words such as 'creativity', 'instinct', 'innovation', 'intuition', 'reflexivity', and 'meta-cognition', have all been used to describe what we do, as has 'experimental practice' (Smith, 1988; Young, 1999). For many years, Donald Schon's (1983, 1987) and Chris

Argyris' (1982) work on reflection 'in' and 'on' action and 'double loop learning' has dominated that professional discourse and still forms a major part of professional youth work practice and training. There may also be other models that capture the reflective and reflexive aspects of youth work, e.g. the 'Bricoleur' (Levi-Strauss, 1962), and, as we shall seek to argue here, the youth worker as improviser.

Reflection in action

At the heart of youth work training lies the notion of 'reflective practice'. Built on the pioneering work of Donald Schon (1983, 1987) this involves two elements. First, 'reflection on action' (i.e. looking back on one's practice after it has occurred and considering it from different perspectives, exploring motives, pinpoint successes, etc.) usually through the use of reflective writing based on critical or exceptional incidents which occur in the field. Schon also presents a picture of a professional simultaneously drawing on experience and reflecting on what they are doing, as they are doing it – 'reflection in action' – and this is the area we want to explore here due to its close relationship to spontaneous conversation.

Skill, competence or expertise in any field, can be understood as a complex sequence of actions that have become so routinised through practice and experience that they are performed almost automatically, accompanied by a reduction in self-consciousness – hence knowledge becomes *tacit* (Polyani, 1958) – like riding a bike, driving a car, or playing football. Indeed most experts may not know what they know – a phenomenon that has been coined as unconscious competence (Nonaka, 1994). Jackson (1968) estimated that a primary school teacher may make 1,000 decisions a day – not deliberative, but interactive decisions made on the spur of the moment. The question is how we keep this process under critical scrutiny lest it become dysfunctional and fails to adjust to new circumstances, develops short cuts and becomes very difficult to change. Interestingly, Schon claims that this kind of tacit knowledge or unconscious competence, and the practice based on it, is only disturbed when the practitioner is confronted with a new, abnormal situation or intuitively feels something is not right. At this point 'reflection in action' begins; a questioning and criticising of the routine nature of the professional's approach and an immediate restructuring of responses. Essentially the worker begins to think on their feet, and works out what to say and what conversation to have.

However, the concept of reflection 'in' action has been critiqued (Eraut, 2007; Russell and Munby, 1989). Michael Eraut (2007: 145) claims that Schon does not have a 'coherent view of reflection'. The efforts of others to describe reflection in action (e.g. Russell and Munby, 1989) Eraut (2007: 74) claims, have led to 'despair'. He concludes that there is 'no elaboration of the psychological realities of reflection in action', and that Schon's work:

. . . is not sufficiently analytical and articulated to enable us to follow the connections that must be made between elements of experience and elements of cognition so that we might see how reflection in action might be understood to occur.

Eraut, 2007: 74

Reflection on action

Eraut also thinks there is confusion about when reflection *in* action becomes reflection *on* action. For this reason it is worth pausing for a critique of reflection on action, because we will go on to look at addressing Eraut's concerns in a way that unifies reflection in and on action. So we need to make sure that our thinking reflection on action is equally robust. Broadly speaking, reflective practice as a mainstay of professional development remains core to training regimes but also problematic. A critique developed by, amongst others, Ecclestone and Hayes (2008) also questions the positioning of reflective practice, both in and on action, as a panacea for student professional development. They maintain that an over emphasis on the emotional and affective aspects of learning can create an unholy alliance between tutor and student, or practitioner and supervisor (particularly non line management supervisors) whereby the student simply regurgitates a pseudo-therapeutic script which they anticipate will gain them academic credit, or in practice the worker elaborately self-justifies their practice to a non-line management supervisor. This collusion, Trelfa (2005) argues, could well be having a corrosive rather than developmental impact on students' and practitioners' professional development, particularly when exacerbated through the use of assessment methods such as reflective writing. David Tripp has raised other questions too:

The problem is that reflection does not take place in a social and psychological vacuum (and) is always informed by our view of the world . . . we construct our world through reflection, but how and on what we reflect is largely determined by our existing world view.

Tripp, 1993: 12

Creativity, intuition and innovation

We wish to offer a way through this that theorises the concept of reflection in action further, and also explores spontaneity in relation to other concepts valued in youth work, like creativity, intuition and innovation, claiming that they are often best expressed, or at least fostered, in the moment. First some exploration of these terms seems appropriate. Creativity (taken here to refer to the invention or origination of something new, original or novel which has value) is a slippery concept that similarly resists categorisation in propositional form. Our interest in creativity here revolves around the potential for fostering creative practice within youth work settings. Such practice incorporates creative (i.e. new and original) thinking in response to situations encountered in practice. From its early beginnings with the work of Wallas (1926), extensive work by Sternberg (2006) and Kaufman (2009) has attempted to theorise the creative process and break it down into its constituent parts. Others such as Nickerson (1999) have attempted to then go on to consider how creativity may be fostered through educational practice and express concerns over how formal schooling may be stifling creativity. Claxton (1999) is adamant that creativity is central to the success of all learners throughout their life, and particularly so in the context of the fast changing, globalised world we now live in. Gibson (2011) has highlighted how, within this political climate, creativity has come to be characterised, as part of a neo-liberal discourse of productivity and labour, as effective market responsiveness within formal education settings. Here we seek to reclaim the term.

Intuition seems highly relevant, as it combines the aforementioned *logos*, with more emotive processes. *Intuitive* practice, for example, is defined here as that which seeks to make decisions and judgements not solely on the basis of reason or rationality alone. Authors such as Gladwell (2006) and Dreyfus and Dreyfus (1986) have highlighted the power of more intuitive thinking within expertise. Rather than referring to prescriptive policies, intuitive judgements are made on the basis of feelings that may be in the realm of the unconscious but still based on extensive experience. Often these decisions are made very quickly on the basis of rapid analysis of the situation:

> *Decisions made very quickly can be every bit as good as those made cautiously and deliberately.* (Gladwell, 2006: 14). *Sometimes we're better off if the mind behind the locked door makes our decisions for us.* (Gladwell, 2006: 61).

The reliability of intuitive practice has been widely debated within the field, for example within the sphere of safeguarding (e.g. Munro, 2011) with most writers agreeing that effective decision-making within complex systems requires a combination of intuition and rationality. Similarly, *innovation* refers to the notion of doing something different to achieve better results or arrive at solutions to problems. Highly valued in the world of corporate business, research, and organisation management for its concomitant advantages in terms of efficiency and competitiveness, innovation is lauded in terms of its potential to lead to breakthroughs in fields of knowledge and the emergence of entrepeneurs.

The related concepts of creativity, intuition, innovation, etc. all express something integral to expert youth work practice but we, as have other authors, struggle to see how it can be learned, and hence improved, particularly in the moment. Ultimately, as youth work educators, we also want to know if and how it can be assessed, if we are meant to be preparing students for the profession, and ultimately acting as gatekeepers to it. We also wish to know how it can inform important aspects which go to the heart of what makes youth work distinct, for instance its commitment to extensive and disciplined engagement with theory as part of preparation for educational practice, above and beyond the making of intuitive decisions or solving of problems.

Improvisation

We think that the notion of *improvisation*, especially as when conceived by jazz musicians, may offer a more appropriate characterisation of youth work practice. There is some evidence of the term improvisation being employed as a metaphor in formal education settings (Sorenson & Coombs, 2007) psychotherapy (Keeney, 1990) and organisation science (Weick, 1998; Pasmore, 1998; Zack, 2000; Hatch, 1998; Crossan, 1998). Michel Eraut (2007:150) uses the term in passing:

> *Plans may exist on paper or in the practitioner's mind, they may be developed or modified during an initiation period; or the practitioner may simply decide to handle the situation in a routine way or even to improvise.*

Jeffs and Smith (1996: 127) briefly employ jazz as a metaphor to illustrate the power of improvised youth work practice:

> *Much as musicians learn to respond to each other to create an intelligible performance, so informal educators must draw out the contribution of others whilst simultaneously making their own . . . it is a delicate balance but one which good informal educators, like good jazz musicians, seek to maintain. Both jazz musicians and informal educators are improvisers.*

Schon, himself an accomplished jazz clarinettist, also employs jazz improvisation as a metaphor claiming 'conversation is collective verbal improvisation' (1987: 30). Importantly, he stresses the way in which the jazz player is heavily influenced by their environment, seeing improvisation as interchangeable with reflection in action:

> *Listening to one another, listening to themselves, they feel where the music is going and adjust their playing accordingly. A figure announced by one performer will be taken up by another, elaborated, turned into a new melody. Each player makes on-line inventions and responds to surprises triggered by the inventions of the other players . . . when good jazz musicians improvise together they . . . display reflection-in-action . . .*

He acknowledges that jazz improvisation is underpinned by deep theoretical knowledge:

The collective process of musical invention is organized around an underlying structure. There is a common schema of meter, melody, and harmonic development that gives the piece a predictable order. In addition each player has at the ready a repertoire of musical figures around which he can weave musical variations as the opportunity arises. Improvisation consists in varying, combining, and recombining a set of figures within a schema that gives coherence to the whole piece. As the musicians feel the directions in which the music is developing, they make new sense of it. They reflect-in-action on the music they are collectively making – though not of course in the medium of words.

Schon, 1983: 55

Schon does not refer to youth work specifically, and his examples are drawn from a wide range of professional contexts. Jazz musicians and youth workers have something distinct in common – *they both improvise, not solely because they have to, but because they positively choose to*. The National Occupational Standards for youth work currently contain no reference to improvisation as a part of youth work practice. However, we argue that the youth workers' readiness, willingness and ability to improvise is so central to the professional task that further exposition of this process is necessary, and that the concept of improvisation, when more coherently expressed, could better serve the field in terms of a model for professional development than other related models. If we are to move beyond mere metaphor and translate across disciplines from art into the intrinsically complex human relations context we will need to first provide a rigorous theorisation of improvisation to withstand that considerable challenge.

The nature of improvisation

The nature of improvisation ultimately involves a number of philosophical questions we have explored, and will explore further, in this book, such as the nature of knowledge and the self, aesthetics, structure and agency, and human freedom. The work of the existentialist philosophers (e.g. Sartre, 1969) challenges us to ask – who or what is the 'self' that improvises? Opinions diverge as to the way to approach the study of improvisation with those such as Derek Bailey (1992) seeking to resist deconstruction of what they see as a 'craft' – a private, idiosyncratic, intuitive, fluid, implicit, mysterious process, 'a transient and irreproducible activity' (Ross and Egea-Kuehne, 2005). Arguably, it is an activity that pervades life itself:

Thinking on one's feet, making spontaneous decisions and responding to the unexpected might be considered generic creative behaviours, essential to a wide variety of creative processes in the arts, sciences and, most importantly, in life.

Neeland, 2011: 171

In lay terms, when we think of improvisation many would immediately think of its application in the arts – whether music, dance, art, comedy or drama. The word improvisation itself is derived from the Latin *improvisus* meaning 'not seen ahead of time' – suggesting that we are talking here of a form of activity that is creative, unplanned and spontaneous. Gary Peters (2009) highlights a pejorative notion of improvisation as a kind of making do, the ability to make something out of nothing – 'the makeshift, the cobbled together'. He quotes Neil Sorrell (1992:9):

> *The word itself poses all kinds of problems . . . because of its usage in everyday speech, conveying something that is insufficiently prepared and of no lasting value (for example an improvised shelter).*

This understanding of improvisatory practice is closer to the Levi-Strauss's (1962) notion of the 'bricolage', a more positive spin, and a term used in several disciplines, among them the visual arts, to refer to the construction or creation of a work from a diverse range of things that happen to be available, or a work created by such a process. The term's core meaning in French is to 'fiddle, tinker' and, by extension, to make creative and resourceful use of whatever materials are at hand (regardless of their original purpose). In many ways this captures the unpredictable world of youth work and the need for the participant to make use of those materials in his or her immediate surroundings for educational purposes. Such a device has been employed by others (e.g. Hatton, 1988) to characterise the work of teachers in school.

Cultural perceptions may also colour our own understanding of creativity and improvisation. Koji Matsunobu (2011) writing on creativity in an eastern paradigm cites Lubart who argues that the eastern concept of creativity is 'less focused on innovative products' (Sternberg and Lubart, 1999: 340). For this reason, East Asians normally underline mastering and perfecting skills through rigid training while often shrugging off new products or ideas. To some extent learning within any artistic domain involves mastery of a basic form that underpins the elements of its artistic expression. Whether the artist's intention is to follow, modify, or break the form, some sort of reference to what has been refined and accumulated as a form is evident in his or her expression of art. In other words, art is no less an expression of the individual artist's mind than a set of cultural, social and historical artefacts available to the artist.

Extensive studies of the jazz musician community (e.g. Berliner, 1994) have begun to shed some light on the process of acquiring these skills of improvisation within jazz music. Detailed imitation and disciplined, repeated practice of this sort form a major part of the jazz musician's education. However this is all in preparation for being able to improvise:

Jazz differs from classical music in that there is no clear prescription of what is to be played . . . given the highly exploratory and tentative nature of improvisation, the potential for failure and incoherency always lurks just around the corner.

Barrett, 1998: 606

In a very real sense this uncertainty creates a freshness, vitality, excitement and edge to the music as well as a sense of peril that arises from an unpredictable outcome – an outcome that is heavily influenced by the ensemble, the environment, the mood of the performers, and the audience. Berliner's work also illuminates how jazz improvisers think. He describes how within the jazz community, pre-rehearsed ideas are seen as a necessary evil (to be avoided if at all possible) and how an attempt is made to incorporate the ideas of others into the performer's own style. A culture exists, which actively seeks the unfamiliar musical situation to avoid habitual thinking. Regulation and control are viewed as restricting interplay. Retrospective sense making is preferred to attempts to plan for anticipated outcomes, an approach mirrored in improvisational approaches to therapy, 'where the score or script comes into play after the performance rather than before' (Tyler, S. and Tyler, M., 1990: xi, in Keeney, 1990). Jazz musicians actively choose to leave space for improvisation within performance so as to avoid reliance on routines and to create vibrancy:

Artists may make decisions about particular features of their renditions outside of performance, but they reserve other decisions for the actual performance.

Berliner, 1994

Youth workers, who are often seeking to engage those young people that have rejected the structure of formal schooling, could arguably see resonance with saxophonist Lee Konitz's approach to performance. He talks of 'delivery' that 'strives to interpret the melody as if performing it for the first time' (Berliner, 1994: 67). Very importantly, if we are to help young people see their existential uniqueness, rote responses are in danger of reinforcing that they are just another young person we have worked with. Chuck Israel, provides an insight into how the seemingly tacit, unconscious process of improvisation is in fact based on a learnable, theoretical framework, whereby basic musical forms which reoccur can be recognised and form the basis of conscious practice regimes:

An essential ingredient in learning to be a musician is the ability to recognise a parallel case when confronted with one. If things remind you of other pieces when you approach a new piece you generally catalogue them very quickly so that you can draw upon your accumulated knowledge.

Berliner, 1994: 78

Teaching improvisation

This process of generalisation could, we suggest, have parallels with how informal educators conduct their conversations, for example in the recognition of Kantian or Utilitarian dimensions to ethical dilemmas, or in seeing educational aspects of the environment or in recognising the underlying issues or 'frame' (Goffman, 1974) of a conversation. Interestingly, according to Purcell (2002) a deeper appreciation of musical improvisation and its range of educational potential has been hindered by the proliferation of study aids in jazz, rock and pop that prey upon the acquisitive nature of students, presenting compendiums of 'hot licks and cool grooves', with little attention to the whole range of processes that characterise musical or artistic development. This is mirrored in approaches to youth work interventions that involve the development of 'toolkits' or pre-prepared activities, often to deal with aspects of curriculum in workshop or other structured activities, and can be delivered, presumably by anyone – an approach that is antithetical to Freirean dialogical educational practice based on worker reflexivity.

Issues still remain, such as how to teach improvisation, and how we can continue to hone it in practice. However, jazz education has a history of trying to do this. Peters (2009: 304) argues for teachers of improvisation in any context to focus on bringing what may be in the realms of students' unconscious competence, back under a degree of critical, reflective control and recognise that in fact improvisation often involves the re-marking, revising or reconfiguring of existing familiar ideas:

> Can improvisation be taught? No. Can the improviser be taught? Yes, but not how to improvise, rather to be made better aware of what improvisation might be, what it might consist of and where it might be found.

Whilst one cannot prepare for specific actions of unknown events, one can become *predisposed* to act in a certain manner regarding unknown events. This predisposition is what Dewey meant by habit, 'an acquired predisposition to ways or modes of response' (Dewey, 1922: 42). This idea stretches back to what Aristotle called 'hexis' and was later elaborated into 'habitus' by Pierre Bourdieu (1977). The individual biographies of all practitioners, their past experiences and values will clearly have an impact on and how they approach uncertainty, their disposition towards learning and ultimately their ability to improvise. Elements of the approach to teaching musical improvisation within jazz education could be adapted to the teaching of improvisation to youth work practitioners, and in so doing, impact on worker disposition, i.e. improve the readiness, willingness and ability of youth workers to improvise in their practice.

Increased sharing between practitioners of experience of improvisation, which requires them to return to and reflect on their 'unconscious competence', may in itself help others to progress towards it. Simply put, describing such things further will not prevent the improvising practitioner from continuing to practice in that manner, but only increase their consciousness of that competence, whilst for those who struggle to improvise, some breaking down of what is involved will, it is hoped, improve their practice.

Conclusion

In conclusion we have seen that the youth work conversation is no ordinary conversation, it seeks to truly engage with the other, as this is how knowledge is created, as well as there being greater mutual understanding between the two parties. In doing this it sees that the youth and community worker has to bring certain values to the conversation and attend to the relationships of those party to it, while acknowledging the impact and restrictions of the outside world on the conversation. As a part of this conversation, youth worker and young person are looking at how we and others are using or abusing logic and rationality to reveal rhetorical and calculatedly emotive devices for what they are.

Seeing youth worker conversations as improvisation in its jazz related guise could have several advantages for youth work practice, and bring together this chapter's opening questions about the youth work conversation.

First, when divorced from its conception as 'making do', it encapsulates how youth workers have to react (or improvise) out of necessity and in order to be effective, but also positively choose to. Rather than viewing youth workers' conditions of practice as restrictive, it allows for a celebratory and theoretically robust articulation of a distinct feature of youth work allied to its stated emancipatory goal. It represents a more fitting response to the conditions in which youth workers operate and the infinite complexity of human relations, thereby preserving the integrity of process based practice. By stressing the need for sustained and extensive preparation, as jazz training does, as well as a commitment to responding in the moment, it avoids the problematic aspects of Schon's work around the distinction between reflection in and on action, identified by Eraut, by conceptually fusing spontaneity and preparedness. By making the abstract process of youth work conversation more concrete it could serve to strengthen practitioners' confidence in their craft. It may also help meet the need for greater public accounting for the value of youth work practice which lies behind policy makers' desire for demonstrable competence.

Furthermore, it ensures that, by focusing on the encounter – the 'existential moment', the conversations between youth worker and young person are not reduced to 'problems'. In emphasising thinking about objects in their immediate environment it mitigates against the temptation for workers to bring preconceived activities from a de-contextualised repertoire to that encounter, thereby casting the young person in the role of passive receptor and 'objectified other' rather than potent co-creator. As a form of youth work practice that positively problematises young people's daily lives and immediate reality, it forces them to recognise what they don't know and actively think reflexively at a time when they are self-motivated to do so, often resulting in the crossing of thresholds of understanding as to the nature of their environment, Gadamer's 'fusion'.

Finally it supports the development of dispositions within students in training so that they begin to actively seek the unfamiliar (rather than simply learn to deal with it) and view impasse as an opportunity for education, rather than an obstacle to growth.

SECTION THREE

CHAPTER 8

'I Treat Everyone as an Individual'

Mike Seal

The human spirituality lives in such solitary confinement that it becomes individuality and individuality becomes a secret that is carried to the grave.

Leunig, 1983: 34

This quote is taken from one of the most striking, and haunting, cartoons I have ever seen. It is by Robert Leunig, an Australian political cartoonist. He is known for his support for Aboriginal causes and is one of the few white people to have open access to Arnhemland, one of their sacred homelands. The cartoon is from an Aboriginal perspective, illustrating their puzzlement at how white people relate to each other, and how the concept of individuality informs this. He starts by saying 'once white people had sacred sites and a dreamtime', accompanied by a picture of some people with a communal dream bubble, going to several people, with people dancing in it. The next scene has a caption that says 'all this was eventually subdivided', accompanied by people with individual dreams dancing alone. The next scene says 'such a subdivision is now called privacy', showing people starting to hide their dreams from each other. The last three scenes use the words above, showing people getting increasingly isolated, with difference and individuality being not something to celebrate, but tragic bi-products of this isolation. The final scene shows someone going to their grave crying and saying 'I'm so lonely'. I sometimes show this cartoon to students when they proudly say that they treat everyone as an individual to illustrate that it is quite a western construct to privilege and celebrate individuality.

Individuality

As youth workers, we explore in our everyday conversations with young people how they make sense of themselves, often couching this in terms of helping them develop a sense of their individuality. More indirectly we touch on ideas of the self through other discussions such as when helping them assess the influence of others on them, when looking at their potential, when discussing the idea of responsibility etc. This is all well and good but I think that, as youth workers, we are in danger of propagating a certain view of individualism, and what the self is, that we need to be aware of, and at times contest. To illustrate: when I ask students how they would react to a situation or scenario, I often get a reaction like 'it depends on the individual situation' or that you 'have to treat each person as an individual' and 'every situation is unique'. Indeed this is how I responded when I was in college. On reflection, while there is a truth to these statements, sometimes I was responding like this to avoid having to answer the question, to pin myself down to how I would respond. It was only when my tutor responded to my stock line about treating every situation as unique by saying 'so you make it up every time then' that I started to think again. More poignantly I remember being stopped in my tracks when a tutor replied to my 'treat everyone as an individual' line with 'why would you want to do something so deeply alienating to them?' I started to question myself and the constructions I was operating in. It therefore seems important to examine what we mean by individualism and concepts such as the self, as they are contested. At the time I was subject to a certain common sense view about it. But any common sense is received, contested and – in the case of individualism – problematic, and there are different concepts, such as collectivism, that may offer us a counter position. Part of my common sense was that it is liberating and developmental to think of oneself as an individual, and part of a journey to being a healthy human being. Burkitt questions the healthiness of such as pursuit:

> *Not only do people in the Western world feel separated from others with whom they live and who make up their society, they also feel divided within themselves, riven between the selves they present in relations with others and the individuals they feel themselves to be deep down inside. The armour that protects and separates us from others appears also to drive a deep wedge between our feelings and our ability to express them in public.*
>
> Burkitt, 1991: 45

At the age of sixteen I remember going down to Glastonbury festival for the first time. I sat on a coach next to woman who for the whole journey talked about her journey to 'find herself', and how she finally had. I remember feeling disconcerted that I had not yet 'found myself', and this sense of unease was exacerbated by an adolescent angst that perhaps I never would. After over 25 years I am still waiting. On reflection, while she told her story, a sense of unhappiness was pervasive; her contentment a mask to cope with layers of anxieties that remained. Reflecting further, perhaps this unhappiness was not because she had not found herself, but, as Burkitt indicates, it was a bi-product of her trying to do so. Buddhists would see the pursuit of self, and individualism, as a source of suffering:

> *Where self is, truth is not. Where truth is, self is not. Self is the fleeting error of our human experience; it is individual separateness and that egotism which begets envy and hatred. Self is the yearning for pleasure and the lust after vanity.*
>
> Carus, 1999

Although disputed in interpretation, Buddhist philosophy has much to say about the fallacy of the self, or of chasing the notion of the self. Suffering is caused by attachment to objects which are inherently transient, and thus condemns us to suffering. The most insidious of the things we become attached to is ourselves, the illusion of self, that we are somehow separate from other things, including our own body. Such ideas are highly influential in Western thinking, with our self, or essence, often being associated with the notion of a soul and an 'indivisible self' (from which the word individualism is derived from the Latin). As Burkitt (1991: 1) goes on the describe:

> *The view of human beings as self-contained unitary individuals who carry their*
> *uniqueness deep inside themselves, like pearls hidden in their shells, is deeply*
> *engrained in our thinking.*

I mention these ideas, not because I recommend discussing with young people whether they have a soul or not, or that we should introduce the idea that individuality and the notion of the self are myths, and dangerous ones at that (although I would not want to preclude such a discussion). We do, however, have a duty to look at how we talk about notions of self and individuality with young people, as we are not neutral. In this chapter, I want to make the claim that youth work is communitarian in orientation, in that we value the individual, and notions such as responsibility and autonomy, but see humans as best fulfilled through the collective. However, we exist in a society that privileges individualism.

I contend that from this privileging of the individual stem three social constructions that need to be contested. First, there is a consequent moral stance that independence and self-reliance are the highest virtues, as opposed to, say, interdependence and collectivism. Second, individualism underpins many political initiatives, or policy considerations for young people and communities. Smith (1996) has written extensively about 'individualisation' of young people in public policy. Such responses blame young people for their predicaments, for instance being in poverty, and so deny more structural causes and inequalities. Responses are then targeted at these individuals, denying the importance of association. Third, there is an assumption that liberal capitalism, politically, and the market, economically, best serve the individual.

The self

Lukes (1973) notes that individualism is an Enlightenment term (individualisme). He also notes that it was originally used, after the French Revolution, by all sides, as a pejorative term for elevation of individual interests above those of the collective, be that the nation, the masses etc. It was associated with selfishness. We also have to see individualism in the context of what came before the Enlightenment, medieval society, where relationships between people in society were rigidly hierarchical, set by god (Williams, 1976) and therefore not to be questioned. The individual did not feature largely in people's thinking. The Enlightenment, and its precursor, the Age of Reason, marked a radical shift with a new stress on a man's personal experience over and above his place or function in a rigid hierarchical society. As Williams says 'there was a related stress . . . on a man's direct and individual relation to God, as opposed to this relation mediated by the church' (Williams, 1976: 135). To the post-Enlightenment mind, one that privileges the individual as king, this medieval construct is easy to dismiss as oppression, and the shift as entirely liberating. However, we should remember the dislocation, as well as the sense of freedom, that accompanied this shift. Williams gives us insight into what this shift must have felt like for ordinary people:

> Before this shift, Men felt more or less linked to God, Man, and the earth around them. They knew their 'place'. Afterwards, they knew only that the earth had moved, and, with it, everything upon it. To some, this was cause for celebration: new possibilities were opened up, old restraints gone. To others, it meant the falling apart of society and the self: an occasion for lamentation.
>
> Mazlish, 1989: 12

As I said, to the modern mind, such a view seems alien, such is the omnipresence of the individualist view. However we need to jolt ourselves from this view, as my tutor did to me, to be able to see it more objectively. To the medieval mind our way of viewing the world must be equally alienating, and our way of viewing the individual as deeply isolating and distant from God.

Multiple individualities

From the Enlightenment on, the views on individualism proliferated, with German, American, French and, to a certain extent, British views predominating. Rather than undertake a tour of the history of ideas, I want to look back on what influence these ideas have now. Smith (1996) identifies four ways that the individual, or self can be considered: as a bounded container; as a part of a community; as a dialogical entity; and as the post-modern self. He produced a taxonomy of how these different views consider questions such as what it is to be human, how they see self and others, their orientation to practice and their educational focus.In this chapter I want to concentrate on the idea of the self being primarily self contained within the individual or within the collective.

I have expanded his division to a continuum, from the individual being entirely self contained, then the individual as primary, but having social aspects, then the group as primary with the individual best fulfilled in the group to, at the other end of the continuum, the individual as only being valid as part of the collective. I think it is important to see it in this way as otherwise we are creating a binary, and binaries have a history in this context. In America in the Fifties, any deviation from 'rugged individualism' as extolled by Herbert Hoover during his presidential campaign in 1928, which he fought on supposed 'traditional' American values of personal freedom, capitalism, and limited government, meant you were a collectivist, and therefore a communist, and anti-American. Conversely on the left there is a danger of what Lenin (1970) called ultra-leftism, which would be a refusal to work with any moderate groups on the basis that these were 'bourgeois individualists'.

The self as a bounded container (rugged individualism)

At one end of the continuum is the idea of the individual as a 'bounded container'. Lukes (1973) sees three beliefs as central to this form of individualism:

- *The supreme value and dignity of the individual.*
- *The individual as independent and autonomous with thoughts and actions not determined by outside agencies.*
- *The onus on individuals to develop their talents to the fullest.*

The idea of the individual as the prime unit goes back to Descartes in his famous dictum 'Cogito ergo sum' (I think therefore I am) whereby the only thing we can be sure of is ourselves because god would not deceive us in this, and this is our starting point. This was developed by the likes of Locke in his 1689 *Two Treatises of Government* (1988) which talked about men as equal, free and independent, which is echoed in the Declaration of Independence, 'all men are created equal; that they are endowed by their Creator with certain unalienable rights; that among these are life, liberty, and the pursuit of happiness; that to insure these rights, governments are instituted among men, deriving their just powers from the consent of the governed'.

This version of individualism, which is probably most closely associated with the United States, had became part of the core American ideology by the 19th Century (Lukes, 1973). Core in this construction is a vision of the aforementioned, rugged individual:

> *An individual emancipated from history, happily bereft of ancestry, untouched and undefiled by the usual inheritance of family and race; an individual standing alone and self-propelling, ready to confront whatever awaited him with the aid of his own unique and inherent resources.*

Of interest here is how we interpret the significance of the individual being the prime unit in society. Nozick, famous for *Anarchy, State and Utopia* argues that 'individuals . . . may not be sacrificed or used for the achieving of other ends without their consent. Individuals are inviolable' (Nozzick, 1969: 23). For him, society must be based on individuals' free exchange of ideas and goods, and any attempt to intervene in this was immoral. This exchange may result in redistribution and equality, but could also justify gross inequalities and even slavery (if freely entered into?). Equality is of opportunity, not of material wealth, and, at an extreme, everyone having the right to exploit one another.

Other authors, such as Ayn Rand (1964), the darling of the American Right, are associated with the idea that selfishness is a virtue, or more accurately, that altruism is amoral. Reminiscent of Nietzsche (1961), she argued that true selfishness is displayed by those who play on altruism to try and create guilt in others. For Rand, even love for others is legitimate only as an extension of love for oneself. Without being able to pursue true self interest we lose our moral compass, and are left only with guilt towards others. If we all ruthlessly pursue self interest then ultimately the best will rise and it will be good for most of us, even if it means that some have to suffer indescribably. In modern culture, Gordon Gekko, played by Michael Douglas in the film *Wall Street* encapsulates this philosophy in his 'greed is good' speech:

> *Greed, for lack of a better word, is good. Greed is right. Greed works. Greed clarifies, cuts through, and captures the essence of the evolutionary spirit. Greed, in all of its forms; greed for life, for money, for love, knowledge, has marked the upward surge of mankind and greed, you mark my words, will not only save Teldar Paper, but that other malfunctioning corporation called the USA.*

As such there are associations with Social Darwinism, although Rand strenuously denied this, saying that allowing the strong to rise does not necessarily imply that the weak should be expunged from society. Critics (Dennett & Steglich-Petersen, 2008) say that this is neither here nor there, the rejection of altruism and embracement of laissez-faire capitalism, which she saw as the only 'moral' economic system, has the same result. The adoption of Rand, and her economic views, by the American Right makes sense in the context of what Lukes sees as a particular American version of individualism which is a fusion of Puritanism, Jeffersonianism and natural rights philosophy, as embodied in the Declaration of Independence, which itself was a rejection of 'state' interference, in this historical case, of the British state. James Bryce, British ambassador to the United States (1907–13) characterised it thus: 'the love of enterprise, and the pride in personal freedom have been deemed by Americans not only their choicest, but [their] peculiar and exclusive possession' (Bryce, 1888: 2). The political manifestation of this view sees capitalism and the free market as the 'correct' economic system, and minimal government, only latterly combined with liberal democracy, as the correct political system.

The question is where and when this vision of individualism arises in the everyday lives of British young people. I would argue often. For instance, in a youth club, should an individual's rights be upheld over the majority? If we give to another, are we really just doing this for ourselves? Does this matter, and if it does, should we perhaps stop doing it? More politically, should people be allowed to accumulate vast wealth; and even if it is at the expense of others? The last one is interesting, especially in the context of debates around Americanisation (Campbell et al., 2004). I have had several debates on these lines in college, about what it is to earn money, and the philosophies behind things like taxation.

The individual as primary but with social aspects

A slightly different tradition and vision of individualism grew directly out of the Enlightenment. It still sees the individual as fundamental, but challenges the bounded container view as, at its extreme, beneficial neither to the individual nor society. Durkheim (1997) made a distinction between the British and American rugged individualism, and a more European rationalist approach, typified by French writers such as Rousseau, encapsulated in his 1789 *Declaration of the Rights of Man and of the Citizen* (1997a), but including writers such as Kant (1724–1804). De Tocqueville (1805–1859) sums up this position saying that individualism can be a 'mild selfishness' that predisposes us to look after our friends and family (2000). He thought that this was bad for the individual as it alienated people from each other, and ultimately from the said friends and family. He saw public life, association and civic virtue as a remedy for this.

This is normally done in the form of a social contract, whereby free autonomous individuals rationally decide to enter into an agreement, normally where they will give up certain 'freedoms' in return for certain guarantees from others. What constitutes such a contract is often based on how people would react if they were all in a 'natural' state, and free to make such choices. A criticism of social contract theories, developed by Hume (1960, 1985), a contemporary of Rousseau, is that this state of being has never happened, and could not happen again, and is therefore unverifiable and a dubious argument. A counter argument is that this does not really matter, we can still rationalise towards such a point, or perhaps just abandon the idea of it coming from a place, as it is a social contract we are rationally agreeing on now.

Social contract theorists argue that people will enter into a contract because it is rationally in their best interests to do so. These rules, such as not murdering each other, will be mutually drawn up and mutually consensual. There are non individual based social contract theories, such as those by Hobbes (1994), who believes humans are naturally aggressive and non co-operative, famously saying that if we had no rules life would be 'nasty, brutish and short'. He believes that in order to avoid this we should submit ourselves to an absolute power who knows better than we do, and will not give into to such cravings; in his case that was the monarchy. Others, such as Locke (1983), had a more benevolent view of people, as we said, whereby the social contract was voluntary, and crucially, negotiable, paving the way for the view that the people should have rights and a say in the government and laws of the contract, i.e. the have to be consulted, or can vote.

Most versions of social contract theory still see the individual as primary and share with rugged individualism (Spencer, 1884) that society and the state are not seen as separate entities. I think this is a crucial distinction and one that makes the distinction between this position and the third position on the continuum, which we will consider in the next section. In this position the state is an expression of a collection of individual wills, and nothing in its own right. Rousseau contested this with his concept of the (luminous) general will. He believed, echoing de Tocqueville, that civil society has a civilising effect on the individual, shaping him, and is thus independent from him. This position seems in danger of mirroring Hobbes' cynical view of human nature, but Rousseau would say it differs in that civil society becomes the greatest expression of individualism, in which the individual does not know their own or others' interests fully, because they do not have the knowledge or collective intellect. Individuals who break the law and descend back into egoism and individual concerns, should be 'forced to be free' by the collective. We can see how this would be the antithesis of, say Rand's view. Hayek (1994) would also see this as 'false individualism', as it over emphasises the rationality of both individuals and the state, and the concept of the general will is far too open to becoming dominance of the state over individuals, leading to Socialism and Serfdom.

Before we move on to this third position it is worth looking for a moment at the work of Proudhon (1994), an Anarchist thinker and French politician in the 19th Century. Proudhon believed that the social contract should not be between the individual and the state, but between individuals, and groups of individuals. To these ends he coined the term 'mutualism', whereby individuals agree not to exploit, coerce or even govern over each other, but that a unified state was not needed for this. Also of interest, as it is one of the ongoing debates in social contract theory, are his views on what the contract should cover. He differs markedly from Locke and other individualists in that he thought that the social contract should not just be expressed in negative terms (i.e. what one would not do, e.g. not interfere) but have positive aspects (i.e. what you would do) including economic redistribution and ownership of the means of production, for it was Proudhon not Marx, who coined the phrase 'property is theft'. Somewhat confusingly he agrees with some forms of private property, and would have approved, say, of private smallholdings. However he disagreed where someone's acquisition of property exploited or impeded on another. Other modern versions of social contract theory exist, perhaps most famously Rawls' (1999) theory of justice, evoking the idea of how we would constitute justice if we drew a veil of ignorance over our own knowledge of the world and looked at what met our interests.

Other criticisms of the social contract tend to focus first on what constitutes the implied consent: e.g. do you have to be born into a society, and if so do you therefore consent to it? Do you have to consent to everything, such as taxation? Second are questions about legitimate expressions of discontent, and more to the point, how far does this discontent go before the social contract is broken. These are again all discussions I have had with young people, with some fascinating responses. Young people I have worked with enter into all kinds of direct and implied social contracts, and are subject to many others for which they feel they have given little consent. A debate about what constitutes anti-social behaviour is pertinent in this context. Going further I have asked whether democracy is the best way of obtaining that consent, and, looking at Proudhon, whether a social contract should extend to people's wealth. At what point accumulating wealth, or pursuing enterprise, constitutes exploiting another individual becomes an interesting discussion when coupled with debates about gangs, illegal businesses, bankers' bonuses and global issues of economic exploitation such as free or fair trade.

The self as best fulfilled through the collective

Humans are always in social relationships from the moment they are born and they remain part of a network of other people throughout their lives.

Burkitt, 1991: 2

This strand of thinking, which I have labelled 'communitarianism' is again multi-stranded and contested. Many of the authors associated with philosophical communitarianism, such as Alasdair MacIntyre (1985), Michael Sandel (1998) and Charles Taylor (1989) would not apply this label to themselves, and indeed the label is often used by their critics. Perhaps a common denominator to the perspective is that indicated by Burkitt, that we are social beings; and it differs from the previous position in that, following on from Rousseau, it would hold that the collective will is more than just a collection of individual wills, it exists in its own right and, if not necessarily better, is a positive influence on individual will. To expand on this, Smith cites Fraser who comes up with some interesting principles behind communitarian beliefs.

> **1. The individual is social or collective** and we must acknowledge the significance of reciprocity, trust, solidarity etc.

Smith, 2001: 263

Communitarians dispute the notion of rugged individualism. As Taylor says, 'Man is a social animal, indeed a political animal, because he is not self-sufficient or alone, and in an important sense is not self-sufficient outside a polis' (Taylor, 1999). This counters the individualist view that we act autonomously, and says that in reality we are subject to habits, routines and views that are embodied in the community, not the individual; and following Rousseau's view, are best expressed in the community and by a general will. There is also a biological strand to this with debates about the 'selfish gene' (Dawkins, 1976) being the basis for the functioning of the mind. In contrast, as Ridley (1996: 249) puts it, 'Human beings are built to be social, trustworthy and cooperative', adding that they:

Come into the world equipped with predispositions to learn how to cooperate, to discriminate the trustworthy from the treacherous, to commit themselves to be trustworthy, to earn good reputations, to exchange goods and information, and to divide labour.

ibid.: 264

On an identity level, debates between liberals and communitarians often centre on whether it is possible to create a sense of oneself, and one's values, outside of a social context or culture (Kymlicka, 1989) and if not, where this leaves notions like autonomy. Communitarians argue that as we are largely socially determined, our decision-making is as well, and that autonomy and autonomous decision-making are largely myths and certainly exceptions. Doppelt (1989) argues that while autonomous decisions might be exceptions, what we *value*, and our standards, or basis, for decision making should be based on those autonomous moments, even if they are exceptions. However, more radical communitarians question this emphasis on autonomy and choice, both psychologically and philosophically. Psychologically certain aspects of our identity, be it our gender, attachment to our mother, sexuality, or even religion, may be fundamental and it would be damaging to say we have a choice in them. Philosophically, returning to Rousseau, there is the question of whether the individual making decisions and exercising choice is desirable. Doppelt implies that decisions are inherently better for being made by autonomous individuals, denying Rousseau's contention that the community has embodied wisdom that the individual does not. I will leave the reader to read Simon's chapter on autonomy (Chapter 9) to look at the other question for autonomy, that perhaps it is a myth in totality, and is always socially determined.

Perhaps the most compelling arguments for a communitarian approach, and that we are social animals, is the idea of social capital, most recently elucidated by Robert Putnam in his book *Bowling Alone*. Building on de Tocqueville's concerns about the dangers of the collapse of civic society, Putnam defines social capital thus:

Social capital refers to connections among individuals – social networks and the norms of reciprocity and trustworthiness that arise from them. In that sense social capital is closely related to what some have called 'civic virtue'. The difference is that 'social capital' calls attention to the fact that civic virtue

is most powerful when embedded in a sense network of reciprocal social rela-
tions. A society of many virtuous but isolated individuals is not necessarily rich
in social capital.

Putnam, 2000: 2

In short, he goes on to say that developing social capital is good for people. He uses a variety of theoretical and empirical data to look at the decline of association and collective activity in America and its impact. He found that where it is strong it impacts positively in terms of child development, public space, economic pros-perity and health. For example, regarding child development, he notes that 'trust, networks, and norms of reciprocity within a child's family, school, peer group, and larger community have far reaching effects on their opportunities and choices, and hence on their behaviour and development' (ibid.: 296–306). In terms of public spaces, areas with high levels of association are 'cleaner, people are friendlier, and the streets are safer'. Perhaps most interestingly factors traditionally associated with risk such as poverty, transport links, etc. are not as determining as often thought. Similarly, in the UK, Johnston et al. (2000) studied a group of young people from an estate in Teeside which 'possesses all of the official, objective indicators of social exclusion' but which was seen as a place of social inclusion by residents. Putnam notes that, conversely, 'places have higher crime rates in large part because people don't participate in community organisations, don't supervise younger people, and aren't linked through networks of friends' (ibid.: 307–18), rather than people not participating because the areas have high crime rates.

Perhaps most significantly he noted that 'where trust and social networks flour-ish, individuals, firms, neighborhoods, and even nations prosper economically. Social capital can help to mitigate the insidious effects of socioeconomic disadvan-tage' (ibid.: 319–25). In the research into violence and gangs I am conducting at the moment we have found high levels of hopelessness in many poor areas, where gangs seem the only viable economic option. However, rather than dwelling on why people join gangs or engage in illegal economic activity, we concentrated on why some young people do not do these things. What seems to be a factor for those who don't engage in such activities is that they have forms of association that are not gang related. Therefore they have alternate sources for their identity and values, which in turn give them other ways of getting often higher levels of self-esteem, self-belief and resilience, and ultimately an advantage in engaging with the few economic opportunities outside of the gang that there are. Finally association has tangible health benefits. As Putnam says, 'as a rough rule of thumb, if you belong to no groups but decide to join one, you cut your risk of dying over the next year *in half.* If you smoke and belong to no groups, it's a toss-up statistically whether you should stop smoking or start joining' (ibid.: 331). This seems powerful.

While authors such as Ladd (1999) and Fukuyama (1999) have critiqued Putnam for both his selective methodology and for not considering the narrowing and oppressive impacts of some forms of association, he makes a powerful argument for the importance of the community and the collective for individual happiness.

2. It is not the case that all there is in the world is individuals, there are also communities, collectives and other institutions.

(ibid)

Following on from this, communitarians say that politically we should not base policies solely on privileging individual development or 'freedom'. We should also have wider political apparatus and not just consult with individuals, and have concerns for their welfare when determining policy. We need to consult with, and emphasise, the family, community groups, religious groups and other representatives of communities. Etzioni (1996), an American who is seen as the founder of American political communitarianism, cites the *truths* that the movement holds:

> We hold that the family – without which no society has ever survived, let alone flourished – can be saved, without forcing women to stay at home or otherwise violating their rights.
> We hold that schools can provide essential moral education – without indoctrinating young people.
> We hold that people can live in communities without turning to vigilantes or becoming hostile to one another.
> We hold that our call for increased social responsibilities . . . is not a call for curbing rights. On the contrary, strong rights presume strong responsibilities.
> We hold that the pursuit of self-interest can be balanced by a commitment to the community, without requiring us to lead a life of austerity, altruism, or self-sacrifice . . .

In this way communitarianism can be seen as economically left wing, supporting universal health care, welfare programmes and co-operatives and localised trading, rather than the market. It is also socially and morally right wing, with support for faith programmes, and pro-family policies. Etzioni is aware of these criticisms and in his statements above seems keen to distance himself from social conservatism. He is also keen to distance himself from communism and even some forms of social democracy, and is anxious to emphasise that there is support for liberty and political freedoms. In this way some communitarians would characterise themselves as 'radical centre'.

Bill Clinton in the 1990s expressed some sympathy with Etzioni's ideas, and its influence could be detected in New Labour policy (Smith, 2001a) with its emphasis on family, embracing religious communities and responsibilities as well as rights.

Perhaps most challenging, and interesting, in communitarian thinking is its relativist position with regards to morality, challenging traditional notions of exten-sive universal human rights. They believe that we have to look at the community and cultural context when assessing the moral values of a society (MacIntyre, 1985; Walzer, 1997). This was not to deny human rights, but that, as Walzer says 'effec-tive social criticism must derive from and resonate with the habits and traditions of actual people living in specific times and places' (Walzer, 1997: 3). However as Mouzelis (2000) notes, this relativist position raises multiple problems about how these community values are derived, and evaluated. Communitarians have not always been successful at giving examples of how and where such values have, and could, arise in a society. Macintyre (1985) developed an Aristotelian model, but that relies on homogeneity, and had little application for multi-faceted modern society. Similarly Walzer's evoking of Hindu Caste societies did not seem to have much resonance outside of the milieu. More recently, examples have arisen with Asian Models of development and Confucian thinking (Bauer and Bell, 1999; Bell, 1993, 2000, 2006, 2008; de Bary, 1998) with its emphasis on family values, social cohesion and education.

However, communitarian thinking is subject to accusations of social conserv-atism, in that by emphasising organic values, it supports status quos (Sennett, 1998). Other authors offer other criticisms, that it overemphasises the positive sides of community, and downplays parochialism, and NIMBYism. (Sennett, 1998; Smith, 2001a) There is also the question of which community, and hence values, we are talking about; and societies are, as we have acknowledged, rarely homog-enous. Etzioni acknowledges that there is more than one type of community, with geographic, psychological and even memory-based communities (close to ideas of national communities), but unfortunately he does not really elaborate on how the competing agendas of these communities can be reconciled, or even established.

Again these are debates that we can have with young people in a multitude of ways. Phrases I have heard young people use that could become discussions include 'that's against my rights' in response to certain challenges. I also think a discussion about the relative importance of family versus other sets of values could be war-ranted; 'that's how we do things in our family', 'that's part of my culture', 'blood is thicker than water' are all challengeable phrases that come to mind. Regarding the benefits of participation, the individualist stance of 'why should I get involved, what am I going to get out of it?' can be challenged. Taking this further, workers should examine their own constructions. When I worked with various homeless organisa-tions trying to encourage user involvement and participation, a common cry from workers was that homeless people would not get involved unless they could directly benefit. When you spoke to homeless people directly they were far more altruistic than they were being portrayed. On a wider scale we need to look at some of the individualist constructions that underpin the concepts of professionalism we operate to.

Take for example the idea of confidentiality. This is something we hold very dear in youth and community work, yet in nature it is a very individualised view of what constitutes good practice. The Fraser guidelines, which are about establishing when a person can act in their own interests, assume that the individual is best placed to do this – Rousseau's idea of the luminous will challenges this. In practice I have worked with colleagues from different parts of the world who find the idea of confidentiality bewildering. That you would not involve the family, if not the community, in making decisions about young people, when they may have their best interests at heart, seemed irresponsible to them. Again, why would you condemn people to this level of isolation and vulnerability?

Similarly I remember sitting on the interview panel of a community group, again from a non-Western culture, who were recruiting for a new worker. We set the question of what the candidate would do if someone came for help last thing on a Friday, and you started to run out of options to house them. In my mind the question was about testing people's boundaries and limits, etc. In the interviews all candidates, when pushed, said that in the last resort they would take people home until things could be sorted on the Monday. The whole panel, apart from me, thought this was the right answer, as they thought the question was about testing people's commitment. It illustrated to me very different ideas about boundaries and commitment, and that mine was very atomised, and in Illich's (1977) parlance, about distancing professionals from the communities they work for.

The collective as paramount

Collectivism in the West, particularly in America, tends to be associated, and tainted, with its political manifestations, and rather hysterical views about, in particular, communism. In this light, the Fleet Foxes' song *Helpless Blues* suggests an interesting counter hegemony. Collectivism can mean different things but as Finkelstein (2011) notes, collectivism stresses interdependence rather than independence and the advantages of 'strong, cohesive in-groups whose members define themselves in terms of their group membership' (Finkelstein, 2011: 598). In terms of individual identity this is often expressed in terms of the groups one belongs to, the area one comes from, etc. As Smith notes (1996, 2001a), in Sanskrit writings individuals introduce themselves with their lineage, then their family, then their address and their personal name only at the end, as this is the least important part of their identity. This notion of identity is worth pausing on as it is a big contrast to the western perspective. This chapters' earlier quote from Buddha illustrates the difference. In Buddhist culture the pursuit of the individual self is often seen as at best chasing a lesser self, or more commonly a delusion to escape from. Similarly in Hindu culture the pursuit of self-revelation is quite different. As Marsella notes, contrasting east-ern and western concepts of self:

The western striving is toward the development of a solid well-functioning ego. The inner experience of self should be clearly delineated from the outside. The Hindu striving goes in the opposite direction – to achieve union with the immutable self, which is ultimately indistinguishable from deity and the totality of the universe.

Marsella et al., 1985: 18

I hear echoes of Rousseau here: our highest self is expressed in the collective self. Looking at the Fleet Foxes' song, and the Leunig quote at the beginning of this chapter, while individualism can be seen as liberating and freeing, it can also be deeply alienating. Marx, well over a hundred years ago, talked about alienation. He mainly saw this in an economic sense, of how modern capitalism was alienating people from their labour and what their labour produced. However, he also saw alienation in a wider sense:

A direct consequence of this alienation of man from the product of his labour, from his life activity and from his species-life, is that man is alienated from other men. When man confronts himself he also confronts other men. What is true of man's relationship to his work, to the product of his work and to himself, is also true of his relationship to other men, to their labour and to the objects of their labour.

Marx, 1844: 125

Since then capitalist production has undergone many shifts but as Jeffs and Smith (2002) noted recently when looking at the individualisation of youth work, individu-alism can in itself become a commodity, and ironically one that does not cultivate the freedom and individual expression it espouses, but unsatisfying conformity:

The individual may gain a spurious independence from the old ties that bound – the family, the local community, even the nation state – but they become manacled to and dependent upon a market that invades every aspect of their lives. They must consume to be free, but that dependency enslaves them to a market bent upon restricting their choice and closing down their options in the interests of efficiency and product standardisation.

Jeffs and Smith, 2002: 40

We have already covered some of the arguments for whether humans being are social beings or not, and this argument will go on. Perhaps one of the most contro-versial, and contested aspect of collectivist thought is that it privileges group goals over individual goals. For some this means that there will be a domination of the minority by the majority, and this is why rights need to be guaranteed. Some of the more hysterical brands of libertarian thought state that collectivism will inevitably lead to slavery (Hayek, 1944) and tyranny (Rand, 1964). Indeed many totalitarian societies have made claims to represent the 'common good' as those on the left acknowledge (Orwell, 1945). However, it is not clear why this 'road to serfdom' is inevitable, an issue we will come back to.

Economic collectivisation

Of relevance here is the notion of economic collectivisation. This is where the means of production i.e. the farms, factories, companies, etc., are held collectively, rather than by private individuals. The modern day manifestation of this is nationalised industries. More radical versions of collectivism will say that the products of labour, i.e. food, clothes, property, etc., should also be held in common, and distributed 'fairly' to all. This is taking communitarian views of positive rights, i.e. the right to food, shelter, or health care, and further saying that their distribution should be more than guaranteed, but equally distributed. Instead of economic decisions being left to the 'market', what is produced should be planned, and not determined by what is profitable, but by other measures. Capitalists would argue that the market is the most effective way of determining what people want, and other mechanisms are inefficient at best and potentially disastrous, favouring only certain people. Libertarian individualists would argue for the rolling back of the state and collective ownership (Hayek, 1944) in favour of private enterprise, or co-operatives of interested parties. Economically there is the claim that the market is neutral and an expression of a democratic system in that people will buy what they want, and not buy what they don't. The logic flows that it allows enterprise, and talented individuals to rise, and ultimately this will benefit all, as their innovations will improve production and there will be a trickle down of wealth (Hayek, 1944). I will leave this section with Emma Goldman who back in the Twenties was insightful as to who 'market interests' and rugged individualism actually served:

> *'Rugged individualism'* . . . *is only a masked attempt to repress and defeat the individual and his individuality. So-called Individualism is the social and economic laissez-faire: the exploitation of the masses by the [ruling] classes by means of legal trickery, spiritual debasement and systematic indoctrination of the servile spirit. 'Rugged individualism' has meant all the 'individualism' for the masters, while the people are regimented into a slave caste to serve a handful of self-seeking 'supermen'* . . . *Their 'rugged individualism' is simply one of the many pretences the ruling class makes to mask unbridled business and political extortion.*
>
> Goldman, 1992: 112

Collective decision-making

Visions of how distribution and economic and political decisions could be made in a collectivist society vary. Triandis et al. (1998) make a useful distinction between 'horizontal' and 'vertical' collectivism. They see 'Horizontal collectivism' as based on mutualism, sharing and cooperation, with an assumption of equality and localised federated decision making. 'Vertical collectivism' is more hierarchical, where one submits to a wider centralised decision making and planning process. It says that people are less equal, in that those who are weaker would suffer and get missed out of more localised decision-making. It can also take advantage of economies of scale. Traditionally horizontal collectivism is associated with variants of anarchism and vertical with communism.

So, does collectivism inevitably lead to tyranny, either of the minority over the majority, or the minority over the majority? Let us look at other famous versions of political collectivism, namely Fascism and National Socialism. Though hotly contested, fascism or more widely nationalism, can be seen to have roots in a German view of individualism. Lukes (1973) notes that the idea of individual uniqueness *Einzigkeit* and self-realisation contributed to 'the cult of individual genius', which by way of thinkers like Nietzsche, Romantics like Wagner and concepts like Social Darwinism, were transformed into a theory of national community, and the superiority of that community. National Socialism, as its name implies, was a peculiar mix of collectivism and individualism. In terms of individualism, they espoused the 'Fuehrer principle', whereby the most gifted acts in the interests of many. As Hitler himself said:

> *Only those should lead who have the natural temperament and gifts of leadership. We must take care that the positions of leadership and highest influence are given to the best men. Hence it is not based on the idea of the majority, but on that of personality. This common interest is surely not served by allowing the multitude to rule, for they are not capable of thinking nor are they efficient and in no case whatsoever can they be said to be gifted.*
>
> Hitler, 1923

At the same time there were collective aspects. Italian Fascism had its concept of 'corporatism' which saw society as divided into different classes, or corporate interests, but propounded that they should collaborate in the collective 'national interest', as opposed to the Marxist concept of class antagonism. There was very much an idea of submission of the individual to the collective. As Goebbels, the Nazi propaganda minister, said, 'to be a national socialist is to submit the I to the thou; national socialism is sacrificing the individual to the whole' (Fromm, 1941), in this case a mythical nationalist, racist whole. There was no notion of equality, in fact particular nations and races were seen as superior, and within that there was a hierarchy. This illustrates the dangers of some forms of collectivism, in that there can be a justification of collective, community or cultural views as being right purely because the community holds them, even to the extent of a creation of such an irrational world view as Nazism which was at pains to create its own folklore, rituals and myths to support its worldview. In fact fascism revelled in its irrationalism, Mussolini famously recognising that it had greater appeal to the Italian Peasantry over communism because of its irrational, yet headily emotive message and nature.

Politically, within fascism and national socialism there was very much a concentration of power and a conscious extension of the state's influence on previously private concerns such as education, religion, the family, youth movements, and an obliteration of value systems that did not agree with the state's moral view. However, this cannot be said, at least initially, of the economic system of these states. Hitler came to power with the promise of business as usual for big business, including large armaments contracts. We must remember that it was Siemens who won the contract to build the ovens in the concentration camps in a competitive bid.

Again discussion of these concepts with young people will be fruitful, perhaps with the Fleet Foxes' song as a start. Debates about what is the right balance between their individualism, and how much that individualism sits within a community or culture context are fascinating debates I have had with young people. Similarly a discussion about the degree to which people hide their values behind their cultures, with the phrase, 'this is part of my culture', or 'that is just the way I was brought up' can bring a lot up. I also think we can still work on the political issues. I have often asked students what they think a fair economic system would look like, and what place guarantees of welfare and individual freedom should play. Similarly we can ask this about collectives we are a part of, such as youth work, and when this creates solidarity, and when it excludes others, such as other agencies, and even demonises them.

Conclusion

However, there is no denying that many atrocities were carried out in collectivist regimes which saw individual and human rights as dangerous (Chomsky, 1973). Even on a local level, Belton (2010) regales against romanticising 'community', talking about how cities were historically seen as places to escape the watchful eyes of one's judging neighbours. He also talks about how communities can be discriminatory and not the progressive forces we like to think they are. It is for this, and other, reasons that I do not think youth and community work is wholly collectivist. As youth workers we talk about values, such as responsibility, relationship, autonomy, etc., that value the individual. Dewey's (1916) position is interesting in this respect. He thought we should not adopt a binary position towards either individualism or collectivism, for we need both. They are in tension, and should be so. As he says,

	Individuals are self contained (rugged individualism)	The individual as primary but has social aspects (social contract)	The self is best fulfilled through the collective (social democracy – communitarianism)	Individualism is valid only as part of the group (collectivism)
What is it to be human?	Human beings as self-contained unitary individuals who carry their uniqueness deep inside themselves.	Humans are primarily individuals but are socially orientated.	Humanity can only be understood as members of a wider community. Individuality is socially based but significant.	Our greatest human fulfilment is as a group. Isolated individuality is a dangerous chimera.
Self and others	Individual and society are separate realms.	We are separate individuals but have a social responsibility and reliance on others.	Humans are always in social relationships and we have a primary responsibility to others and they to us to develop each other.	Our primary responsibility is to other people, the collective is more important than any individual.
Practice orientation	Practitioners look to what is inside the individual.	Practitioners look to developing socially responsible individuals.	Practitioners focus on the whole and look to the individual as an aspect of that.	Practitioners focus on the whole, seeing individuality as a part of this.
The educational focus	Educators seek to develop the individual as independent and autonomous. They have a concern for self-development.	Educators privilege independence, autonomy and self-development, but also emphasise social responsibility.	Educators privilege inter-dependence and social responsibility. Individual development is best done through community development.	Educators look to develop the capacity of the community as a whole. Individuality is to be challenged unless it directly benefits all.

Figure 8.1

'the individual in his isolation is nothing; only in and through an absorption of the aims and meaning of organised institutions does he attain true personality' (Dewey, 1916: 94). And yet at the same time he says that 'society is strong, forceful, stable only when all its members can function to the limit of their capacity' (Dewey, 1933: 208).

This is perhaps the central debate we need to have – what is the right balance? Moreover, as the confidentiality and boundary discussion illustrates, it is worth looking at what impact these debates have on practitioners as a whole, their orientations, their practice and how they see education. Smith (1996, 2001a) developed a taxonomy that looked at the two ends of the spectrum and I have expanded on this as summarised in Figure 8.1. It is intended as a point of reflection for workers as to how their world view impacts on their practice. Having reflected on it myself I recognise that I move between these positions, and have different positions on different aspects according to the situation. Again this seems fine, but it made me reflect more on when this flexibility became inconsistency.

CHAPTER 9

'You Can't Tell Me What to do!' Autonomy, Free Will and Coercion

Simon Frost

As a youth worker I am sure you are accustomed to young people not wanting to do what is asked of them. Perhaps given the level of instruction and direction that is enacted on children and young people you are able to empathise with the sentiments expressed in the title of this chapter.

Think about the way young people are spoken to by those in positions of authority and power. As an adult would you accept being told what to do all the time? There is something about our desires which is innately human. In the main we are all capable of knowing what we desire most of the time. However what we desire and what we ought to do are not always one and the same. Here we might find ourselves in a situation where we are subjected to the authority of another against our will. So when is this acceptable, and when should we be respected and encouraged as autonomous agents capable of rationalising how it is we ought to behave?

There are many arguments for the need of governance of some sort. The philosopher Hobbes (1994) thought that without governance our natural state would be solitary, nasty, brutish and short. For Locke (1988) the role of government is to serve people, namely by protecting life, liberty, and property. Whether you agree with Hobbes or Locke or somewhere in between, the significance of governance as a way of maintaining both social control and promoting liberty is an issue that affects us all. That said, there is an argument to be had that we can govern ourselves and at the same time be capable of working together. Central to this discussion is the idea that we should be able to live our lives according to what we think is right, rather than living under the authority of others, which is what makes this subject an important one. If we have free will and the ability to reason we are somehow obliged to take responsibility in determining our actions (Wolff, 1970).

It is with this in mind that I will be asking you to separate out self-governance and collective governance, or what Kant (1948) describes as autonomy and heteronomy. Elsewhere in this book we look at heteronomy in the context of democracy and democracy's critics, but for now we are going to focus on the idea of autonomy and its necessary conditions. As practitioners you will often be working with young people as they make their own choices. Encouraging young people to think and reason their own desires against the expectations of others is likely to be a feature in your interventions as a youth worker whatever the context of your practice might be. So what is autonomy exactly? Whilst there are literal definitions of the word, and we will come to those shortly, as a concept there are number of ways in which autonomy can be approached. What does it mean is a good starting point, but going further we also need to think about the components of autonomy as well as the necessary conditions for autonomy to exist. This chapter will explore the following aspects of autonomy:

- What is autonomy?
- The components of autonomy.
- The value of autonomy.
- Autonomy and coercion.

What is autonomy?

The word 'autonomy' comes from the Greek *auto-nomas* meaning 'one who gives oneself their own law'. This sounds relatively straightforward, but as with many philosophical ideas there are a number of criteria that have to be considered in order to fully understand what is meant. In what might appear a backwards way of doing things it is helpful to start by thinking about what autonomy is not. It is not the same as freedom. This is an important distinction to make as the idea of autonomy and free will are often used interchangeably. Whereas autonomy concerns the independence and authenticity of our desires and choices that move us to act in a particular way, freedom is concerned with the ability to act, without external or internal constraints whilst at the same time having sufficient resources and power to make our desires effective (Blackburn, 1999). Whilst freedom and autonomy mean different things the former is a condition of the latter. If autonomy refers to the capacity of a rational individual to make a choice then that choice has to be acted upon freely.

We might think of an autonomous person as being concerned with determining their own path, whereas those who accept the authority of others are in effect in less control. By accepting authority, Wolff (1970) argues, we are accepting the assertion of another that they have the right to be obeyed. Whether this ought to be the case is another matter but, for now, the idea of allowing someone else to reason on our behalf potentially weakens our ability to take full responsibility for our own actions. But what happens to our autonomy if we are coerced into doing something we do not want to do? The way in which philosophy deals with this dilemma is to distinguish between freedom of will and freedom of action. In this sense it is possible to force someone to act against their will, but it is much harder to affect someone's will so that it changes. You don't have to agree with the action you are being forced into. I am sure you are familiar with the phrase 'you can lead a horse to water but you can't make it drink'. Similarly in the context of compulsory education, whilst a child might have to be in a classroom and comply with the norms of acceptable school behaviour, it can be very difficult to make a child want to learn.

What is less clear is whether someone is acting autonomously when they choose to do something because they want to, whilst at the same time technically living in a state of authority. For example, consider those young people you know who go to school because they choose to go of their own free will as compared to those who go to school because they are scared of the sanctions they will face if they do not attend. Question – Is a child with a reasonable level of maturity, through a process of reasoning their own behaviour, acting autonomously if they want to go to school if they are at the same time compelled to go to school?

I think the answer to this question is yes and I shall now try and convince you of my reasons why, but before I do I would like us to consider briefly Wolff's (ibid.) description of the relationship between a patient and their doctor. A patient might rationalise that it is in their best interest to accept the wisdom and knowledge of their doctor and follow their prescribed course of action. We might think of this as being persuaded even to the extent that we are in some way deferent to the knowledge of a doctor. That said the patient is autonomous in that they are choosing, having deliberated, to follow their doctor's advice. Wolff's example of the patient and the doctor is not exactly the same as the child who both has to attend school and who wants to attend school, in that a patient under normal circumstances does not have to do what their doctor advises. However the argument that a child with a level of maturity might be persuaded by the state's argument that they 'ought to' attend school, in the ethical sense of the term, is similar in that the child is persuaded by the idea that the state is acting in their best interest when it says that children ought to attend school. If we now return to look at our two groups of children side by side we see that they are acting with different motivations. The difference in the two is that the former is persuaded by the argument of the state as an autonomous agent, and the latter is persuaded by the authority of the state and therefore acts out of fear of coercion. As practitioners this leaves us several questions to ask ourselves. Is it possible to be autonomous within a state of authority? In what ways does our practice facilitate and encourage freedom of choice, and in what way does our practice restrict freedom of choice?

Summary
- Autonomy, put simply, means: being one's own person, to live one's life based on one's own motivation and reasons rather than being answerable to the manipulation and/or oppression of others.
- Autonomy requires freedom of choice.
- To coerce a person's actions is to take away their autonomy.

- To reason whether to be persuaded by another's ideas may not necessarily weaken a person's autonomy.

The components of autonomy

To give oneself one's own law is more than simply saying I choose to do this because it is something I desire. The idea of self-rule contains two components: the capacity to rule oneself and the independence of one's deliberation and choice from manipulation by others (Dworkin, 1988). Think of an important decision you have had to make recently. How did you assess and weigh the reasons for your action? What considerations did you have to make that spoke for and against alternative courses of action that were open to you?

Capacity to reflect and evaluate

At one level all adults are autonomous, broadly speaking. We are held accountable in law for our actions in the sense that we choose how to behave, based on our beliefs, our desires and our understanding; for example I am free to follow a religion or not, providing my beliefs do not infringe on the liberty of others. In contrast paternalistic approaches to working with children and young people presume that some sort of decision may be required against their will for their own good. To be fully autonomous then is more than making choices and being held accountable. To be able to make these choices as human beings we require the capacity to rationalise or think about our behaviours. The ability to reflect on one's desires is an important part of being autonomous. According to Frankfurt's hierarchy of desires (Cuypers, 1995), the process of reflection on first order desires is evidence of personal autonomy in that the individual is able to reflect, evaluate and choose in response to both their own desires and the expectations of others. This is not simply a case of doing what one wants to do. To be able to self-govern implies that as individuals we need to govern ourselves – to be able to rationalise our behaviour rather than simply following our own instincts and desires.

> *Autonomy is volitional harmony . . . autonomy is self-rule; a person rules her or himself by evaluating her or his desires of the lower order according to her or his desires of the higher order. This self-evaluation amounts to self-government: the government of a person by the person her or himself.*
>
> Cuypers, 1995: 12

According to Kant, as individuals we all have a will through which we can choose rationally and independently of irrational desires. Kant (1948) stated that this is possible, through 'practical reason'. As human beings we are capable of knowing the right thing to do. Duty in this sense means to follow reason and/or morality, rather than the arbitrary authority of another person. It is on this premise that Kant develops the idea moral autonomy; law given by the moral, rational person to him or herself; moreover it is the will that motivates one to perform duty for its own sake and not because of any natural inclinations or benevolent inclinations towards others.

Whilst Kant includes us all in his argument he also recognises the issue of immaturity in both children and some adults; moreover whilst we all have the capacity to be autonomous, the capacity itself needs to be encouraged and disciplined. Herein the capacity to reflect and evaluate is called into question. Whilst we all have the capacity to choose, to be able to deliberate and reflect implies a higher level of cognition. At the same time the ability to reason our behaviour is seen as something that develops, particularly during the stages of late childhood and adolescence. In western educational philosophy there is an argument that in working with children there is a need to steer them towards what is socially valuable, constituted in part by personal autonomy. The extent to which we have the capacity to be autonomous is encouraged through restricted and guided choices; therefore to achieve autonomy one must first be subjected to outside intervention.

This creates a paradox in that children and young people are treated as subjects before they can attain personal autonomy.

> *If personal autonomy is to come out of this, it cannot run counter to all social constraints since these constraints are built in from the start . . . Educators need to work confidently on laying these foundations, untroubled by the thought that they are illicitly moulding children after a preconceived pattern.*
>
> White, 1991: 2

> *Education consists essentially of the initiation of others into a public world picked out by language and concepts of a people and in encouraging others to join in exploring the realms marked out by a more differentiated form of awareness.*
>
> Peters, 1971: 52

Let us think about this in the context of practice. For many practitioners working with young people interventions are targeted: for example reducing the number of young people who are not in employment, education or training, or tackling what is seen by some as anti-social behaviour. Such interventions are predetermined and value-laden with ideas about what is good for young people. The dilemma here for practitioners is around the impact of their interventions on the development of autonomy in the young people they work with. Do interventions respect and encourage the autonomy of the young people that are being targeted or are young people being treated in a way that others think good for them? From a paternalistic perspective this amounts to the justification of restricting the autonomy of a young person and interfering in their freedom in order to advance their welfare (Dworkin, 1988). Such an approach stands as something of a contrast to the liberal educational values which aim to encourage children and young people to determine for themselves the right path within an ever changing society.

> *Radical liberal educators emphasise the role of education in preparing young people to make choices that potentially challenge the values and beliefs of the society in which they live.*
>
> Winch & Gingell, 2004: 43

There are those of course who challenge the idea that values and beliefs are fluid and cannot be universalised. Given the current political fixation with targets in youth work we see an emphasis on the idea that young people ought to behave in a particular way. For philosophers a number of distinctions emerge here. Is there such a thing as absolute truth which is not bound by relative cultural understanding of what is right? Is it possible to know truth objectively, or is all knowledge subjective to our own existence? Moreover, is it important for the functioning of a society that certain values are held by all? Should youth workers approach values education from the point of view that there are certain values that should be transmitted? In terms of the development of autonomy these ethical distinctions are significant. The extent to which children and young people should be given choices, and the range and type of choices, is closely connected with the pedagogy of youth workers. Is it enough to instruct young people on what is good, or should educators be thinking about how the experiences of young people will inform their development of autonomy?

> *The role of the school as an institution can inspire or depress its students and staff. For institutions too can induce in their members feelings of inadequacy and dependence – the phenomenon of so-called learned helplessness – or they can in some cases make members feel competent and confident.*
>
> White, 1991: 26

People who feel that they have both choices and a voice in a democratic society founded on respect for autonomy will want to fulfill their role within a liberal society. Youth workers need to think about how confidence in one's ability to self-determine and reason one's own actions is gained or lost, and the part that youth work plays in this. A practitioner must consider the elements of their practice which reflect a paternalistic approach to working with young people. We must also consider whether all young people have the capacity to reflect and evaluate on the choices they make or whether some are more capable than others. Do we agree with the liberal aim of education that we should question everything, and if so, does this include the claim that we should challenge the liberal aim that we should question everything? Finally as an educator how might we facilitate the development of a young person's autonomy?

Choice and influence

Hitherto then we have been concerned with the idea of autonomy in terms of the capacity of a person to reflect and evaluate in relation to the aims of our work with them and other young people and the opportunity and encouragement required to develop autonomy. The second condition of autonomy is the extent to which someone's choices are their own. Are the choices we make independent and authentic or are our choices merely a causal response to our environment and our experiences? To address this question we need to return to the idea of free will. But before we do that, consider the important decision we asked you to consider at the beginning of this section. Ask yourself whether the choice you made was an independent one, or was dependant on the judgement of others. Are you able to separate yourself from those others who may have been involved in your deliberations?

Arguably it is in our choices that we are conscious of our freedom. For some though, personal autonomy is compromised by external influences in our decision-making. In his works on Wittgenstein and autonomy Cuypers puts forward the idea that social interference in whatever way poses a serious threat to personal autonomy.

> How can a person be called autonomous, if what (s)he is and does necessarily depends upon the judgments of other people, if her or his identity is radically moulded under the influence of the social environment?
>
> Cuypers, 1995: 252

Central to this argument is the relationship between the self and its environment. If the self is a product of the environment then any choices a person might make about what they see as their own desires is caused by what is going on around them. In philosophical terms there are essentially three responses to this issue. First, there is the origination argument which suggests that as human beings we are capable of acting independently; moreover as human beings we are the original source of our actions. Second, there is the counter argument which is known as causal determinism: when the laws of nature combine with events from the past, there is only one course of action (Blackburn, 1999). And finally there are those who argue for the coexistence of free will and causal determinism. These people are called compatibilists. Compatibilists argue that it is the presence of choice that is important. A person must be able to make their own choices free of any coercion (free will) but the choice that is made has already been determined by the laws of nature, beliefs, desire and character.

We act freely if our acts are voluntary – in accordance with our natures and desires – even if those acts are causally originated in past events.

Baggini & Fosl, 2003: 67

Let's stop to think about what that means for a moment. Think about what you are doing right now. What are the events that led you to do what you are doing now? I assume you are reading this chapter because you are a youth worker or you are interested in the values that inform youth work, maybe having a cup of tea or trying hard not to stare out of the window. Maybe you are on a train or at work or in a library. Whatever you are doing there will be a chain of events that led to this particular moment in time. Can you then say categorically that your decision to read this chapter now is entirely your idea or is there a sort of inevitability that who you are, the choices you have made and the experiences you have had have led you to this point in time?

Summary
- Autonomy is based on two components – the ability to reflect and evaluate and the freedom to self-govern without interference.
- There is always a causal component in the choices we make. Whether we are the originators of our choices or our choices are causally determined is a matter of debate.
- Whilst it is not possible to predict the future it is possible to understand the causation of our actions through hindsight.

The value of autonomy
To have respect for another person as an individual requires an appreciation of their autonomy. According to Kant we should never treat others merely as a means to an end but also as ends in themselves. Kant (1948) considers the duty to the self and others in terms of what he describes as the duty to develop oneself morally, intellectually and physically, so as to attain one's own perfection, yet at the same time ensuring that we do not prevent others from pursuing their function and purpose in life. In essence he is saying that our relationships should permit everyone to work towards their own perfection and the happiness of others.

Every action is right if it or its maxim allows each person's freedom of choice to coexist with the freedom of everyone in accordance with a universal law.

Kant, 1948: 230–1

There are a number of important points being made here. First, that we should regard people as valuable in themselves not because of what they can contribute, but simply for their value and worth as human beings. Second, that which makes us human is our ability to reason and deliberate. This is an interesting argument in the context of the instrumental value of youth work. Politically much of youth work is now seen as a way of engaging with young people with a view towards developing their participation in employment and education. There is a risk here that an over emphasis on outcome focused work with young people detracts from the value of young people as ends in themselves. In contrast, intrinsic aims do not need to appeal to external justification.

Kant has much to say on the value of autonomy but there are other philosophical perspectives which recognise the importance of being able to self-govern which are equally important. Mill (1985) and his famous 'harm principle' argued that we should be free from interference so long as we do not harm others; society should leave people alone to pursue their own ends subject to certain rules. Mill's argument is based on the premise that the main aim for people is happiness which in part is constituted by autonomy. Happiness without autonomy would just mean being in a pleasant mental state. If autonomy is a part of happiness and well-being and this is our most desirable state of mind then autonomy should be something that is promoted in a utilitarian state (Lindley, 1986). From an egalitarian perspective Mill is concerned with having a state of affairs in which the maximum amount of pleasure is experienced by the maximum number of people, which leads to his advocating the idea of democracy as a method in which all are free and equal in value. Central to Mill's ideas is the individual who should be at liberty to participate in democracy. With this in mind the contribution of the autonomous person can be seen in the context of promoting happiness beyond the scope of self-interest.

Summary
The value of autonomy is both intrinsic and instrumental. Intrinsic in the sense that it highlights the importance of the individual as one who should be free to self-determine, and instrumental on the premise that having autonomy maximises the greatest amount of pleasure for the greatest number of people. As a practitioner we need to consider how we might encourage young people to reason as a means of making moral choices. Can we see a link between happy young people and autonomous young people, and between the autonomy of individual young people and the greater good of the groups of which they are a part?

Autonomy and coercion
Hitherto the focus on autonomy in this discussion has been positive. Arguments for autonomy and working towards the promotion of autonomy, in the main, have emphasised the importance of freedom and choice. There are however situations when one might want to consider restricting a person's freedom to self-govern.

This is something that the philosopher Aquinas (1920) is concerned with when he talks about the necessity of coercion. Can there be a time when it is right to force someone to act in a particular way? The following formula offered by Nozick (1969) demonstrates how coercion can take away a person's freedom to choose:

1. P coerces S if and only if:
2. P aims to keep S from choosing to perform action A;
3. P communicates a claim to S;
4. P's claim indicates that if S performs A, then P will bring about some consequence that would make S's A-ing less desirable to S than S's not A-ing;
5. P's claim is credible to S;
6. S does not do A;
7. Part of S's reason for not doing A is to lessen the likelihood that P will bring about the consequence announced in (3).

What Nozick provides here are number of conditions on which coercion is dependent. First, we need a coercer, someone who is able to force or threaten another to act against their will. Second, we need someone or a group to be coerced. Third, the threat has to be powerful enough to make a person act against their will. There are also degrees of coercion dependant on the severity of the threat to the person being coerced, the likelihood of the coercer to carry out the threat and finally the ability of the coercer to carry out the threat.

At a basic level coercion is taking away a person's choice. We make many choices, not all of which are based on rational thinking. Our feelings and desires often compel us to choose a particular path as much as the cognitive processes of reasoning and reflection. With this in mind, to coerce a person to the extent that their autonomy is taken away implies a restriction on a certain type of choice, particularly those choices concerned with the way in which we govern ourselves.

There are certain conditions under which it may become necessary to restrict a person's autonomy, particularly if the choices they make restrict the freedom and well-being of others. Again the thinking of Aquinas considers the right time to use what he describes as 'force and fear' in order to restrain those who are 'found to be depraved, and prone to vice, and not easily amenable to words' (Aquinas, 1920: 20). This may sound harsh but I am sure you will agree that its sentiments are still reflected in Britain's criminal justice system today. There are however counter perspectives that challenge the need for coercion. If we look again at education policy there is a clear compulsory element that can be seen to be coercive if we agree with Nozick's criteria for coercion. With this in mind it is important as educators that we look at alternatives to coercion. Are there times when coercion should be avoided in favour or reasoning, persuasion or plea? Is it ever possible to justify coercion? In what way does your policy and practice restrict the autonomy of young people?

[An individual] cannot rightfully be compelled to do or forbear because it will be better for him to do so, because it will make him happier, because, in the opinions of others, to do so would be wise, or even right. These are good reasons for remonstrating with him, or reasoning with him, or persuading him, or entreating him, but not for compelling him, or visiting him with any evil in case he do otherwise.

Mill, 1859: 12

Summary

• Coercion is dependent on the presence of genuine threat, someone who is able to carry out the threat and the threat has to be significant enough to force a person to act against their will.
• Not all autonomous acts are good. In certain conditions it may be necessary to coerce another person.
• Whilst it may be necessary to challenge the autonomy of a person, coercion isn't necessarily the only option.

Conclusion

Throughout this chapter a great deal has been made of reasoning and self-determination in relation to the development of autonomy and its necessary conditions. To round off then I would like to introduce a series of brief challenges to the arguments made thus far. Firstly the cognitive emphasis on reasoning one's moral decisions has been vilified particularly by those concerned with emotion and sentiment and its relationship with ethical behaviour (Noddings, 2005). That is not to say that reason has no place in moral behaviour; rather it is but one part, and for some it is not the most important part. Contrary to the idea of following rules based on reasoned principles is the philosophy of Hume who argued that we cannot know *a priori* (knowing something independently from experience), but we can interpret or try to make sense of our experiences (a more empirical view of knowledge). Moreover, moral choice should be based on sentiment rather than reason (Hume, 1978). Here Hume argues that our passions should be considered as an alternative to reasoning as a way of basing one's actions. Hume goes on to argue that sentiment can only be challenged by another sentiment. Sentiment cannot be changed by reason. Given this perspective, morality is exercised in our sympathy for one another. The relationship of sentiment is then acted out through the ability to sympathise with another person's sentiments. For Hume reason does not give us our morals, rather they come from our passions. Such an approach to morality is significantly different to approaching moral philosophy using solely reason and deliberation. Whilst I don't have space to go into Hume's ideas in detail you might want to look at how empiricists determine moral behaviour compared to the *a priori* approach of rationalists like Kant.

Another critique of the emphasis on reasoned autonomy can be found in the thinking of Aristotle. Unlike Hume, Aristotle does have something to say about the importance of reason; however for Aristotle it is not enough to simply reason; virtue was equally important. It isn't enough to reason how we should behave, we need to be good people as well. Consider this: if you see a situation which requires some sort of moral response, how do you act? I don't mean what do you do to rectify the situation you find yourself in, rather how do you feel, and in turn how are your feelings affected by your reasoning? Imagine someone lies to you. Do you simply rationalise it is wrong to lie and therefore challenge the person who has lied to you, or do you feel as well that you should challenge the person? Is there something in your character or disposition as a human being that directs you to respond? For Aristotle being virtuous was as important as reasoning. Whilst reasoning is a part of being virtuous, so are our emotional response, our choices, our values, our desires, our perspectives, our attitudes, our expectations and our sensitivities (Hursthouse, 2012). In essence, Aristotle thought that we should 'be' good people.

Hitherto we have seen how Hume and Aristotle challenge the view of reason alone. By way of signing off this chapter I would like to offer a link back into Mike's chapter on individualism and communitarianism. In communitarianism greater emphasis is placed on shared identity within people's communities. Rather than choosing one's own way independent of associations, people should think more about how they are linked to their communities:

> It is not the case that all there is in the world is individuals. We have also to look at the significance of collectives, institutions etc. Communitarians take issue with the idea that the individual stands and should stand in direct unmediated relationship with the state and with society.
>
> Frazer, 1999

The downside of an individualised autonomous society, what some describe as atomised society, is a lack of social cohesion and social capital:

> Whereas physical capital refers to physical objects, and human capital refers to the properties of individuals, social capital refers to connections among individuals – social networks and the norms of reciprocity and trustworthiness that arise from them. In that sense social capital is closely related to what some have called 'civic virtue'. The difference is that 'social capital' calls attention to the fact that civic virtue is most powerful when embedded in a sense network of reciprocal social relations. A society of many virtuous but isolated individuals is not necessarily rich in social capital.
>
> Putnam, 2000: 19

What started out as a justification for the liberal value of free independent rational self-governance has found its limits in communitarianism. I think it would be fair to say that the contra-positions we have here would not dismiss the importance of autonomy, rather that autonomy should be considered as a feature of a collective exercise rather than an act of purely self-governance. This is an important distinction given the emphasis that is placed on autonomy in youth work. For now though how are you going to respond to this chapter – rationally, sentimentally, individually or collectively? All or none of the above?

CONCLUSION

CHAPTER 10

Philosophies of Youth Work: Post-Modern Chameleons or Cherry-Picking Charlatans

Mike Seal and Simon Frost

It [youth work] is seemingly naive, romantic, anti-intellectual and metaphysical, to say the least; a simplistic, pseudo-philosophical, incomplete mix of existential, phenomenological, Buberian and other metaphysical ideas!

Baizerman, 1989: 1

On face value Baizerman, an American writer on youth work, seems a little harsh. We explored in an earlier chapter the accusation that youth work is anti-intellectual, but we need to consider whether his wider criticisms have validity. He has an important point to make – there is a difference between saying our practice is a 'bricolage' (Levi-Strauss, 1962) a conscious, spontaneous, fusion of multiple influences and perspectives (at best) and it being a confusing, inconsistent, made-up-as-we-go-along practice – a collection of tricks and ideas that sound good. Many practitioners over the years almost pride themselves on the jackdaw approach. To illustrate with an example from my own practice, a game often used as an icebreaker is a trust game, asking people to fall back into the arms of strangers. Many youth workers use it, but if we look into its history, it was developed within psycho-drama (Gale, 1990). Gale is explicit that this is a specific device to be used in a therapeutic setting, and dangerous outside of it. Presumably it was encountered by a youth worker who adopted it, and passed it on to others because it sounded 'good', and it has now become common practice. By not investigating the implications of this particular activity, we fail to consider this wisdom, given levels of abuse in society, of asking people to be physically held by strangers in a situation where they have to place trust in them.

In the light shed by this example, it does seem to be an important project to look at what the philosophical underpinnings of youth work are, or more accurately what the different philosophical traditions that inform it are, and whether there are any consistencies between them.

On one level, any attempt to define our philosophical influences is doomed to accusations of bias or partiality, as we do not even have a common definition of youth and community work. Davies (2003) points out the difficulties of normative definitions, which rarely justify their claims or map well against practice, and of descriptive definitions, where realities do not necessarily reflect the descriptions or leave room to contest them, with youth work as a result becoming whatever is done in its name. Instead he cites MacIntyre (1984) who says we should consider any concept by 'a consideration of its trajectory through time, its tradition' (Davies, 2003: 2). We must look at its 'historically extended, socially embodied argument'. This gives us a chance to trace youth and community work's tradition, with an understanding that there is an interplay between idealism and reality, between theory and practice. In short, we need to look at its praxis.

There have been numerous attempts to look at, claim, and define our history and development, and we do not wish to repeat that task here. All historical accounts, including this one, are inevitably partial, and it would be even more partial to try and second guess what the philosophical underpinning of previous practice was. With this in mind, it is possible to trace the tradition of youth work through looking at what has been taught on, and what has appeared on the reading lists of, JNC courses. One could question whether what we teach has anything to do with workers' practice, and this, as Holmes (2008) points out, is one of our tensions. For some though, this is the nature of praxis. As qualified workers, we live those tensions, as have all those who were practitioners and are now lecturers, or were students and are now practitioners. We remember fellow practitioners questioning the relevance of some teaching to everyday practice, and whether it was too idealistic, or not idealistic enough. However, it is hard to remember questioning the philosophical basis of what was taught.

This is the subject of this chapter – to lay out youth work's philosophical traditions concisely, but with rigour.

One has to also appreciate that taking this approach can only cover, at best, the work of those who have undertaken JNC training, and that the majority of youth work, as (Smith, 2004) points out, happens where unqualified workers predominate. However, the literature that underpins the JNC qualification is useful, with valid reference points, even to those without the qualification. It is possible to identify with practice as unqualified workers and debates around the nature of youth work, both with JNC qualified workers and with others not qualified, and the youth work literature featured in our debates. In these days of integrated services and partnerships these debates carry on. Some effort is made here to look at the youth ministry literature, but no claims are made to cover all philosophers who feature in their canon. We do not intend to enter into seemingly eternal debates, such as that of youth and community work's relationship to informal education, or to re-rehearse Davies' tensions (Davies, 2008, 2009, 2010). Instead it is important to identify those philosophical tensions that cut across and inform these debates.

In laying out a stall it is important to recognise the influence of Marxism and communitarianism in our thinking, as well as recognising the relevance of humanism, critical theory, feminism, post structuralism and existentialism. Indeed, it is also important to remember that it is these influences that give youth and community work its appeal, whilst appreciating that not all would agree.

There is a broad claim that we are a communitarian project of the left, and that our project is not compatible with certain free market and libertarian strands of thought, although we will undoubtedly have elements of common cause. In our experience, youth and community workers see that existing economic structures maintain poverty and discrimination, and that the political state uses its apparatus, sometimes bolstered by fellow travellers such as the media, to maintain a delusion about the ethical and non-discriminatory nature of its operation. We think this is a hegemony that needs to be countered. The form this challenge may take will differ, as will the alliances made to make that challenge, but ultimately it is a political enterprise of the left.

In terms of exposure to the youth and community work canon, between us we have taught on three JNC courses over 12 years, as well as being subject to different courses when qualifying and acting as external examiners on eight others. In this time, because of exposure to philosophy at both undergraduate and postgraduate study, we have taken an interest in the philosophical aspect of the courses, and often taught to this expertise. There have also been opportunities of working with seminal thinkers like John Holmes, who has been involved in JNC courses for almost 40 years and was editor of a *Youth and Policy* special edition on youth work training. His article *Youth and Community Work Qualifying Courses: Living with the Tensions?* (Holmes, 2008) and *Practices, Policies and Professionals: Emerging Discourses of Expertise in English Youth Work, 1939–1951* by Simon Bradford, were of particular relevance. Time has also been taken to look back at previous editions of *Youth and Policy*, which at is best is an interesting interface between youth work academics and practitioners, to see who we make reference to.

Humanism

We can group our influences into four main strands. First, there is the influence of humanism, in its widest sense of a concern with human nature, behaviour and spirit. We have debts here to Aristotle (1976) for his concepts of 'the good life' as a driving principle, virtue ethics as a basis for decisions about action, the importance of reason in debate, and the dynamic nature of knowledge. Building on this has been the work of Dewey (1916, 1933) with its emphasis on practical wisdom and the importance of reflection and education. Finally there has been the influence of Rogers (1961, 1980) and Maslow (1968, 1970). While their analysis, particularly Maslow's, is deeply flawed, they have been important in defining the nature and conditions of our relationship with young people, and providing a framework for what we mean by their 'needs'. They also stress the importance of education, not instrumentally, but to being a human being. Later youth work authors such as Smith

(2001a, 2008) stress the importance of association, understanding others, and our-selves. All of these humanist influences have given us a strong picture of how we should live life, whereas the other three strands have been more powerful in explor-ing what is problematic in society.

Marxism

The second major strand of influence has been Marxism, directly through concepts established by Marx himself and early Marxists, such as alienation, the importance of class and the nature of societal and economic relationships (Burke, 2000). However, an even greater influence has come from the later Marxists who attempted to escape the more deterministic elements of some interpretations of Marx. Gramsci (1971) was particularly important in his analysis that ideology and hegemony are powerful agents of social control, but that this hegemony can be countered. He stressed the importance of the organic intellectual, which some view as the proto-type youth worker. Of course the major influence on youth work has been Freire (1972, 1995) whose concepts of conscientization, of an emphasis on education as a mutual conversation, and of locating education within the lived experiences of people gave us a framework for working with Marx's ideas.

   An interesting crossover between humanism and Marxism is the work of Habermas (1984), whose ideas of the 'ideal speech situation' added to the frame-work of what makes for reflection, conversation and the relationship that we should try to foster with young people. He also indicated the limits of conversation, by get-ting us to think about those with whom a conversation is not possible, those with a vested interest in not hearing our side, or letting our side be heard. Alinsky (1971) is an interesting figure in our lexicon, and not one who would describe himself as a Marxist, but certainly one on the side of the oppressed. He proposed using tactics with the oppressors that go against many of the values of youth work including the use of threat, deception and ridicule, saying that:

> *Only two kinds of people can afford the luxury of acting on principle, those with absolute power and those with none and no desire to get any . . . every-one else who wants to be effective in politics has to learn to be 'unprincipled' enough to compromise in order to see their principles succeed.*
>
> Alinsky, 1971: 42

We will come back to this cross-cutting debate when considering Utilitarianism, virtue ethics and deontological approaches.

Phenomenology and existentialism

Another major strand of influence, particularly on American youth work, and an acknowledged influence on Freire himself, in *Pedagogy of Hope*, has been phenomenology and existentialism. Phenomenology, particularly through the ideas of Noddings (1984, 1992) on care and education, emphasises the relativity of experience and the importance of truly trying to understand the perspective and 'life world' of others. The influence of existentialism is more subtle, and probably most evident with Christian existentialists, in developing what we are doing in the moments where we engage with others, and what we are trying to create in those moments. Buber (1958), who was Jewish, but influential in existential Christian thought, has emphasised the importance of 'encounter' and being 'present' in the moment with people. Friedman (1981), and later Baizerman, note that central to encounter is *confirmation*, which places a duty on youth workers to enable a process in others that makes them 'present in their uniqueness' (Baizerman, 1987) to 'induce their innermost self-becoming'. There is an interesting combination here that the worker is there to aid young people to understand and escape their biographies and their common sense, in a way that is akin to countering hegemony and developing conscientisation, but also in way that young people have agency, to become free to create their own meanings and flourish, echoing humanist and Aristotelian concerns.

Feminism, postmodernism and poststructuralism

A forth and final strand of influence has been feminist, postmodern and post structural thought. The girls work battles of the 1970s and 1980s, where youth work 'open spaces' were challenged as really being masculine spaces, and that there was a need for separate work with women, still has relevance today, and the argument has been extended to BME young people's, and LBGTQ young people's marginalisation. The author bell hooks developed the ideas of Freire further, breaking down the barriers between the personal and the private, saying that an engaged educator needed to look to the well-being of all, including themselves. This challenged youth work to examine a culture of accepting burn out, and neglecting our own lives and families, which was a further manifestation of a macho culture that pervaded (and still pervades) youth work. As such it had become clear that we needed to look again at our practice, and our everyday personal interactions, as the 'personal is political'. Postmodern thinking has taken this idea of deconstruction further, questioning all boundaries, binaries and claims of absolute truth, including gender, sexuality, race, class, etc. (Lyotard, 1984). Suddenly identity politics was being challenged. Did we not all have multiple identities? To buy into any fixed ideas was to play into the hands of the social constructors. There was a questioning of any claim to 'truth', particularly the 'grand narratives' (Lyotard, 1984), those ideas which claimed to explain everything, from Christianity, to Marxism, to youth work itself, in favour of multiple subjectivities. Some of this desire to develop 'local narratives' was in our tradition, but to lose our political, religious or ethical certainties was a direct challenge both to

faith-based and to political youth work. Perhaps most challenging, philosophically, as we explored in the chapter on conversation, was postmodernism's refusal
to accord reason a sovereign status. According to Lyotard, the enlightenment
project had failed; the idea that humans, or 'mankind', could, and should, shape
society through its own vision had ended in tyranny.

So where does this smorgasbord of influences leave us? Does our work have
any philosophical basis, or coherence, or are we just nowadays cherry-picking
the bits that seem to have resonance, leaving us permanently at the mercy of the
'fads, fashions and moral panics' that Smith worries about (Smith, 1988: 2). There
are points of convergence, but also points of tension, but we need not worry. If
postmodern thought has taught us anything it is the fallacy of seeking a 'grand
narrative', the thing that unites us all. At best we seek to find a series of ideas with
'family' resemblances (Wittgenstein, 1972) something we can recognise. Hopefully
youth and community workers are a functional rather than a dysfunctional family
(depending on your view of 'functional', or of 'family' for that matter). In fact to
seek total agreement would be against one of our unifying themes, that knowledge
is a dynamic evolving force. As Eldridge Cleaver said 'too much agreement kills the
chat' (Cleaver, 1970: 55) and it is precisely that youth work commitment to conversation and dialogue which defines us. We see the tensions between ideas as part
of that dynamic, which, at best, lets each idea enrich each other rather than clash,
but which also keeps ideas in check, should one seek to dominate, or be pushed to
the fore by current trends.

Tensions

Essentialism vs intersubjectivity
This tension has, and will, necessarily play out throughout youth work. An essentialist would say that a thing, and often in youth and community work a person,
has an essential essence whereas a subjectivist would say they do not, and what a
thing or person is depends on their situation. It could work on an individual level
as in 'so and so is like this', on a wider level such as 'women are like this', or more
subtly that 'we have an essential sexuality, rather than it being fluid'. In its earliest
forms youth work was engaged in a political battle with policy makers and politicians to say you could 'trust' poor people with the vote, to become educated, to
have a say – as opposed to the underclass argument, whereby working class people
are essentially untrustworthy, and that there was a 'natural' order to people's position in society that should not be disturbed. This would seem to put youth and
community work firmly in the subjectivist camp, rejecting such constraining con-
structs as confining. However it is more subtle than that. In later years subjectivists
argued that categories like men and women, young and old, and class divisions are

similarly essentialist and socially constructed. As Kumar notes, 'identity is not unitary or essential, it is fluid or shifting, fed by multiple sources and taking multiple forms' (Kumar, 1997: 98). Therefore identity politics is called into question – should we unify behind an identity, such as gender or race that is a social construction, and is ultimately hollow? The danger with such subjectivist positions is their potential to be de-politicised. As Cohen says, there is a danger that 'in the wrong hands it can quickly degenerate into collage and pastiche in which everything is rendered equivalent in the cultural supermarket of ideas' (Cohen, 1997: 390/1). In reality, there is discrimination on the basis of race, sexuality, gender, etc. whether they are hollow categories or not, and groups may initially need to find common bond in those identities, be they socially constructed, to understand their positions and oppressions. As Marcus Garvey recognised (Garvey, 1986) such unity is a necessary stage, there being a need to counter a cultural hegemony that a people have been subject to. Only then, with confidence and pride, can a group of people find unity with other social movements, to see that these categories and identities are ultimately constraining. A unity through difference, and difference within unity, as Giroux would understand it.

Agency vs structure

Again there has always been a tension over the degree to which we see individuals as having agency within a highly structured hegemonic society. If we over emphasise agency, we are in danger of denying the extent of social closure (Parkin, 1978) in our society. If we minimise, or deny, agency, where does that leave the people we work with? Marx himself, and later Marxists such as Marcuse (1964) and Foucault (2002), have been accused, not unjustly, of being pessimistic about individual agency – of being deterministic. Early Marxists saw the collapse of capitalism as inevitable as a result of its own internal contradictions playing out (dialectical materialism). Marx himself always placed great emphasis on the need for human agency, but that the economic conditions had to be right. Later orthodox Marxists recognised that the historical economic development of caplitalism did not play out quite as Marx had predicted, as Callinicos in *Marxism Today*, the theoretical journal of the British Communist Party, expressed in 1989:

> *Mass production, the mass consumer, the big city, big-brother state, the sprawling housing estate, and the nation-state are in decline: flexibility, diversity, differentiation, mobility, communication, decentralization and internationalisation are in the new era.*

Callinicos, 1989: 4

If the revolution was to happen, and it was no longer certain, there was a lot more onus on individual and collective action, rather than on waiting for the right economic and historical conditions. At the same time Foucault, in all his writings, and Marcuse in *One Dimensional Man*, were very pessimistic about the possibility of the individual 'escaping' their hegemonic environment, although both of them saw discourse as sites of resistance and struggle. However, 'the end of history' (Fukuyama, 1992) did not happen, and Liberal democracy turned out to be another grand narrative that could not unite and explain everything. Other forms of left politics, forms of resistance, have emerged, that have not fallen into the old power traps of thinking that if the rebellion does not take power, the revolution does not succeed, and has failed. Foucault taught us that power plays out at lots of levels, so by definition it can be contested at those levels – and will eventually start to falter at them. There is power in symbolic resistance, just as there is reality in the symbolic violence (Bourdieu, 1983) of the state. Symbolic resistance becomes part of a mythology that others take up and carry as expressions of hope. As those on the left who have seen its failures, successes and 'defeats' over many years might suggest, only the deluded or selfish think the revolution will happen in their lifetime, it is a greater project we are all a part of.

Within this we have learnt how to combine Freirean ideas with existential ideas, helping people see that they can have freedoms and escape their own biographies, but that they are still subject to social forces and will have to make autonomous decisions about what and when to resist, and hopefully, having experienced it themselves, they will be enabled to, in turn, help free others, hopefully within an ethical framework that sees the importance of others, and of association.

Utilitarisanism vs virtue ethics vs deontology

The ethical basis on which youth workers act has also been a cause of constant debate and tension. Should we have universal rules (deontology), such as never lying, treating everyone as equal, or holding the view that all perspectives have a right to be heard, even when it means the majority suffering to preserve the rights of the few? Or should we be strictly democratic, looking for the interests of the majority, even if it means the minority have to suffer injustices (Utilitarianism)? Or are both of these perspectives too flawed and should we instead concentrate on cultivating virtuous youth workers (Virtue ethics) who will weigh things up, and decide on what the most ethical decision is at the time? Such decisions will often be in the moment, as we have explored, and be different from one day to the next. It is possible to maintain all three of these perspectives, but acknowledge their tensions. We can say that we will uphold some universal ethical positions, being mindful of the viewpoint of minorities. However we will also be mindful of the majority, who are often the young people and communities we are fighting for anyway, particularly when they are being oppressed by powerful minorities, those in power, who cannot, will not, or should not, engage in our conversations

(Habermas, 1984). In those situations we have to employ different tactics (Alinsky, 1971), in the short term, which go against our universal principles, for example when bringing a large group of homeless people into a council meeting to protest about a motion the council had passed banning them from public space. Doormen had deliberately excluded them from a public meeting about it because of their appearance, and the homeless people wanted to cause a public embarrassment – they also wanted to draw attention to the irony of their exclusion. It worked where discussion had failed. The decisions about when we will do these kinds of action, to whom, when and why is mediated by cultivating ethical, virtuous and reflective youth workers.

Individualism and communitarisnism

In the same way that we have guiding principles, but do not follow them unquestioningly, we value the individuals, but do not see the notion of the individual as sovereign. This is where Communitarians would nail their colours to the mast. Youth work does not have to be viewed as a libertarian project. Rather, it believes that the individual flourishes best through the collective, but neither should the collective be sovereign over the individual. They should remain in tension. For instance, youth work does have a tendency to romanticise community (Belton, 2010) and to underestimate the conservative, limiting and discriminatory tendencies it can have towards those not in the group, and towards those who do not conform within the group. We also romanticise young people as being somehow beyond these tendencies in their collective endeavours, or as not yet encultured into it. Valuing critique, dialogue and the importance of autonomy should be a good check and balance to our own tendencies towards privileging communitarianism. The balance to be struck will vary at different times and in different places but youth and community work should resist political structures that are based on the primacy of 'rugged individualism', but also those that see individuals as irrelevant or dangerous, and subservient to, or even absorbed into, the state.

Pragmatism and idealism

Again, we seem to exhibit both of these traits at the same time. In an earlier chapter we traced our anti-intellectualism and pragmatism, but also the firm principles that we feel we should not waver from. We place heavy emphasis on what we call 'being real', but, drawing on Baizerman and Freire, this should be about staying rooted in the worlds and understandings of those we work with and, at times, represent. At the same time we are idealistic, seeking to develop these ideas, to make connections that they might not, to abstract, in a word, to theorise. In fact we go beyond this, we are not content to understand, but seek to create new understandings and knowledge. In this way we move beyond the confines of phenomenology, believing it is not enough to really understand people who are different from us. We want to change their, and our, perspective and lives, to engage their, and our, imagination about what the world could be like. As Einstein (1931) says:

> *Imagination is more important than knowledge. For knowledge is limited to all we now know and understand, while imagination embraces the entire world, and all there ever will be to know and understand.*

This is where our combining of our philosophical strands comes into its own. Marxism, post-Marxism and postmodernism, give us great tools for de-constructing the present, and existentialism for working with individuals on their own agency in this deconstructed world. Marxism also gives us, again combined with postmodernism's insights, a way of developing forms of resistance to the forces we are subject to.

However, it is humanism, and its visions of the 'good life', that give us something to fight for, a vision for the future. This is something that Marxism can be silent on, other than vague references to the withering away of the state. The way we run our clubs and projects and how we conceive of education can give us models for how society could operate, but it can also remind us that we are responsibile for the gaps and inconsistencies in how we portray ourselves, and our 'lived lives'. This is where Christian and other faith-based youth work have great contributions to make. While personally we do not agree with their ontological and metaphysical claims, their codes and sets of moral precepts are often the basis of a debate that needs to happen.

Conclusion

Strangely, in identifying our philosophical tensions, we have outlined our commonalities. Also, we take note of the post-structural critique. To talk about tensions is to buy into the idea of binaries, as is to contrast tensions with commonalities. Therefore we have only one over-arching theme still to mention. It is the aforementioned epistemological belief that knowledge is a dynamic force created by humans. This idea is common to all the thinkers and schools of thought mentioned. Aristotle, Marx, Freire, Dewey, feminism, postmodernism and others all propound that knowledge is something that is created by humans. The names for the processes of knowledge's creation, and interpretations of who has power in this, vary, but the idea of knowledge being a dynamic force is common. Moreover, there is the idea of common sense, but this is something we create, or is created for us, and it is never static. To be a part of this knowledge creation, and enabling others to take their part, is the essence of what it is to be a youth worker.

Returning to the challenge set out in the introduction, there is some coherence between our philosophical influences and the outlined themes, and tensions, that emerge from this. We are not cherry-picking charlatans, but there is always the danger that we become so. It is for us and others in our community or 'family' to pull ourselves back when we start doing this. A part of doing it should be to value philosophy and to recognise what it has to offer us in our day-to-day practice. If nothing else it clarifies the basis of our arguments, but it also looks at how we argue. It minds us to pay attention to the language we use, for this is our major medium, and reminds us that our speech is laden with concepts, ideas and assumptions, that need unpacking and re-packing. We need to move away from the separation of practice and theory, for it dumbs us down, does not allow us to display our rich theoretical and philosophical heritage, and means we are not involved in knowledge creation, one of our mainstays. As Socrates said over two millennia ago

The unexamined life is not worth living.

Socrates (470–399 BCE)

Let the dialogue and debate continue.

Glossary

We have provided a glossary, as philosophy often uses quite specific terms, and we have not shied from using them in the book. Sometimes we need to use complex terms to explain complex concepts, and if they were easy to grasp, then they would not be reflecting the complexity of the world. It is not exhaustive, but is intended as a starting place.

Capitalism
An economic system based on private ownership of business and economic enterprises. Tends to be accompanied by beliefs such as the 'free market', where people can trade without interference, and that what thrives is what people want; and the need for profit, to act as an incentive, but to be re-invested, making for innovation.

Catagorical imperative
Immanuel Kant's rules for acting morally: act only according to the maxim by which 'you can also will that it would become a universal law, act in such a way that you always treat humanity, whether in your own person or in the person of any other, never simply as a means, but always at the same time as an end'.

Communitarianism
At its heart this is the belief that we are social animals. It says that the individual is best fulfilled through the community, which can define and shape them. It questions the assumption that the community is made up of individuals who choose to participate in it. It tends to value things like association, solidarity and mutual gain.

Critical theory
Developed by post-Marxists of the 'Frankfurt school'. Whereas traditional Marxism sees the economic structure as being the dominant force in society, they emphasised the importance of 'ideology' as a form of control, which is reinforced through ideological forces such as literature, the media, etc. It is linked to Gramsci's concept of hegemony. It seeks to expose the power structures and assumed knowledge in many art forms and writing.

Conscientization
The process of developing a critical consciousness of one's social and political situation. Recognising that oppressed people may need to be 'educated' to believe in themselves, develop consciousness of their situation – to see what is happening to them and why, and – most importantly – to take action. It implies that people are deliberately kept ignorant of the reasons for their situations by other parties.

Deontology

This is a normative ethical position (see below) that judges an action according to whether it adheres to a set of rules, e.g. the Ten Commandments or Kant's categorical imperative.

Epistemology

The study of the nature and limits of knowledge. It is concerned with how, and under what conditions, we can say that we know something. Different traditions, such as science and humanities, have very different views on what it is to know something, with some saying it is impossible to know anything with certainty.

Essentialism

A belief that any phenomena will have essential characteristics. Often associated with postmodernists and existentialists who reject it, saying humans in particular do not have anything that is essential, e.g. what it is to be a woman, what sexuality is, etc.

Existentialism

Hotly contested, but an essential belief is that existence precedes essence, i.e. that we are an autonomous, conscious, individual before we are the labels, stereotypes and received identity that make up our essence (what we are seen as). It says that we are free to make our own meanings in life.

Feminism

Philosophically it looks at the nature of gender, how it is socially constructed, and more broadly women's experiences of inequality – socially, politically, economically and spiritually.

Hegemony

The concept is associated in its modern form with Gramsci. It holds that a particular set of values, beliefs and morals permeates society, perpetuated through all institutions, social relations, education, etc., that support the status quo, and specifically the dominance of the ruling class. It becomes common sense that the existing social, political and economic structures are 'natural'.

Humanism

In terms of youth and community work this is a philosophy concerned with what it is to be human. It is often concerned with ideas like motivation and self-development, but is also a counter to scientific trends to reduce people to animals and their behaviour and biological drives. It is often concerned with the whole human experience, including the intuitive, emotional and spiritual aspects of people, as well as the rational.

Ideology
A way of looking at the world – ideologies tend to be comprehensive, encompassing ideas, beliefs and actions. It is often used in the context of someone, or the 'state', trying to portray something as the truth, when it is only actually one world view.

Intersubjectivity
The interaction and relationships between people, normally spoken of in terms of trying to find some common ground, although all experiences are relative – normally used in contrast to individualism and solipsism.

Marxism
Wide ranging and again contested, but Marx's central belief was that the economic base, how industry or agriculture is organised, determines the political and social structures of a society, and even individual consciousness, and not the other way round (historical materialism). He also believed that these structures served the interests of a dominant 'class' of people, this being determined by how they related to the economy, e.g. workers on the land or in industry (working class), landowners (upper/ruling class), or merchants and professionals (middle class). He proposed that over time as the nature of the economy changed, through inherent contradictions in its organisation, different classes would dominate. Eventually the working class would take over and class distinctions would wither away.

Metaphysics
Broadly the study of the nature of reality, although it is more commonly used to look at the study of things that are beyond the normal everyday life, or things that cannot be proved, or disproved by material science – such as spirituality and the existence of god.

Meta-narrative
A narrative that attempts to explain the nature of the world, to be all encompassing, or to be a narrative that explains other narratives. It tends to be used pejoratively by postmodernists who believe we cannot explain everything, and who rejected meta-narratives such as religion, capitalism and communism.

Normative ethics
Concerned with how one *ought* to act in a moral situation. It considers the rightness and wrongness of a particular action or intended action.

Ontology
Broadly the study of the nature of being, existence, and sometimes reality.

Phenomenology

Broadly the study of human subjectivity and consciousness. In terms of research it tends to say that all knowledge is relative, and places an importance on understanding the 'life worlds' of humans.

Postmodernism

Broadly a rejection of the modernist project with its emphasis on science, an assumption of progress, and a belief that we can know the material world, and more widely, absolute truth. Instead, postmodernism emphasises fluidity, seeing most truth and knowledge as subjective, and resists essentialism, which tries to define the essence of things.

Post-structuralism

Similar to postmodernism. Specifically it rejects structuralist explanations of human nature, society and even language, and its attempts to systematise, and account for the totality of human experience.

Praxis

The idea that theory and practice cannot be separated, but is instead a dynamic, and that knowledge is evolving. It tends to see knowledge as action orientated, defined by how it impacts on the material world.

Social constructionism

The belief that reality, particularly social reality, is not objective, but is created by dominant social groups. Sexuality, gender, class, etc. have all been called social constructions.

Utilitarianism

The belief that we should take moral decisions based on what benefits the largest number of people, or creates the greatest happiness. This may mean breaking moral codes if it favours the majority. Issues include how happiness calculations are to be made, and when the minority suffers for the benefit of the majority.

Virtue ethics

The belief that we cannot provide consistent rules, or mechanisms such as utilitarianism, by which to make moral decisions. Instead we should cultivate people to be virtuous so that they will make the appropriate decision, weighing up the different factors, when the decision has to be made.

For further definitions see the Stanford online encyclopedia of philosophy at http://plato.stanford.edu/

References

Alinsky, S.D. (1971) *Rules for Radicals: A Pragmatic Primer for Realistic Radicals.* New York: Vintage.

Anyon, J (1981) Social Class and School Knowledge. *Curriculum Inquiry,* 11(1): 3–42.

Aquinas, T. (1920) The Summa Theologica of St. Thomas Aquinas. [1273] 2nd Revised Edition. Translated by Fathers of the English Dominican Province. Online text is available at http://www.newadvent.org/summa/.

Archer, L. (2003) *Higher Education and Social Class: Issues of Exclusion and Inclusion.* London: Routledge.

Argyris, C. (1982) *Reasoning, Learning, and Action: Individual and Organizational.* San Francisco: Jossey-Bass.

Aristotle (1976) *The Nicomachean Ethics.* London: Penguin.

Baggini, J. & Fosl, P.S. (2003) *The Philosopher's Toolkit: A Compendium of Philosophical Concepts and Methods.* Oxford: Blackwell.

Baier, A.C. (1986) Trust and Antitrust. *Ethics,* 96: 231–60.

Baier, A.C. (2004) Demoralisation, Trust, and the Virtues. In Calhoun, C. (Ed.) *Setting the Moral Compass: Essays by Women Philosophers.* New York: Oxford University Press.

Bailey, D. (1992) *Improvisation, Its Nature and Practice in Music.* Ashbourne: Da Capo Press.

Baizerman, M. (1989) Why Train Youth Workers? *The Child Care Worker,* 7: 1, July.

Baker, J. (1987) Trust and Rationality. *Pacific Philosophical Quarterly,* 68: 1–13.

Barrett, F. (1998) Creativity and Improvisation in Jazz and Organisations: Implications for Organisational Learning. *Organisation Science,* 9: 5.

Bauer, J. and Bell, D. (Eds.) (1999) *The East Asian Challenge for Human Rights.* New York: Cambridge University Press.

Becker. L.C. (1996) Trust as Noncognitive Security about Motives. *Ethics,* 107: 1, 43–61.

Beetham, D. (1999) *Democracy and Human Rights.* Cambridge: Polity Press.

Bell, D. (1993) *Communitarianism and Its Critics.* Oxford: Clarendon Press.

Bell, D. (2000) *East Meets West: Human Rights and Democracy in East Asia.* Princeton: Princeton University Press.

Bell, D. (2006) *Beyond Liberal Democracy: Political Thinking for an East Asian Context.* Princeton: Princeton University Press.

Bell, D. (2008) *China's New Confucianism: Politics and Everyday Life in a Changing Society.* Princeton: Princeton University Press.

Belton, B. (2010) *Radical Youth Work: Developing Critical Perspectives and Professional Judgement.* Lyme Regis: Russell House Publishing.

Bender, T. (1993) *Intellect and Public Life.* The Johns Hopkins University Press.

Beneditt, T. (2008) Why Respect Matters. *The Journal of Value Inquiry,* 42: 487–96.

Benn, S.I. (1988) *A Theory of Freedom.* Cambridge: Cambridge University Press.

Berliner, P. (1994) *Thinking in Jazz: The infinite Art of Improvisation.* Chicago: The University of Chicago Press.

Birk, A. (2000) *Learning to Trust.* Autonomous Agents 2000 Workshop on Deception, Fraud and Trust in Agent Societies, Barcelona: June 4.

Blackburn, S. (1999) *Think.* Oxford: Oxford University Press.

Boggs, C. (1976) *Gramsci's Marxism.* London: Pluto Press.

Bornmann, L., Mutz, R. & Daniel, H-D. (2010) A Reliability-Generalization Study of Journal Peer Reviews: A Multilevel Meta-Analysis of Inter-Rater Reliability and Its Determinants. *PLoS ONE*, 5: 12.

Bourdieu, P. (1977) *Outline of a Theory of Practice*. Cambridge and New York: Cambridge Univ. Press.

Bourdieu, P. (1983) Forms of Capital. In Richards, J.C. (Ed.) *Handbook of Theory and Research for the Sociology of Education*. New York: Greenwood Press.

Bourdieu, P. (1989) *The Corporatism of The Universal: The Role of Intellectuals in The Modern World. Telos 81*. New York: Telos Press

Bowman, D. and Spicer, J. (2007) *Primary Care Ethics*. London: Radcliffe Publishing.

Boxill, B.R. (1976) Self-Respect and Protest. *Philosophy and Public Affairs*. 6: 58–69; Reprinted In Dillon, R. S. (Ed.) (1995) *Dignity, Character and Self-Respect*. New York: Routledge.

Braaten, J. (1991) *Habermas's Critical Theory of Society*. State University of New York Press.

Bradford, S. (2007–8) Practices, Policies and Professionals: Emerging Discourses of Expertise in English Youth Work, 1939–1951. *Youth and Policy Special Training Edition*, 97–98: 13–28.

Brody, B.A. (1982) Towards a Theory of Respect for Persons. In Green, O.H. (Ed.) *Respect for Persons*. Tulane Studies in Philosophy, Vol. 31. New Orleans: Tulane University Press.

Brookfield, S.B. (1994) Self Directed Learning. In YMCA, *Adult and Community Education Unit 2: Approaching Adult Education*. London: YMCA George Williams College.

Bryce, J.B. (1888) *The American Common Wealth, Vol 2*. Indianapolis: Liberty Fund.

Buber, M. (1949, 1958, 1996) *Paths in Utopia*. Trans. Hull, R.F.C. London: Routledge; Boston: Beacon Press; Syracuse, NY: Syracuse University Press.

Burawoy, M. (2005) For Public Sociology. *American Sociological Review*, 70: 1, 4–28.

Burbules, N. (1993) *Dialogue in Teaching. Theory and Practice*. New York: Teachers College Press.

Burke, B. (1999, 2005) Antonio Gramsci, Schooling and Education. *The Encyclopedia of Informal Education*, http://www.infed.org/thinkers/et-gram.htm.

Burke, B. (2000) Karl Marx and Informal Education. *The Encyclopaedia of Informal Education*, www.infed.org/thinkers/et-marx.Htm.

Burkitt, I. (1991) *Social Selves: Theories of the Social Formation of Personality*. London: Sage.

Burton, J. (Ed.) (1990) *Conflict: Human Needs Theory*. London: Macmillan.

Buss, S. (1999) Respect for Persons. *Canadian Journal of Philosophy*, 29: 517–50.

Calhoun, C. (1984) Cognitive Emotions? In Calhoun, C. and Solomon, R. C. (Eds.). *What Is An Emotion?* New York: Oxford University Press.

Campanario, J.M. (2004) Challenging Dominant Physics Paradigms. *Journal of Scientific Exploration*, 18: 3, 421–38.

Campbell, N., Davies, J. & Mckay, G. (2004) *Issues in Americanisation and Culture*. Edinburgh: Edinburgh University Press.

Carey, J. (1992) *The Intellectuals And The Masses: Pride And Prejudice Amongst The Literary Intelligentsia, 1880–1939*. London: Faber and Faber.

Carus, P. (1999) *The Gospel of Buddha*. London: One World.

Chomsky, N. (1973) *For Reasons of State*. New York: Pantheon.

Christian, C. & Kitto, J. (1987) *The Theory and Practice of Supervision*. London: YMCA National College.

Clauson K. A. et al. (2008) Scope, Completeness, and Accuracy of Drug Information in Wikipedia. *Annals of Pharmacotherapy*, 42 (12): 1814.

Claxton, G. (1999) *Wise Up*. London: Bloomsbury.

Cleaver, E. (1970) *Soul on Ice*. New York: Delta.

Coady, C.A.J. (1992) *Testimony: A Philosophical Study*. Oxford: Clarendon Press

Cohen, P. (1997) *Rethinking the Youth Question: Education, Labour and Cultural Studies.* London: Macmillan.

Collini, S. (2006) *Absent Minds: Intellectuals in Britain.* Oxford: Oxford University Press.

Cook, K. R., Hardin, R. & Levi, M. (2005) *Cooperation Without Trust?* New York: Russell Sage Foundation.

Cooley, M. (1987) *City Aphorisms.* New York: Fourth Selection.

Cranor, R.S (1975) Toward a Theory of Respect for Persons. *American Philosophical Quarterly,* 12: 309–320.

Crossan, M (1998) Improvisation in Action. *Organization Science,* 9 (5).

Cummiskey, D. (2008) Dignity, Contractualism, and Consequentialism. *Utilitas,* 16: 629–44.

Curren, R. (Ed.) (2007) *Philosophy of Education: An Anthology.* Oxford: Blackwell Publishing.

Cuypers, S. (1995) What Wittgenstein Would Have Said About Personal Autonomy. *Studies In Philosophy And Education,* 14 (2–3).

Dahl, R. (1989) *Democracy and its Critics.* New Haven, CT: Yale University.

Darusenkov, O. (1975) *USSR – Cuba: Fifteen Years of Fraternal Friendship and Co-operation.* Moscow: Novosti Press.

Darwall, S. (1977) Two Kinds Of Respect. *Ethics* 88: 36–49. Reprinted In Dillon, R.S. (Ed.) (1995) *Dignity, Character and Self-Respect.* New York: Routledge.

Darwall, S. (2004) Respect and the Second Person Standpoint: Presidential Address, Central Division of the American Philosophical Association. *Proceedings and Addresses of the American Philosophical Association,* 78 (2): 43–59.

Dasgupta, P. (1988) Trust as a Commodity. In Gambetta (Ed.) *Trust: Making and Breaking Cooperative Relations.* Oxford: Oxford University Press.

Davies, B. (2005) Threatening Youth Revisited: Youth Policies Under New Labour. *The Encyclopaedia of Informal Education,* www.infed.org/archives/bernard_davies/revisiting_threatening_youth.htm.

Davies, R. (2003) *Education, Virtues and The Good Life.* Unpublished PHD thesis.

Dawkins, R. (1976) *The Selfish Gene.* Oxford: Oxford University Press.

De Sousa, R. (1987). The Rationality of Emotion. Cambridge: MIT Press.

De Bary, T.W. (1998) *Asian Values and Human Rights: A Confucian Communitarian Perspective.* Cambridge: Harvard University Press.

DeCremer, D. (2002) Respect and Cooperation in Social Dilemmas: The Importance of Feeling Included. *Personality and Social Psychology Bulletin,* 28, 1335–41.

DeCremer, D. & Tyler, T. (2005) Am I Respected or Not? Inclusion and Reputation as Issues in Group Membership. *Social Justice Research,* 18, 121–53.

Dennett, J. & Steglich-Petersen, S. (2008) *The Philosophical Lexicon.* Denmark: Aarus University.

De Tocqueville, A. (2000) Democracy In America, Trans. and Eds., Harvey C. Mansfield & Delba Winthrop. Chicago: University of Chicago Press.

Dewey, J. (1916) *Democracy and Education: An Introduction to The Philosophy of Education.* 1966 edn. New York: Free Press.

Dewey, J. (1922) *Human Nature and Conduct: An Introduction to Social Psychology.* New York: Holt.

Dewey, J. (1933) *How We Think: A Restatement of The Relation of Reflective Thinking to The Educative Process.* Boston: D.C. Heath.

DfES (2006) *Widening Participation in Higher Education.* London: HMSO.

Dickson, J. (2005) Oscar Romero of El Salvador: Informal Adult Education in a Context of Violence. *The encyclopedia of informal education,* www.infed.org/thinkers/oscar_romero.htm.

Dillon, R.S. (1997) Self-Respect: Moral, Emotional, Political. *Ethics,* 107: 226–249.

Dillon, R.S. (2001) Self-Forgiveness And Self-Respect. *Ethics,* 112: 53–83.

Dillon, R.S. (2003) Kant On Arrogance And Self-Respect. In Calhoun, C. (Ed.) *Setting The Moral Compass: Essays By Women Philosophers.* Oxford: Oxford University Press.

Dillon, R.S. (2010) *Respect.* At http://plato.stanford.edu/entries/respect/ (Accessed July 2012.)

Doppelt, G. (1989) Is Rawls' Kantian Liberalism Coherent and Defensible? *Ethics*, July, 820–1.

Downie, R.S. and Telfer, E. (1969) *Respect for Persons.* London: George Allen and Unwin.

Doyle, M.E. and Smith, M.K. (1999) *Born and Bred? Leadership, Heart and Informal Education.* London: YMCA George Williams College/The Rank Foundation.

Dreyfus, H and Dreyfus, S. (1986) *Mind Over Machine: The Power of Human Intuition and Expertise in the Era of the Computer.* New York: Free Press.

Dryzek, J.S. (2000) *Deliberative Democracy and Beyond. Liberals, Critics, Contestation.* Oxford: Oxford University Press.

Du Bois, W. E. B. (1903) *The Souls of Black Folk.* Reprinted in 1994, New York: Gramercy Books.

Duck, S. (1999) *Relating to Others.* 2 edn. Buckingham: Open University Press.

Durkheim, E. (1997) *The Division of Labor In Society.* Trans. Lewis A. Coser. New York: Free Press.

Dworkin, G. (1988) *The Theory and Practice of Autonomy.* New York: Cambridge University Press.

Ecclestone, K. and Hayes, D. (2008) *The Dangerous Rise of Therapeutic Education.* London: Routledge.

Einstein, A (1931) *Cosmic Religions: With Other Opinions and Aphorisms.* London: Covici-Frierdi.

Ellemers, N., Doosje, B. & Spears, R. (2004) Sources of Respect: The Effects of Being Liked by Ingroups and Outgroups. *European Journal of Social Psychology*, 34, 155–72.

Eraut, M. (2007) *Developing Professional Knowledge and Competence.* Abingdon: Routledge Farmer.

Etzioni, A. (1995) *The Spirit of Community: Rights, Responsibilities and the Communitarian Agenda.* London: Fontana Press.

Evans, G. (2007) *Educational Failure and Working Class White Children in Britain.* Palgrave Macmillan.

Everitt, A. (1995) Monitoring and Evaluation: A Culture of Lying? *Paper Presented to the Conference on Researching the Voluntary Sector.* National Council for Voluntary Services.

Falcone, R. & Castelfranchi, C. (2001) Socio-cognitive Dynamics of Trust: Does Trust Create Trust? In *Trust in Cyber-societies: Integrating the Human and Artificial Perspectives.* Springer: Lecture Notes in Computer Science Volume 2246.

Feinberg, J. (1970) The Nature and Value of Rights. *Journal of Value Inquiry*, 4: 243–57.

Finkelstein, M.A. (2011) Correlates of Individualism and Collectivism: Predicting Volunteer Activity. *Social Behavior and Personality*, 39: 5, 597–606.

Foucault, M. (2002) *The Archaeology of Knowledge.* London: Penguin.

Foley, R. (2005) Universal Intellectual Trust. *Episteme*, 2 (1): 5–11.

Fook, J. et al. (2000) *Professional Expertise.* London: Whiting and Birch.

Forst, R. (2012) Toleration. *The Stanford Encyclopedia of Philosophy.* (online) Available at: http://plato.stanford.edu/archives/sum2012/entries/toleration/ (Accessed 13 June 2012)

Frank, R. (2007) *Falling Behind.* Berkeley, CA: University of California Press.

Frazer, E. (1999) *The Problems of Communitarian Politics.* Oxford: Oxford University Press.

Frei, J.R. & Shaver, P.R. (2002) Respect in Close Relationships: Prototype Definition, Self-Report Assessment, and Initial Correlates. *Personal Relationships*, 9, 121–39.

Freire, P. (1972) *The Pedagogy of the Oppressed.* Harmondsworth: Penguin.

Freire, P. (1995) *The Pedagogy of Hope.* London and New York: Penguin.

Fricker, E. (1995). Telling and Trusting: Reductionism and Anti-Reductionism in the Epistemology of Testimony. *Mind*, 104 (414): 393–411.

Friedman, M.S. (1981) *The Worlds of Existentialism.* New York: Random House.

Fromm, E. (1941) *Escape From Freedom.* New York: Farrar.

Frost, S. (2003) *Democracy.* London: YMCA George Williams College.

Fukuyama, F. (1992) *The End of History and the Last Man.* New York: Free Press.

Fukuyama, F. (1999) *The Great Disruption: Human Nature and The Reconstitution of Social Order.* London: Profile Books.

Furedi, F. (2004) *Where Have All The Intellectuals Gone?* Continuum.

Gadamer, H-G. (1979) *Truth and Method.* London: Sheed and Ward.

Gale, D (1990) *What Is Psychodrama?* London: Penguin Books.

Gambetta, D. (Ed.) (1988). *Trust: Making and Breaking Cooperative Relations.* New York: Basil Blackwell.

Garvey, A. (Ed.) (1986) *The Philosophy and Opinions of Marcus Garvey.* Majority Press.

Gaus, G.F. (1998) Respect for Persons and Environmental Values. In Kneller, J. and Axinn, S. (Eds.) *Autonomy and Community: Readings in Contemporary Kantian Social Philosophy.* Albany: State University of New York Press.

Gerth, H. H. & Wright Mills, C. (Eds.) (1991) *From Max Weber: Essays in Sociology.* London: Routledge.

Gibbard, A. (1990) *Wise Choices, Apt Feelings: A Theory of Normative Judgment.* Cambridge, MA: Harvard University Press.

Gibson, H. (2011) Management, Skills and Creativity: The Purpose and Value of Instrumental Reasoning in Education Discourse. *Oxford Review of Education,* 37: 6, 699–716.

Giles, J. (2005). Internet Encyclopaedias Go Head to Head. *Nature,* 438 (7070): 900–1.

Gilmore, J. (1991) All This and More: Analysis and Practice in Youth Work. *Transitions,* 1: 3, 27–30.

Gladwell, M. (2006) *Blink: The Power of Thinking Without Thinking.* London: Penguin.

Goddard, M (2005) *Public Confidence in National Statistics.* London: Office For National Statistics.

Goetschius, G.W. and Tash, M.J. (1967) *Working with Unattached Youth. Problem, Approach, Method.* London: Routledge and Kegan Paul.

Goffman, E. (1974) *Frame Analysis.* Cambridge: Harvard University Press.

Goldman, A. I., 1992. *Liaisons: Philosophy Meets the Cognitive and Social Sciences.* Cambridge, MA: MIT Press.

Gonsalez, J. (2004) *Cuba After Castro: Legacies, Challenges, and Impediments.* New York: Rand.

Govier, T. (1997). *Social Trust and Human Communities.* Montreal and Kingston: McGill-Queen's University Press.

Gramsci, A. (1971) *Selections from the Prison Notebooks.* London: Lawrence and Wishart.

Grattan, A. & Morgan, S. (2008) 'Organic Intellectuals' as Catalysts of Change: Working with Young People in Conflict and Post Conflict Environments. *International Journal of Interdisciplinary Social Sciences,* 2: 6.

Guevara, C. (1989) *Socialism and Man in Cuba.* New York: Pathfinder Press.

Habermas, J. (1984) *The Theory of Communicative Action Volume 1.* Cambridge: Polity Press

Hampshire, S. (1983) *Morality and Conflict.* Cambridge: Harvard University Press.

Harden, J. et al. (2000) Scary Faces, Scary Places: Children's Perceptions of Risk and Safety. *Health Education Journal,* 59, 12–22.

Hardin, R. (1996) Trustworthiness. *Ethics,* 107: 26–42.

Hardin, R. (2002) *Trust and Trustworthiness.* New York, NY: Russell Sage Foundation.

Hardwig, J. (1991) The Role of Trust in Knowledge. *The Journal of Philosophy,* 88 (12): 693–708.

Harris, P. (2005) Curriculum Debate and Detached Youth Work. *Youth and Policy,* 87, 57–84.

Hart, H.L.A. (1958). Legal and Moral Obligation. In Melden, A.I. (Ed.) *Essays in Moral Philosophy.* Seattle: University of Washington Press.

Hatch, M. (1998) Jazz as a Metaphor for Organizing in the 21st Century. *Organization Science,* 9: 5.

Hatton, E. (1988) Teachers' Work as Bricolage: Implications for Teacher Education. *British Journal of Sociology of Education*, 9: 3.

Hayek, F. (1944) *The Road to Serfdom*. London: Routledge.

Herman, E, S. & Chomsky, N. (1988) *Manufacturing Consent*. New York: Pantheon Books.

Hill, T.E (1973) Servility and Self-Respect. *Monist* 57: 12–27. Reprinted in Dillon, R.S. (Ed.) (1995) *Dignity, Character and Self-Respect*. New York: Routledge.

Hitler, A (1923) *Mein Kampf*. Berlin: Eher Verlag.

Hobbes, T. (1994) *Leviathan*. (with selected variants from the Latin Edition of 1668, Curley, E (Ed.)) London: Hackett.

Holmes, J (2007–8) Youth and Community Work Qualifying Courses: Riding the Tensions? *Youth and Policy Special Training Edition*, 97–98: 1–5.

Honderich, T. (1991) *The Oxford Companion to Philosophy*. Oxford: Oxford University Press.

Horsburgh, H.J.N. (1960) The Ethics of Trust. *Philosophical Quarterly*, 10: 343–54.

Horton, J. (1996) Toleration as Virtue. In Heyd, D. *Toleration, an Elusive Virtue*. Princeton: Princeton University Press.

Hume, D. (1978) *A Treatise Of Human Nature*. Edited By L.A. Selby-Bigge, Revised By P.H. Nidditch (Second Edition). Oxford University Press.

Hume, D. (1985) *Essays Moral, Political and Literary*. Miller, E.F. (Ed.) Indianapolis: Liberty Press.

Hursthouse, R. (1991) After Hume's Justice. *Proceedings of the Aristotelian Society*, 91: 229–45.

Hursthouse, R. (*2012)* Virtue Ethics. *The Stanford Encyclopedia of Philosophy, Summer,* Zalta, E.N (Ed.) URL = <http://plato.stanford.edu/archives/sum2012/entries/ethics-virtue/>. Accessed Sept 2012.

Illich, I. et al. (1977) *Disabling Professions*. London: Marion Boyars.

Jackson, L.M., Esses, V.M. & Burris, C.T. (2001) Contemporary Sexism and Discrimination: The Importance of Respect For Men and Women. *Personality and Social Psychology Bulletin*, 27: 48–61.

Jackson, P. (1968) *Life in Classrooms*. New York: Holt, Rinehart and Winston.

Jefferson, T. et al. (2002) Effects of Editorial Peer Review: A Systematic Review. *Journal of the American Medical Association*, 287: 2784–6.

Jefferson, T. et al. (2007) Editorial Peer Review For Improving The Quality of Reports of Biomedical Studies. *Cochrane Database of Sytematic Reviews*, Issue 2.

Jeffs, T. (1990) *Educating Informal Educators: Using Informal Education*. Buckingham: Open University Press.

Jeffs, T. (2005) Citizenship, Youth Work and Democratic Renewal. *The Encyclopaedia of Informal Education*, http://www.infed.org/association/citizenshp_youth_work_democratic_renewal.htm

Jeffs, T. & Smith, M.K. (1996) *Informal Education: Conversation, Democracy and Learning*. Derby: Education Now Books with the YMCA George Williams College.

Jeffs, T. & Smith, M. K. (1997, 2005, 2011). What Is Informal Education? *The Encyclopaedia of Informal Education*. http://infed.org/mobi/what-is-informal-education/ Retrieved: July 2012

Jeffs, T. & Smith, M.K. (2002) Individualization and youth work. *Youth and Policy*, 76: 39–65.

Jetten, J. et al. (2005) Suppressing the Negative Effect of Devaluation on Group Identification. *Journal of Experimental Social Psychology*, 41, 208–15.

Johnson, P. (1988) *Intellectuals: From Marx and Tolstoy to Sartre and Chomsky*. Harper Perennial.

Johnston, L. et al. (2000) *Snakes and Ladders: Young People, Transitions and Social Exclusion*. Bristol: The Policy Press and The Joseph Rowntree Foundation.

Jones, K. (1996) Trust as an Affective Attitude. *Ethics*, 107: 4–25.

Jones, K. (1999) Second-Hand Moral Knowledge. *Journal of Philosophy*, 96 (2): 55–78.

Kant, I. (1948) Groundwork of the Metaphysics of Morals. In Patton, H.J. (Ed.) *The Moral Law.* New York: Harper and Row.

Kaufman, J. C., & Beghetto, R. A. (2009). Beyond Big and Little: The Four C Model Of Creativity. *Review Of General Psychology,* 13: 1–12.

Keeney, B. (1990) *Improvisational Therapy.* London: Guilford.

King, A. (2010) In Search of Respect: A Qualitative Study Exploring Youth Perceptions. *International Journal of School Disaffection,* 1 (1): 6–11.

Kosfeld, M. et al. (2005) Oxytocin Increases Trust in Humans. *Nature* 435 (2): 1,4.

Kumar, K. (1997) The Post-Modern Condition. In Halsey, A. H. et al. (Eds.) *Education: Culture, Economy and Society.* Oxford: Oxford University Press.

Kymlicka, W. (1989) *Liberalism, Community and Culture.* Oxford: Clarendon Press.

Ladd, E. (1999) *The Ladd Report: Bowling with Others.* New York: Free Press.

Lahno, B. (2001) On the Emotional Character of Trust. *Ethical Theory and Moral Practice,* 4: 171–189.

Langdon, S. W. (2007) Conceptualizations of Respect: Qualitative and Quantitative Evidence of Four (Five) Themes. *The Journal of Psychology,* 141: 5, 469–84.

Ledwith, M. (2007) Reclaiming the Radical Agenda: A Critical Approach to Community Development. *Concept,* 17: 2, 8–12.

Lehrer, K. (1997) *Self-Trust: A Study of Reason, Knowledge and Autonomy.* New York: Oxford University Press.

Leithner, A. et al. (2010). Wikipedia and Osteosarcoma: A Trustworthy Patients' Information? *Journal of The American Medical Informatics Association,* 17 (4): 373–4.

Lenin, V. (1970) *Left Wing Communism: An Infantile Disorder.* Peking: Foreign Languages Press.

Leunig, M. (1983) *A Bag of Roosters.* London: Penguin.

Levi, P. (1947) *If This is a Man.* Paris: Desilva.

Levi-Strauss, C. (1962) *The Savage Mind.* Oxford: Oxford University Press.

Lindley, R. (1986) *Autonomy.* London: MacMillan Education.

Locke, J. (1983) *A Letter Concerning Toleration.* Tully, J.H. (Ed.) Indianapolis: Liberty Fund.

Locke, J. (1988) *Two Treaties of Government.* Laslett, P. (Ed.) Cambridge: Cambridge University Press.

Louden, W. (1991) *Understanding Teaching. Continuity and Change in Teachers' Knowledge.* London: Cassell.

Luhmann, N. (1979) *Trust and Power.* Toronto: Wiley.

Lukes, S. (1973) *Individualism.* Oxford: Blackwell.

Lyotard, J-F. (1984) *The Postmodern Condition: A Report on Knowledge.* Manchester: Manchester University Press.

MacIntyre, A. (1985) *After Virtue.* Notre-Dame: University of Notre Dame Press.

Mackenzie, C. and Stoljar, N. (Eds.) (2000) *Relational Autonomy: Feminist Perspectives on Autonomy, Agency and the Social Self.* New York: Oxford University Press.

Marcuse, H. (1964) *One Dimensional Man.* Boston, MA: Beacon Press.

Marsella, A.L. Devos, G. & Hsu, F. (Eds.) (1985) *Culture and Self: Asian and Western Perspectives.* London: Tavistock Press.

Martin, B. (1997) *Suppression Stories.* Wollongong: Fund for Intellectual Dissent.

Marx, K. (1844) *Political and Economic Manuscripts.* Moscow: Progress Publishers.

Maslow, A. (1968) *Towards a Psychology of Being.* New York: Van Nostrand.

Maslow, A. (1970) *Motivation and Personality.* New York: Harper and Row.

Matsonobu, K. (2011) In Sefton Green et al. *The Routledge International Handbook of Creative Learning.* Abingdon: Routledge.

Mayer, J., Davis, J. & Schoorman, D. (1995) An Integrative Model of Organisational Trust. *The Academy of Management Review*, 20 (3).

Mazlish, B. (1989) *A New Science: The Breakdown of Connections and the Birth of Sociology.* Pennsylvania: Pennsylvania State University Press.

McDowell, J. (1979) Virtue and Reason. *Monist*, 62: 331–50.

McGeer, V. (2008) Trust, Hope, and Empowerment. *Australasian Journal of Philosophy*, 86: 2, 237–54.

McLeod, C. (2002) *Self-Trust and Reproductive Autonomy.* Cambridge, MA: MIT Press.

McLeod, C. (2011) Trust. *The Stanford Encyclopedia of Philosophy.*

Mill, J.S. (1958) *Considerations on Representative Government.* Shields, C.V. (Ed.) Indianapolis: Bobbs-Merrill.

Mill, J.S. (1985) *On Liberty.* London: Penguin.

Moody-Adams, M.M. (1992) Race, Class, and the Social Construction of Self-Respect. *The Philosophical Forum*, 24: 251–66. Reprinted in Dillon, R.S. (Ed.) (1995) *Dignity, Character and Self-Respect.* New York: Routledge.

Mouzelis, N. (2000) Communitarianism: The Issue of Relativism. In Lehman, E.W. (Ed.) *Autonomy and Order: A Communitarian Anthology.* Oxford: Rowman & Littlefield.

Mullin, A. (2005) Trust, Social Norms, and Motherhood. *Journal of Social Philosophy*, 36: 3, 316–30.

Munro, E. (2011) *The Munro Review of Child Protection.* DfE.

Neeland, J. (2011) Drama as Creative Learning. In Sefton-Green, J. et al. *The Routledge International Handbook of Creative Learning.* Abingdon: Routledge.

Nickel, P.J. (2007) Trust and Obligation-Ascription. *Ethical Theory and Moral Practice*, 10: 309–319.

Nickerson, R.S. (1999) Enhancing Creativity. In Sternberg, R.J. (Ed.) *Handbook of Creativity.* Cambridge: Cambridge University Press.

Nietzsche, F. (1961) [1883–85] *Thus Spoke Zarathustra: A Book for All and for None.* Trans. Hollingdale, R.J. New York: Penguin Classics.

Noddings, N. (1984) *Caring: A Feminine Approach to Ethics and Moral Education.* Berkeley: University Of California Press.

Noddings, N. (1992) *The Challenge to Care in Schools: An Alternative Approach to Education.* New York: Teachers College Press.

Noddings, N. (2005) Caring in Education. *The Encyclopedia of Informal Education.* At http://infed.org/mobi/caring-in-education/

Nonaka, I. (1994) A Dynamic Theory of Organizational Knowledge Creation. *Organization Science*, 5: 14–37.

Nozick, R. (1969) Coercion. In Morgenbesser, S., Suppes P. and White, M. (Eds.) *Philosophy, Science, and Method: Essays in Honor of Ernest Nagel.* New York: St. Martin's Press.

NYA (2010) *Valuing Youth Work.* Available at http://nya.org.uk/dynamic_files/policy/valuing%20youth%20work%20lo%20res%5B1%5D.pdf

O'Neill, O. (1993) Kantian Ethics. In Singer, P. (Ed.) *A Companion to Ethics.* Oxford: Blackwell.

O'Neill, O. (2002) *Autonomy and Trust in Bioethics.* Cambridge: Cambridge University Press.

Orwell, G. (1945) *Animal Farm: A Fairy Story.* London: Secker and Warburg.

Orwell, G. (1949) *Nineteen Eighty-four.* London: Secker and Warburg.

Padian, K. and Matzke, N. (2009) Darwin, Dover, 'Intelligent Design' and Textbooks. *Biochemical Journal*, 209 (417), 29–42.

Page, S. and Woskett, V. (1994) *Supervising the Counsellor. A Cyclical Model.* London: Routledge.

Palmer, P.I. (1998) *The Courage to Teach: Exploring the Inner Landscape of a Teacher's Life.* San Francisco: Jossey-Bass.

Parkin, F. (1979) *Marxism and Class Theory. A Bourgeois Critique.* London: Tavistock.

Pasmore, W. (1998) Organizing for Jazz. *Organization Science*, 9: 5, 562–8.

Perlman, H.H. (1979) *Relationship: The Heart of Helping People.* Chicago: University of Chicago Press.

Perry, E. & Francis, B. (2010) *The Social Class Gap For Educational Achievement: A Review Of The Literature.* London: RSA.

Peters, G. (2009) *The Philosophy of Improvisation.* Chicago.

Peters, R. S. (1971) *Ethics and Education.* London: George Allen & Unwin.

Pincoffs, E. (1971) Quandary Ethics. *Mind*, 80: 552–71.

Plato (1987) *The Republic.* Harmondsworth: Penguin.

Polanyi, M. (1958) *The Tacit Dimension.* New York: Anchor Books.

Pollard E, Pearson R, & Willison, R. (2004) *Next Choices: Career Choices Beyond University, Report 405.* Institute for Employment Studies.

Popper, K.R. (1966) *The Open Society and its Enemies.* London: Routledge & Kegan Paul.

Posner, R, A. (2002) *Public Intellectuals: A Study of Decline.* Cambridge, MA: Harvard University Press.

Potter, N. N. (2002) *How Can I Be Trusted? A Virtue Theory Of Trustworthiness.* Lanham, Maryland: Rowman & Littlefield.

Proudhon, P.J. (1994). *What is Property: An Inquiry into the Principle of Right and Government.* Trans. Tucker, B.R., New York: Humbold, 1890; New York: Dover, 1970; Cambridge, Cambridge University Press, 1994.

Purcell, S. (2002) *Improvisation and the Improvisational Practice Cycle in Musical Patchwork: The Threads of Teaching and Learning in a Conservatoire.* London: Guildhall School of Music and Drama.

Pusey, M. (1987) *Jurgen Habermas.* London: Ellis Harwood/Tavistock.

Putnam, R.D. (2000) *Bowling Alone: The Collapse and Revival of American Community.* New York: Simon and Schuster.

Rand, A (1964) *The Virtue of Selfishness.* New York: New American Press.

Rawls, J. (1999) *A Theory of Justice.* Oxford: Oxford University Press.

Raz, J. (1986) *The Morality of Freedom.* Oxford: Oxford University Press.

Reavley, N.J. et al. (2012): Quality of Information Sources about Mental Disorders: A Comparison of Wikipedia with Centrally Controlled Web and Printed Sources. *Psychological Medicine*, 42 (8):1753–1762.

Reay, D., Crozier, G. & Clayton, J. (2010) 'Fitting In' or 'Standing Out': Working Class Students in UK Higher Education. *British Educational Research Journal*, 36 (1): 107–124.

Rennie, D. et al. (2003) Fifth International Congress on Peer Review and Biomedical Publication: Call for Research. *JAMA*, 289: 11, 1438.

Richardson, V. (1990) The Evolution of Reflective Teaching and Teacher Education. In Clift, R.T. et al. (Eds.) *Encouraging Reflective Practice in Education: An Analysis of Issues and Programs.* New York: Teachers' College Press.

Ridley, M. (1996) *The Origins of Virtue.* London: Viking.

Robeyns, I. (2011) The Capability Approach. *The Stanford Encyclopedia of Philosophy.* (online) Available at: http://plato.stanford.edu/entries/capability-approach/ (Accessed 17 January 2013)

Rogers, C.R. (1961) *On Becoming a Person. A Therapist's View of Psychotherapy.* Boston: Houghton Mifflin.

Rogers, C.R. (1967) The Interpersonal Relationship in The Facilitation of Learning. reprinted in Kirschenbaum, H. and Henderson, V.L. (Eds.) (1990) *The Carl Rogers Reader.* London: Constable.

Rogers, C.R. (1980) *A Way of Being.* Boston: Houghton Mifflin.

Rosenthal, M.A. (2010) Tolerance as a Virtue in Spinoza's Ethics. *Journal of the History of Philosophy*, 39: 4, 535–57.

Ross, D. & Egea-Kuehne, D. (2005) Ad-Liberal Education – Improvisation And Open Curricula. *International Journal Of Learning*, 12 (6)

Rousseau, J. J. (1997a) *'The Social Contract' And Other Later Political Writings*, Trans. Victor Gourevitch. Cambridge: Cambridge University Press.

Rousseau, J.J. (1997b) *'The Discourses' And Other Early Political Writings*, Trans. Victor Gourevitch. Cambridge: Cambridge University Press.

Russell, R. & Munby, H. (Eds.) (1989) *Teachers and Teaching: From Classroom to Reflection*. London: Falmer.

Sandel, M. (1998) *Liberalism and the Limits of Justice*. Cambridge: Cambridge University Press.

Sartre, J.P. (1969) *Being and Nothingness*. London: Routledge.

Scanlon, T. (2003) *The Difficulty of Tolerance*. Cambridge: Cambridge University Press.

Schon, D. (1983) *The Reflective Practitioner, How Professionals Think In Action*. London: Temple Smith.

Schon, D. (1987) *Educating the Reflective Practitioner*. San Francisco: Jossey-Bass.

Seal, M. (2005) *Resettling Homeless People: Theory and Practice*. Lyme Regis: Russell House.

Seal, M. (2008) *Not About Us Without Us: Client Involvement in Supported Housing*. Lyme Regis: Russell House.

Seal, M. (2009) *Youth Workers' Cultures Around Conflict*. London: YMCA George Williams College.

Seligman, M.E.P. (1975) *Helplessness: On Depression, Development and Death*. San Francisco: W.H. Freeman.

Sen, A. (1999) *Development as Freedom*. New York: Knopf.

Sennett, R. (1998) *The Corrosion Of Character. The Personal Consequences Of Work In The New Capitalism*. New York: Norton.

Skyrms, B. (2008) Trust, Risk and the Social Contract. *Synthese*, 160: 21–25.

Smith, H. (2002) Seeking out the Gift of Authenticity. *Youth and Policy*, 77, 19–32.

Smith, M.K. (1988) *Developing Youth Work: Informal Education, Mutual Aid and Popular Practice*. Milton Keynes: Open University Press.

Smith, M.K. (1996, 2001a) Selfhood. *The Encyclopaedia Of Informal Education*, at www.Infed.Org/Biblio/B-Self.Htm.

Smith, M.K. (2001b) Communitarianism and Education. *The Encyclopaedia of Informal Education*. At http://www.infed.org/biblio/communitarianism.htm

Smith, M.K. (2001c) Relationship. In *The Encyclopaedia of Informal Education*. At www.infed.org/biblio/relationship.htm

Smith, M.K. (2004) *The Case for Youth Work*. Presentation to the Prime Minister's Strategy group.

Solomon, D. (1988) Internal Objections to Virtue Ethics. In French et al., 428–41.

Sorenson, N. & Coombs, S. (2007) *Towards an Improvisation Based Pedagogy: Using a Four-Phase Framework For Teacher Development to Identify Individual Staff Training Needs*. International Professional Development Association.

Sorrell, N (1992) Improvisation. *Companion to Contemporary Musical Thought, Vol 2*. London: Routledge.

Sowell, T. (2010) *Intellectuals and Society*. London and New York: Basic Books.

Spence, J. (2009) In Defence of Rigorous Youth Work. At http://indefenceofyouthwork.wordpress.com/2009/08/19/in-defence-of-intellectually-rigorous-youth-work/ (Accessed July 2012).

Spence, J. and Devaney, C. (2006) *Youth Work: Voices of Practice*. Leicester: NYA.

Spencer, H (1884) *Man Vs The State*. London and Edinburgh: Williams And Norgate.

Sternberg, R.J. and Lubart, T.I. (1999) The Concept Of Creativity: Prospects And Paradigms. In Sternberg, R.J. (Ed.) *Handbook Of Creativity*. London: Cambridge University Press.

Sung, K.T. (2004) Elder Respect Among Young Adults: A Cross-Cultural Study of Americans and Koreans. *Journal of Aging Studies*, 18, 138–215.

Swift, A. (2005) *Political Philosophy.* Oxford: Blackwell Publishing.

Taylor, C. (1989) *Sources of the Self: The Making of the Modern Identity.* Cambridge: Cambridge University Press.

Tolstoy, L. (1967) *The Great Short Stories of Tolstoy.* New York: Grove Press.

Trelfa, J. (2005) Faith in Reflective Practice. *Reflective Practice*, 6 (2), 205–12.

Triandis, H. C. & Gelfand, M.J. (1998). Converging Measurement of Horizontal and Vertical Individualism and Collectivism. *Journal of Personality and Social Psychology* 74 (1): 119.

Trinder, L. (2000) A Critical Appraisal of Evidence-Based Practice. In Trinder, L. & Reynolds, S. (Eds.) *Evidence-Based Practice: A Critical Appraisal.* Oxford: Blackwell.

Tripp, D (1993) *Critical Incidents in Teaching: Developing Professional Judgement.* London: Routledge.

UCU (2009) *Statement On Academic Freedom* http://www.ucu.org.uk/3672 Accessed 3/3/2012.

Uslaner, E. M. (1999). Democracy and Social Capital. In Warren, M. (Ed.) (1999) *Democracy and Trust.* Cambridge: Cambridge University Press.

Wallas, G (1926) *The Art of Thought.* New York: Harcourt Brace.

Walter, M (1997) *On Toleration.* Yale: Yale University Press.

Warren, S. (2007) Migration, Race and Education: Evidence-based Policy or Institutional Racism? *Race, Ethnicity and Education*, 10 (4): 367–385.

Webb, M. O. (1993) Why I Know About As Much As You: A Reply to Hardwig. *The Journal Of Philosophy*, 90 (5): 260–270.

Weick, K (1998) Improvisation as a Mindset for Organisational Analysis. *Organisation Science* 9 (5): 543–553.

Wenger, E. (1999) *Communities of Practice: Learning, Meaning and Identity.* Cambridge: Cambridge University Press.

White, Stephen (1991) *Political Theory and Post Modernism.* Cambridge: Cambridge University Press.

Williams, R. (1976) *Keywords: A Vocabulary of Culture and Society.* London: Fontana.

Willis, P. (1981) *Learning to Labour: How Working Class Kids Get Working Class Jobs.* New York: Columbia University Press.

Winch, C. & Gingell, J. (2004) Introduction. *Educational Philosophy and Theory*, 36 (5): 479–483.

Wittgenstein, L. (1922) *Tractatus Logico-Philosophicus (TLP)*, C.K. Ogden (Trans.), London: Routledge & Kegan Paul. Originally Published As 'Logisch-Philosophische Abhandlung', In *Annalen Der Naturphilosophische*, XIV (3/4), 1921.

Wolfe, M. & Richardson, L.D. (2001) *Principles and Practice of Informal Education: Learning through Life.* London: Routledge.

Wolff, R. (1970) *In Defence of Anarchism.* California: University of California Press.

Young, K. (1999) *The Art of Youth Work.* Lyme Regis: Russell House.

Zack, M. (2000) Jazz Improvisation and Organizing: Once More from the Top. *Organization Science*, 11 (2): 227–234.

Radical youth work
Developing critical perspectives and professional judgement
By Brian Belton

978-1-905541-57-7

'Refreshing, honest, provocative, unapologetic, irritating, often challenging and highly recommended... a catalyst for reflection, debate and experimentation in the youth work field at a time when this is sorely needed.' *Addiction Today.*

How can youth workers support young people while delivering policy?
What makes a 'positive activity' positive?
When is an 'informed choice' truly informed?
Why is politics in education discouraged?
How can we make sense of all of this?

Belton encourages workers to help young people – through questioning – to forsake ready-made ideas and products and reawaken their own – and our – imaginations, sense of wonder, and faith in dynamic possibilities.

'What a breath of fresh air to read this book. Not an easy or comfortable read as it pushes the brain to do some work, but definitely worth the effort.' *Youthwork.*

Includes Tania de St Croix's consideration of a foundation literature of radical youth work, and how new theories could be engendered.

The art of youth work
Second edition
By Kerry Young

978-1-903855-46-1

The Second Edition reaffirms this established book's commitment to youth work as an exercise in philosophy, not because young people are troubled or troublesome, but because they are people in the process of reconciling reason and passion in ways that make sense to them. You will find here a:
- *clear theory of youth work*
- *framework for making sound judgements about practice and the training of youth workers*
- *reaffirmation of youth work, at its best, as a powerful educative and developmental process.*

'Young's description of the way in which good youth work can instil the key features of critical thinking that underpin educational attainment and the sense of citizenship is about as good as it gets... an eloquent, poetic and philosophical reassertion of the unique contribution of the youth work purpose.' *Rapport.*

Reappraisals
Essays in the history of youth and community work
Edited by Ruth Gilchrist, Tony Jeffs, Jean Spence, Naomi Stanton, Aylssa Cowell, Joyce Walker and Tom Wylie

978-1-905541-88-1

The range of material in this volume reflects the editors' hope to encourage practitioners and academics to reflect upon the earlier forms of practice and, via that process, reappraise what they are currently doing within both fieldwork and teaching.

Roots and wings
A history of outdoor education and outdoor learning in the UK
By Ken Ogilvie

978-1-905541-84-3

Driven by those who believe that a traditional academic approach to education is both too narrow and ignores important aspects of the whole person, the history of outdoor learning is here fleshed out to explore these and the many other factors influencing its evolution.

In the first 200 pages of this book, the author traces the evolution of man's relationship with the outdoors from prehistory onwards, focusing on the key movements and thinkers, including Rousseau and Ruskin, and the influence of the Renaissance, the Reformation, the Enlightenment and Romanticism.

The remaining 600 pages explore the blooming of outdoor education/learning in the twentieth century, setting the development of ideas and practice in social and political contexts.

Social pedagogy in the UK
Theory and practice
By Kieron Hatton

978-1-905541-89-8

Social pedagogy is an approach to service delivery that is common across Europe. This accessible text explores and explains:
- *why it is attracting increasing interest in the UK*
- *its influence on UK debates about – and its potential contribution to – UK welfare practice.*

Focusing on practice situations within which social pedagogy can be seen to be effective, it:
- *investigates how European and UK services could benefit from a better mutual understanding of what each other does*
- *discusses how social pedagogy is already making a contribution in children's residential services in the UK, and could do so in other areas, including youth work, adult social care and community development.*

Power and empowerment
By Neil Thompson

978-1-903855-99-7

Empowerment has become a well-used term across a wide variety of work settings that involve dealing with people and their problems. But is it a central part of good practice or an empty word? And what of power? It is a central theme of human services practice but, like empowerment, is often only loosely examined.

'A useful gateway to the complexity of power and empowerment... as succinct an introduction as one could wish for... It is a book which speaks a strong commitment to social justice and which also provides a welcome antidote to the tendency to polarise 'powerful' and 'powerless' – Neil Thompson provides an altogether more subtle and compelling analysis... I can see experienced practitioners and practice teachers enjoying it. This is a book that goes well beyond the rhetoric.' Professor Mark Doel, Sheffield Hallam University.